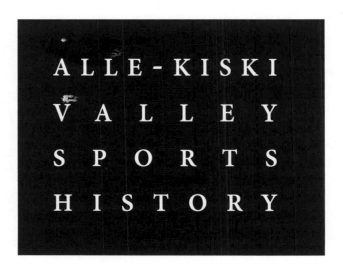

ALLE-KISKI
VALLEY
SPORTS
HISTORY

A CENTURY OF SPORTS IN WESTERN PENNSYLVANIA'S A-K VALLEY

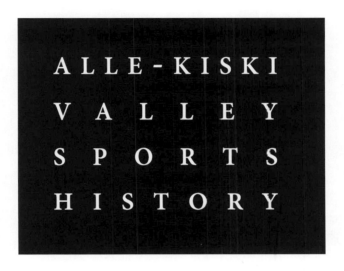

ALLE-KISKI VALLEY SPORTS HISTORY

A CENTURY OF SPORTS IN WESTERN PENNSYLVANIA'S A-K VALLEY

GEORGE GUIDO

Printed in the United States of America.

ISBN: 978-1-59571-464-0
Library of Congress Control Number: 2010921682

WORD ASSOCIATION PUBLISHERS
205 Fifth Avenue
Tarentum, Pennsylvania 15084
www.wordassociation.com
1-800-827-7903

Design: Word Association Publishers (Gina Rinchiuso Datres)

DEDICATION

THIS BOOK IS DEDICATED
TO MY DEAR WIFE, BRENDA.

HONEY, WHILE MOST WIVES
ARE A HIGH SCHOOL SPORTS WIDOW
ONE SEASON OF THE YEAR,
YOU SPEND TIME AT HOME NIGHTLY WHILE
I'M OUT COVERING EVENTS YEAR-ROUND.

I CAN'T THANK YOU ENOUGH
FOR YOUR SUPPORT.

ACKNOWLEDGMENTS

TO PUT THIS PROJECT TOGETHER TAKES THE HELP OF MANY PEOPLE.

Chief among them is Sam Buffone, former general manager of Westmoreland Cable Co., who gave me my start broadcasting high school sports on Feb. 19, 1971. Bob Tatrn and Joe Falsetti, broadcasting legends who I worked with for many years.

My editors at the *Valley News Dispatch*, including Rick Starr, who gave me my first newspaper job, to Kevin Smith, and Bill Beckner, Jr.

Sue Eddy, Jason Bridge and Lou Ruediger of the *Valley News Dispatch* who spent considerable hours processing the many photographs in this book.

Managing editor Jeff Domenick of the *Valley News Dispatch*. Dom Corso and Al Uskuraitis of the A-K Valley Sports Hall of Fame.

From Vandergrift: The Victorian Vandergrift Museum, Rudy Minarcin, retired Kiski Area football coaches Dick Dilts and Frank Morea.

From New Kensington: People's Library, Bill Englert, George 'Cub' France, Dan Thimons, Kenny Russell, Valley High School athletic director Frank Campbell.

From Lower Burrell: Shirley Seben, Mary Spagnolo, Dave Abate, Scott Covert, retired police officer Al Chamrad.

From Springdale: Commander Jim Anderson of American Legion Post 754, the Free Public Library, Sam Renaldi Sr. & Jr.

From Ford City: Bill Oleksak and Tom Dinga

From Tarentum: Mickey Cendrowski of the
A-K Historical Society

From Freeport: Bob Fair and Randy Scott from Rock-A-Fellas
Restaurant

From Oakmont: John Fitzgerald of the Oakmont Country Club
Historical Dept., Riverview High librarian Lynne Madden
From Plum: Nick & John Veltri of Veltri's Restaurant, sports
enthusiast Frank Furko

West Deer historian Dan Angeloni; Stan Watychowicz of
Natrona Heights; Bonnie Berzonski of the Fox Chapel Area
School District; Neila Riggle of Bell Township; Apollo-Ridge
High School librarian Robert Fello; Mike Mackin of the John
Heinz Historical Center; the University of Pittsburgh Sports
Information Office; the Harry Truman Memorial Library of
Independence, Mo.; the National Baseball Hall of Fame &
Library of Cooperstown, N.Y.; Eric Westerndorf of Lernerville
Speedway; Ron Musselman of the *Pittsburgh Post-Gazette*; Rich
Vetock of *Pennsylvania Football News*; and to the countless
athletes, coaches, administrators, political and civic figures who have
provided interviews and background information over the years.

Last but not least, my parents Evelyn and the late William S.
Guido, who helped cultivate my interest in sports, particularly
local sports. Thank you for sending me to broadcasting school
while I was in high school which enabled me to get an early start
covering high school games at 17. Before I got my driver's
license, you somehow got me to the big high school games
despite having to divide your attention between 4 children, for
which I remain eternally grateful.

West
Franklin

East Franklin

Kittanning

Rayburn

Valley

BUTLER COUNTY

West
Kittanning

Penn

Jefferson

Winfield

North
Buffalo

Applewold

Manor

Ford
City

422

Cacogan

Ford
Cliff

Kittanning
Township

Saxonburg

356

28

South
Buffalo

Clinton

Freeport

Bethel

Buffalo

Gilpin

66

ARMSTRONG COUNTY

Brackenridge

Leechburg

Parks

Burrell

West
Deer

Fawn

West
Leechburg

Tarentum

Hyde
Park

East
Vandergrift

56

ALLEGHENY COUNTY

Frazer

East Deer

56

Allegheny
Township

Vandergrift

North Apollo

Arnold

Lower
Burrell

Apollo

Kiskiminetas

Indiana
Township

New
Kensington

Upper
Burrell

Avonmore

Harmar

Oklahoma

Springdale Twp.

Fox
Chapel

28

Springdale

Washington

Bell

Cheswick

Oakmont

Verona

76

Plum

Blawnox

66

Sharpsburg

Penn
Hills

WESTMORELAND COUNTY

Aspinwall

Murrysville

Map area

Credit: Denise Shean, Trib Total Media Graphics

3 miles

INTRODUCTION

The Allegheny River valley and Kiskiminetas River valley areas aren't necessarily wealthy in terms of dollars.

Many families and governmental bodies continue to struggle, financially, toward the end of the first decade of the 21st Century.

But the wealth of the geographic area known as the Alle-Kiski Valley is in terms of its sports teams, particularly high school sports teams, and the memories of a century of success is rich and plentiful.

Community pride in these sports teams is fierce and unwavering. Those in the media who cover these teams will relate stories of how fans will complain if they feel their team isn't getting enough coverage, or if the rival school's games are getting larger articles in the newspaper than their team.

Loyalty has many faces.

It's the loyalty of the Plum fans whose automobile caravan stretched for miles and miles in 1983 to and from Three Rivers Stadium when their Mustangs shocked favored New Castle in the WPIAL football title game.

When a Springdale High School sports team returns home after a huge win, a convoy of fire trucks await at Exit 11 of the Allegheny Valley Expressway in Harmar, ready to escort the team along old Route 28 with sirens blaring.

It's the Kiski Area fans during the heyday of Cavaliers football who would stand in line for an hour Thursday nights at Pugliese's Florist in Vandergrift, making sure they got tickets for Friday's big game.

During the 1930s and 40s when not everybody owned a car, it was a Ford City ritual where a clerk from the Pennsylvania Railroad would show up at the school selling tickets. Fans rode the rails into Pittsburgh for many WPIAL basketball playoff games held at the Pitt Pavilion, located underneath Pitt Stadium.

When the wrecking ball visited the former New Kensington High School on Ridge Avenue in 2006 to make way for an apartment complex, former students - by then retirees - stood on the sidewalk and watched the demolition with tears in their eyes.

The Alle-Kiski Valley is generally considered to be 47 munic-ipalities on the edges of four counties – Allegheny, Westmoreland, Butler and Armstrong. The population of those communities in the 2000 census was 262,000.

The Alle-Kiski Valley is so typical of Western Pennsylvania, dotted with many small, riverfront industrial towns from a bygone era where nearly every community had its own high school. Many schools still play football in old, downtown stadiums, where fans can still walk to the games, even though the high school campus is located elsewhere.

Part of being a Western Pennsylvanian is visiting a friend's house and using the back door or the side door. Who wants to track through and mess up the living room unnecessarily?

Part of being a Western Pennsylvanian is employing a dialect all its own.

"The roads were slippy (not slippery) coming home from last night's basketball game."

"Apollo-Ridge plays its home games at Owens Filled (not field)."

"That quarterback has a strong arm, I used to work with his dad at the still mill."

Also, part of being a Western Pennsylvanian is enjoying history. So, enjoy!

Credit: Valley News Dispatch

Burrell (right) and Freeport square off on their first play from scrimmage in the WPIAL Class A title game on Nov. 18 1967 at Ken High Memorial Stadium. Burrell won, 6-0. This is one of the most famous photos taken by the late *Valley News Dispatch* chief photographer Bill Larkin, who died in 2003.

Credit: Valley News Dispatch

Boxing was a big deal in 1950. It was an even bigger deal when the world heavyweight champion came to town on Oct. 1, 1950 as Ezzard Charles was paraded through the downtown area of New Kensington and followed by fans. Charles' manager was Arnold's Tom Tannas, seated at left in the back seat. It was safe to say shirts with horizontal stripes were in style for boys that fall.

Credit: Harry Truman Library, Independence, Mo.

The 1952 Army-Navy game had plenty of Western Pennsylvania flavor. At left is Ford City graduate John Gurski, captain of Navy, and Al Paulekas, a native of Farrell. It was President Harry Truman's last Army-Navy game as Commander-in-Chief.

Credit: A-K Valley Sports Hall of Fame

Tarentum native and Pirates broadcaster Albert K. 'Rosey' Rowswell tries out his new wheels at Forbes Field. In the back seat is the mythical 'Aunt Minnie.' When Rowswell was re-creating games on radio via a Western Union te eticker, Rowswell would often describe a home run by saying "Open the window, Aunt Minnie,"only to have the sound of shattering glass follow as Aunt Minnie couldn't get to the window fast enough.

CHAPTER 1
THE KING OF (NEW) KENSINGTON

After New Kensington High School suffered through a winless season in 1938, the call for a new coach went out to Windber High School where Don Fletcher was guiding the Ramblers, a Somerset County power at the time.

Fletcher took the job at New Kensington, popularly known as Ken High, or, simply, the contraction "Ken-Hi."

With Fletcher in command, the sour memories of an 0-9 campaign quickly turned into a 6-2 success in 1939. But more than that, Fletcher started a 22-year reign in which Ken High would become not only a WPIAL powerhouse, but a nationally-known program.

Fletcher used innovative techniques at the time like taking the team away to summer camp and using multiple formations in the old single wing offense with an unbalanced line. During his tenure, he compiled a record of 113-65-12 playing solely in the largest enrollment classification.

Ten of his 22 teams lost two games or less. From 1945-48, the Red Raiders went 31-3-1, including two WPIAL championships and a runner-up.

Born on June 12, 1905, Fletcher learned football as a youth in one of the nation's all-time football hotbeds – Massillon, Ohio. An end, he was named to Massillon's 100th anniversary team in 1994, a notable achievement, considering the fact that Massillon is the second-winningest high school football program in U.S. history and the Tigers have won 22 Ohio state titles.

In fact, to understand Massillon is to understand how Fletcher's formative years were the seed to his success. The town is part of America's industrial heartland, where hard work in the factories was preceded by hard work on the football field.

Football tradition is so embedded at Massillon that when a baby boy is born in the town's hospital, the Boosters Club puts a tiny orange and black football in the baby's bassinet.

Fletcher never brought any footballs into the maternity ward at the former Citizens General Hospital in New Kensington, but he always knew that discipline and hard work translated into victories.

It's been said that behind every good man is a quality woman, and Fletcher was no exception. His married Marjorie "Billie" Fletcher in 1932. She was the daughter of John T. Taylor, the founder of the Allegheny Mountain Association of the Amateur Athletic Union (AAU).

Mrs. Fletcher, who died on Oct. 11, 2006, was strong-willed and supportive of the program. The Fletchers had no children, but Billie always considered her players "my boys." Long after Don Fletcher died in 1984, former Red Raiders kept in contact with her, even visiting her at the family farm.

The farm?

In this day of each school trying to establish a glitzier weight and training room than the school next door, Fletcher's conditioning program was simple: His players came out to the farm located in Hampton Township over the summer and got into shape by working out in the fields.

Unconventional? Yes, but it also built team camaraderie.

Fletcher's great teams, however, were forged in pre-season training camp. Starting in 1945, Fletcher obtained the use of an old Civilian Conservation Corps (CCC) camp near Salisbury, Somerset County. No electricity, no telephones, no radios – just solitude and football.

After returning from camp, the Red Raiders lost the first game of the season to North Catholic, then a non-WPIAL member. After that defeat, Ken High then went on a roll, winning the remaining seven regular season games and qualified for the WPIAL title game.

In those days, a team that lost or tied a game in its enrollment classification was out of WPIAL title consideration. The WPIAL played a one-game, winner-take-all championship contest.

Teams qualified for the game by collecting Gardner Points. The Gardner Point System was devised in 1927 by Ralph Gardner, a mathematics teacher from New Castle High School. The system was based on strength of schedule, where teams earned points from the number of games a defeated opponent won.

The 1945 title game pitted Ken High against the Donora

Dragons at St. Vincent College, Latrobe. Donora was led by quarterback Arnold Galiffa, who went on to become an All-American at Army, Lou 'Bimbo' Cecconi later a star at Pitt and 'Deacon' Dan Towler, the fullback who played six years with the Los Angeles Rams.

The championship game belonged to Donora, as the Dragons rolled to a 38-6 victory.

The defeat would be the final setback for Ken High for nearly three seasons, as the Red Raiders would go 26 games without losing, including WPIAL championships in 1946 and '47. New Kensington was headed for a three-peat in 1948, but an upset loss late in the season sent Ken High tumbling from the title race.

The 1946 Season

Of all the great Ken High teams, Fletcher always considered the 1946 team the best. With a number of key players returning from the 1945 runner-up, the Red Raiders got a taste of what it took to be a championship-caliber club.

The 1946 season started with a 26-0 victory over Pittsburgh Central Catholic. Convincing victories over Beaver Falls (25-7) and Pittsburgh Schenley (45-0) followed. That set up a showdown against cross-river rival Har-Brack. In the closest game of the season, the Red Raiders prevailed, 19-6.

New Ken's rampage continued with victories over Baldwin, Sharon and North Braddock Scott. At the same time, some 10 miles from New Kensington, Vandergrift High School also was piling up the wins.

The Blue Lancers were building toward a showdown with New Ken to conclude the regular season. Interest was intense as the big game loomed. That caused the WPIAL to move the game from the relatively small George Leslie Memorial Stadium in Arnold to Forbes Field, despite the protests of Vandergrift coach Johnny Karrs.

Davis Field, Vandergrift's home venue, had just installed lights for the first time in anticipation of the arrival of minor league professional baseball in 1947. The first two nocturnal contests proved to be a hit, as 7,000 fans showed up for the Blue Lancers victory over Penn Hills (19-0) and the win the following week over Har-

Brack, 13-0.

But the game between the two unbeaten squads would serve as the de facto WPIAL championship game.

A crowd of 17,967 watched Tony Kotowski score three touchdowns and an extra point as the Red Raiders prevailed, 21-0. Kotowski, who wore a specially-constructed face mask to protect his thick eyeglasses, scored on an 11-yard run using the Statue of Liberty play.

After Vandergrift back Dick Veitch was tossed into the end zone for a safety by Dick Tamburro, George France fired a 20-yard touchdown pass to Kotowski.

Later, the Red Raiders concluded the scoring as Kotowski hauled in a 40-yard scoring pass from Willie Thrower.

Sour Oranges

By the time Ken High was declared the WPIAL champion because it was the only undefeated, untied team in Class AA, then the largest enrollment classification, the Red Raiders had become known nationwide.

The team's success caught the eye of a promoter in Florida. New Kensington was invited to play in what was called the Peanut Bowl, pitting high school squads from different parts of the country at Miami's Orange Bowl stadium.

There was just one caveat.

Because the Jim Crow Laws of Florida and other Southern states prohibited black and white players from performing on the same field, Ken High was told it could come if the team left its two black players behind.

The players voted to decline the bid to play in sunny Florida. "If they couldn't go, then we would not go," said Vince Pisano, Red Raiders halfback.

Fletcher told the promoter what he could do with his game, and McKeesport High School made the trip South.

1947 & The New Stadium

As the football program grew in popularity, demand to see the team in person increased.

Ken High had played its home games for several years at nearby George Leslie Memorial Stadium in Arnold. The stadium got its name from the first serviceman from Pennsylvania to be killed in the Japanese attack on Pearl Harbor on Dec. 7, 1941.

But the Arnold facility, built in a residential neighborhood, had a limited seating capacity.

Before that, Ken High played in Herr Stadium, located in the Parnassus section of New Kensington and named after Benjamin Herr, a long-time school director in the community. The field was the first to host a night game, as Parnassus High School introduced Friday night football to the Alle-Kiski Valley in 1929, renting a set of arc lights, crude when compared to modern standards.

Located at least 10 feet below ground level, the stadium playing surface was slow to dry after a rainstorm. The facility, somewhat ahead of its time because it was designed for both football and baseball, was affectionately called "The Duck Pond" by fans.

After eight years on the job, Fletcher had amassed significant influence in the community. He was one of the driving forces behind the construction of Memorial Stadium, built about one-half mile from the city's downtown area on a small flood plain abutting Little Pucketas Creek.

The stadium, built to seat 8,000-plus, could easily accommodate 10,000 fans for a big game. Construction proceeded swiftly so the new facility would be ready for the 1947 season. A grand entrance in the end zone closest to the creek was a major feature of the new home site, and the field would be named Memorial Stadium in honor of the many area veterans who never returned home from World War II.

It was a festive atmosphere on opening night at the new stadium on Sept. 6, 1947 against Pittsburgh Central Catholic. The school band, under the direction of Frank Oliver, entertained before the game. An honor guard representing the VFW Post 92 from what was then a nearly-rural Lower Burrell Township, also was on hand.

Pisano appeared to have scored the first touchdown in the new stadium, but a penalty against the Red Raiders nullified the score. Three plays later, however, Pisano scored on a 9-yard run.

Ken High would win the game, 20-6. The following week, the

Pittsburgh Steelers played a preseason game at the new stadium against the Richmond Rebels of the Dixie League, an NFL affiliate at the time

One night earlier, the Red Raiders were one play away from changing history. New Kensington held off a late Beaver Falls rally, 7-6, stopping the Tigers at the 2-yard line. A Ken High loss would have eliminated the team from WPIAL title consideration. The close call spurred the Red Raiders to six more victories, setting up a must-win against Sharon to conclude the regular season. Ken High passed the final test with flying colors, 38-6, setting up a title game date with neighboring Har-Brack, New Kensington's biggest rival.

School officials didn't schedule a game during the regular season, sensing the rivalry had become too heated.

It was back to Forbes Field for the Red Raiders - this time for the official WPIAL title game. The pre-game hype was huge. It was Thanksgiving Day, and a trainload of local fans headed toward the Oakland ballpark, despite snowy and cold conditions.

Early in the game, Thrower picked off a Ralph Atkinson pass and returned it to the Har-Brack 16. Thrower scored soon after and Ken High followed that with a Thrower lateral to Pisano that resulted in a 25-yard scoring run.

Thrower intercepted another Tigers pass, setting up a 7-yard scoring strike from Thrower to Pisano. New Ken finalized the scoring with a 3-yard plunge by Harold Vestrand late in the fourth period to put the finishing touches on a 28-0 romp before nearly 16,000 fans.

After the game, the Red Raiders, their families and friends were treated to a holiday feast at the Kenmar Hotel in downtown New Kensington. Meanwhile, across the river, brothers and future NFLers Ed and Dick Modzelewski were so embarrassed by the loss that they didn't even show up at the local soda fountain hangout, Ye Pickett, for several days.

No Three-Peat

The sky seemed to be the limit for the New Kensington football program as the 1948 season approached.

Fletcher's Marine drill sergeant-style approach was working. Even the townsfolk were helping out, telling the coach if they saw his players out after curfew. Fletcher even visited players' residences himself, checking to make sure the Red Raiders were in bed.

One night, Thrower was out and received word that Fletcher was making the rounds. The all-stater sneaked into his bedroom and got under the covers, seemingly, just in time. When Fletcher opened the door for the bed check, Thrower's young cousin, whom he shared the room with, blurted out that Willie was there, but still had his shoes on.

Many of the players from the first two WPIAL title teams had graduated, but Thrower, Renaldo 'Kosi' Kosikowski, Dick Tamburro and George 'Cubby' France remained. Ken High came into the new season breathing fire, shutting out two of its first six opponents.

In Week Seven, Ken High played Allentown to a 7-7 tie, thus halting the winning streak at 24 and giving future opponents the feeling that the Red Raiders weren't invincible, after all. In Week Eight, Ken High survived a bruising, 25-19 encounter at Ambridge.

The game was punctuated by Ambridge players punching and getting in cheap shots. The fact that the officiating crew wouldn't call any penalties only encouraged the Bridgers.

Renaldo Kozikowski suffered a broken jaw and all-state linemen Dick Tamburro an ankle injury. Ambridge reserve Al Sefek started a tussle with Thrower late in the game and both were tossed out.

New Kensington School Board member James Patterson was among the 15,000 in the stands at Ambridge and was appalled at what he witnessed. He said after the game that Ken High wouldn't play Ambridge again if he had anything to say about it.

Kozikowski would not play against Vandergrift. The Blue Lancers came into the game with a 2-6 record, making Ken High a heavy favorite. With Vandergrift trailing, 14-13, early in the fourth quarter, a Ken High muff of a punt at the 7 was recovered by John Minarcin. Two played later, fullback Lou Cherre crashed into the end zone and Vandergrift emerged with a 20-14 victory.

By the time the team bus had returned to Vandergrift, jubilant fans had clogged the streets to the point where vehicles couldn't move.

Meanwhile, Ken High's 26-game unbeaten streak was over and New Castle knocked off Monongahela, 43-14, for WPIAL honors.

Felled By the Flu

By the time the 1957 season rolled around, it appeared as though the Red Raiders were ready to make another run at another WPIAL title.

New Kensington had won the final three games of the 1956 campaign against Har-Brack, McKeesport and Latrobe. Excitement also surrounded the pre-season because New Kensington was ready to open its new high school on Stevenson Boulevard, next door to the stadium, which was ready to start its 11th season. The high school had been located on Ridge Avenue since 1913.

After another grueling training camp in Somerset County, Ken High had an open date as the season got underway. In those days, relatively few schools had conference affiliations and most teams simply had to find games on their own.

The actual opener was Sept. 20 at home against Vandergrift. The Red Raiders breezed to a 39-0 victory and headed to Johnstown for a big Week Two clash. New Kensington led, 7-6, as the Trojans drove for a potential winning touchdown late in the game. Linebacker Gene Collodi, however, intercepted a pass and raced 48 yards to seal the upset, 14-6.

Things seemed to be falling into place for the Red Raiders. But a deadly strain of the Asian flu was circulating throughout Western Pennsylvania. Leechburg students, attending the annual Alle-Kiski band festival at Memorial Stadium were the first to fall ill. Soon, 20 Ken High players missed practice and major industries such as ALCOA and PPG had their employees inoculated. Games were being postponed throughout the region as doctors used up vaccine almost as quickly as it became available.

"It was really devastating," Collodi said. "Players came and went and the ones that were healthy practiced."

Ken High would have its next three games against Turtle

Creek, Hempfield and Greensburg postponed because of flu-related high absenteeism. WPIAL Football Steering Committee chairman Tony Bazard, the principal at Har-Brack, announced a one-week extension of the regular season to Nov.23 as schools scrambled to make up games.

Finally on Oct. 25, New Kensington played its third game of the season, a 14-0 shutout over Har-Brack. Consider that in 2008, the regular season ended Oct. 25.

The following week, Ken High needed two goal line stands to defeat McKeesport on the road, 25-16, before 5,401 fans.

Large crowds followed the Red Raiders everywhere. Getting fuel was no problem because there were 32 gasoline stations at the time within the New Kensington city limits.

A 14-12 victory at Latrobe was supposed to end the regular season. But makeup games against Turtle Creek and Hempfield loomed. New Kensington blanked the Creekers, 31-0 and belted Hempfield, a second-year school, 34-7. The WPIAL offered to extend the regular season two more days to Nov. 25 in order to make up the game against Greensburg and play the finals at Forbes Field Nov. 29.

But New Kensington school officials said that would force the team to play three games in eight days and the plug was pulled on the season with Wilkinsburg and Clairton heading to the championship game.

Wilkinsburg won the title, 13-0.

Fletcher would coach three more seasons before calling it quits after the 1960 campaign, when the Red Raiders posted a 5-4 mark. By then, Ken High had joined the fledgling All-West Conference, made up of some of the largest WPIAL schools such as Har-Brack, Turtle Creek, Johnstown, Chartiers Valley and Penn Hills.

Top assistant Dick Brown took over for Fletcher and won the All-West Conference in his first season, the final football title for the school. New Kensington failed to post a winning season in its final five seasons before it consolidated with Arnold High School.

On Nov. 4, 1966 Ken High triumphed in its final contest over Plum, 40-7, with Brown on the sidelines. Brown died in 2008.

Ken High's final tally was 249 wins, 206 losses and 38 ties in 59 seasons.

Brown died in 2008.

Credit: Kenny Russell

This is a look at the Ken High-Vandergrift game of Sept. 22, 1945 at Davis Field. Ken High stopped a late Vandergrift drive to eke out a 21-20 victory. Note the absence of lights at Davis Field. Lighting would not be installed until Oct., 1946.

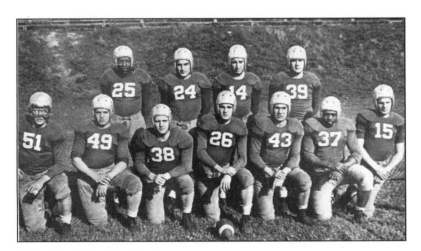

Credit: George France Family

Here are the starters for the 1946 Ken High Red Raiders.
Front row, from left: Tony Kotowski, Bill Horrell, Sonny Ciancutti, Dick Tamburo, Fred George, Flint Greene, Harry Tamburo.
Rear: Willie Thrower, Vince Pisano, George 'Cub' France, Harold 'Hawk' Vestrand.

Credit: Courtesy A–K Valley Hall of Fame

In this 1972 photo, Don Fletcher holds the game ball from the 1947 WPIAL title game. Fletcher is flanked by captains Harold Vestrand (left) and Vince Pisano.

Here is a look at the program fans bought on Nov. 1, 1946 when Ken High played Vandergrift at Forbes Field.

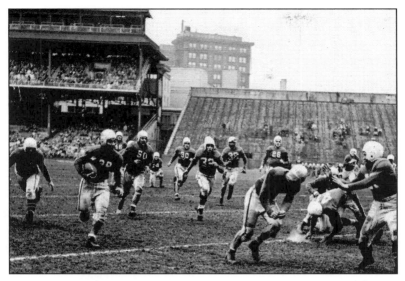

Credit: 1948 Ken High Yearbook

Vince Pisano (28) runs a sweep against Har-Brack on Nov. 27, 1947 in the WPIAL Class AA title game at Forbes Field. Note the William Pitt student union building in the background, which still stands.

Credit: George France Family

George 'Cub' France was a key, four-year starter for Ken High. France later went to Michigan Sate and was an educator for 38 years in the Freeport Area School District.

Credit: Dan Thimons

Joe Giordano takes a breather on Oct. 29, 1948 after a 97-yard touchdown run that proved to be the difference in Ken High's 25-19 victory at Ambridge.

Credit: Valley News Dispatch

Marjory 'Billie' Fletcher admires a bust of her husband Don, dedicated on Aug. 29, 1986 at Valley High Memorial Stadium. The bust was sculpted by Marlein Harrison of Fox Chapel and is erected near the Willie Thrower statue at the stadium.

Credit: Dan Thimons

It's father-son day at Ken High Memorial Stadium in 1948. Front row from left: Rocco Cartisano, Frank Kwiatkowski, Renaldo Kozikowski, Jr., Renaldo Kosikowski Sr., Dick Tudor, Frank Kwiatkowski, Sr., Rocco Cartisano, Sr. Rear: Joe Girdano, coach Don Fletcher, Dominic Girdano, Richard Tudor

chapter 2

THE FORD CITY BASKETBALL DYNASTY

Just a few years after basketball was invented by Dr. James Naismith in 1891 at the Springfield (Mass.) YMCA, John B. Ford opened the first plate glass factory in the country in what would come to be called Ford City.

Ford's idea of manufacturing plate glass took off, but there was one vital ingredient missing – workers. The call then went out to immigrants of eastern European descent and Blacks who were already emigrating to the northern industrial states to create a better life.

The game of basketball then grew to the point where high schools were beginning to sponsor the sport. When Ford City High School decided to sponsor basketball, little did anyone know at the time how successful the school would be at this purely American game.

Since coming onto the hardwood scene, Ford City has won three WPIAL titles, finished a runner-up five times and has entered postseason play an astounding total of 44 times, with 32 of those postseason trips coming as a section champion.

Ford City once won 12 consecutive section titles, losing a chance at a 13th in a tiebreaker game. The school has won over 1,200 basketball games as of Jan. 1, 2009.

Assimilation, Ford City Style

Besides all that winning, basketball was also important for a variety of reasons other than numerical success. Basketball helped immigrants assimilate more easily into American life. With names like Kovolovsky, Signorella, Petroncheck, Panchot and Holizna dotting the early Ford City rosters, it didn't take long for immigrant families, many of whom worked at Ford's Pittsburgh Plate Glass (PPG) plant, to become Americanized.

For Black families looking to escape the shadow of the Jim Crow Laws that permeated the Old Confederacy, Ford City was a quality destination. If you wanted to learn basketball or play in a neighborhood pick-up game, the door of opportunity was wide open.

"I have to give credit to the parents who raised us and to PPG, who had mixed-race softball teams from various plant departments," said Tom Dinga, a 1973 Ford City graduate and principal of Lenape Elementary School in nearby Manor Township. "If there was a pick-up game or a team of any type, race just was not an issue."

In 1932, Odeal Pryor was named captain of the school's undefeated football team, something close to unheard of in that era.

When Ford City would go on basketball trips of four or five days duration, some hotels forbid Black players to register, even though Western Pennsylvania is above the Mason-Dixon Line. At times, Ford City's team would form a tight circle while entering the hotel lobby, hiding the Black players in the middle while the coach registered the team to an unsuspecting desk clerk.

In the Beginning

Ford City inaugurated basketball on Jan. 12, 1910, losing to Punxsutawney 28-12. The first coach was Archie Hilliard and the team consisted of Tillman Scheeren, Harry 'Dutch' Drury, James Miller, Henry Roberts, Eugene Bryan, and a player named Peters.

The school had limited success at first, playing in the Alle-Kiski League until joining the WPIAL in 1919. Two years later, Ford City was a section champ for the first time, posting a 12-2 Section 6 mark in 1920-21 under coach Roy R. McIntosh.

Ford City repeated in 1924-25, though the school played only nine section games.

Abraham Sharadin by then had taken over head coaching duties. Sharadin took his team off the floor at Leechburg, because that school played a 21-year-old. Sharadin filed a protest with the WPIAL, and won. Largely because of the incident, Ford City refused to participate in WPIAL play during the 1925-26 campaign.

A Dozen Dandy Teams

In 1926-27, Ford City was back in WPIAL competition. At the time, home games were played in a barn several blocks from the high school. Hube Rupert, who would later go on to become the school's winningest coach, made an notable play in 1927, driving to the hoop to bank in a shot. Rupert's momentum took him through a doorway and outside into a snow bank.

As the regular season ended, Ford City was part of a 3-way tie with Vandergrift and Kittanning for first place in Section 5. Ford City beat Kittanning in a tiebreaker game, 33-16. But Vandergrift won the decisive game, 25-24, over Ford City and entered the WPIAL tournament, where only section champions qualified until 1977.

After that, however, Ford City went on to reel off 12 consecutive section titles.

In 1929, Ford City and Kittanning tied for the section title and had to have a tiebreaker game, which was scheduled for New Kensington. Interest in the game was intense as 11 Pennsylvania Railroad coaches were filled for the trip to see the big tiebreaker game, won by Ford City, 16-10.

After the first four titles, Sharadin left and was replaced by Cornelius 'Neenie" Campbell, who led the team, by then known as the Glassers, to eight more titles.

In Campbell's first season, 1931-32, Ford City beat North Union and Mt. Lebanon in the WPIAL playoffs before losing to in the finals to Braddock, 26-10. During the 1930s, the Glassers, dominated section play and the trips to the WPIAL playoffs were like a ritual of early spring. In fact, the Pennsylvania Railroad ticket clerk was almost like a faculty member from being at the school so often.

But train travel was the way to go to the playoffs, then held in a small gym beneath the grandstand at Pitt Stadium. After losing a semifinal round playoff game to Rankin in 1934, the Glassers went on the win the 1937 WPIAL championship against Duquesne, 20-19, on a late foul shot by Milan Dvorsky. That triumph was followed by a repeat title run in 1938.

Repeating was a bit difficult. First of all, the Glassers and Vandergrift tied for first place in Section 5 with identical 8-2 records. The teams had split the season's series, setting the stage for the tiebreaker game at the Har-Brack gymnasium.

Ford City needed to win the game not only to defend its WPIAL championship, but a win was needed to garner the 12th consecutive section title. Getting to the tiebreaker game wasn't easy. The team bus was involved in a traffic accident on Route 66 south of Ford City near the old Gable's Inn, about a mile from the present entrance to Crooked Creek State Park. Players were shaken up, but had to await a replacement bus with the temperature hovering near 7 degrees.

The team arrived at Har-Brack and the start of the game was delayed 15 minutes. For a gym that sat about 800 fans, nearly 1,000 had crammed their way in and watched the Glassers dispose of Vandergrift with relative ease, 41-24. Ford City also won its next game, 35-29, over North Braddock Scott in the WPIAL quarterfinals.

A semifinal encounter with New Castle loomed at the Pitt Pavilion. In an era where more and more high schools were taking on nicknames or mascots, New Castle had recently adopted the moniker Red Hurricanes. During a football game, the dominant New Castle team was consistently marching down the field when a radio announcer said "New Castle is moving down the field like a red hurricane." The name stuck.

Now the basketball version of the Red Hurricanes was set to battle the Glassers. New Castle led, 31-28, with 27 seconds left in the game. Dvorsky was fouled in the act of shooting and made both free throws. New Castle was getting set to take the ball out of bounds, a new wrinkle to the 1937-38 basketball season. Prior to that, a center jump would take place after each basket.

The Glassers defense forced New Castle into a 10-second violation, giving possession to Ford City. With 15 seconds to go, Coley Jackson dribbled past two opponents near the foul circle and let fly a running jumper just before the buzzer to give Ford City a 32-31 victory, setting off a wild celebration on the floor by Ford City fans.

The championship game was against Har-Brack in the only time two A-K Valley teams would meet in the finals. Har-Brack had a 14-12 halftime lead but Ford City scored 10 points each in the third and fourth quarters to come away with the gold, 33-26. Jackson led Ford City with 12 points.

Ford City won its 12th straight section title in 1939, but there would be no WPIAL title three-peat as Homestead defeated the Glassers, 34-22. In 1940, Kittanning won the section with a 6-0 mark, as Ford City and Leechburg settled for 3-3 records.

That Dream Season

Campbell left after winning section titles in 1941 and '43, heading for McKeesport High School where he added to his coaching legacy. The stewardship of the Ford City program was turned over to assistant Hube Rupert.

After finishing a game behind frontrunning Ken High in 1944, Rupert went off to fight in World War II, serving from 1944-46 in the Navy as a Lieutenant Junior Grade in the Pacific Theatre. James Davis took over the team and won two section titles in Rupert's absence.

Rupert returned in time for another section title. The 1947 team had a record of 20-5, losing to Aliquippa in the WPIAL semifinals, 39-37.

Though the players didn't make it to the WPIAL title game, they felt something special was brewing. There were six weeks of practices held following the Aliquippa loss. As summer approached, John Gurski asked Rupert if the team could convene during the summer months. While most athletes were enjoying their summer vacations, the Glassers were out practicing three times a week, wherever they could find a hoop.

When the backyards were soggy after a rainstorm, the players would get sawdust from a nearby lumberyard so they could continue practicing. They would burn tires to ward off the nighttime chill.

By the time the 1947-48 season got underway, the Glassers were ready. The season opened in Brentwood on Dec. 2 with a 37-29 victory. WPIAL powerhouse Farrell provided the opposition in Ford City's home opener, but the Glassers dominated with an astounding 53-31 decision.

With a trip to Brookville on the horizon, the school acquired a modern, Harmony Short Line bus for the road game, replacing what had become the "monoxide special." The new bus made traveling a pleasure as victories at Brookville, Indiana Area and Beaver Falls followed.

Former coach Neenie Campbell brought his McKeesport Tigers to town. Since leaving Ford City, Campbell's Tigers had beaten the Glassers by 1, 2, and 2 points. The story would be different this time as Ford City took the measure of McKeesport, 44-

33. Following a win over Turtle Creek right after Christmas, the Glassers sported a 7-0 mark, but a 33-30 loss to New Castle tumbled the Glassers from the undefeated ranks. Next came section play and a trip to New Kensington to play the pre-season favorites in the opener. After trailing for three quarters, the Glassers blanked Ken High in the fourth quarter to record a 36-26 victory. That set the stage for wins over Vandergrift and Kittanning. With a 3-0 section start, Ford City squeaked by Har-Brack, 25-23. Bill Englert scored all eight Ford City points in the fourth period. Arnold handed Ford City its first Section 1 setback, 27-25. The Glassers then reeled off seven consecutive victories for the second time that season, clinching the section title with a 48-30 win over Arnold. A loss to Butler in the final section contest was followed by a loss to Sharon in a playoff tune-up game. The Sharon setback was the only homecourt loss in four seasons. Added to that setback was the fact that Archie Brumbaugh was declared ineligible because he had played with the Company C team at the Ford City Armory.

The WPIAL playoffs finally arrived and Ford City made quick work of Brentwood, th team the Glassers opened the season with. In the WPIAL semifinals, Ford City faced a solid Wilkinsburg team that included Alexander Jaffurs, who would later become mayor of Wilkinsburg and, in the 1970s, was chief counsel for the Pennsylvania Liquor Control Board (PLCB).

Always one to do things by the book, Jaffurs was forced out of the liquor board when he protested politicians getting free booze. After graduating from Wilkinsburg, Jaffurs played football and basketball at the University of Pennsylvania.

After Ford City circumvented Wilkinsburg's upset plans, 47-40, the Glassers would play none other than McKeesport for the WPIAL championship. Once a nemesis, Ford City defeated McKeesport handily, 41-30.

The first PIAA tournament game was against the Conemaugh Iron Horses, sporting a 27-1 record. Ford City sent the Horses trotting away from Pitt Pavilion, 51-33. A 37-29 victory over Pittsburgh City League champ Westinghouse gave the Glassers a date for the PIAA title at the Penn Palestra in Philadelphia.

The team was treated royally in the big city.

"We went to the Click Night Club and saw Gene Krupa perform," Englert said.

A crowd of 8,200 jammed the historic hoop cathedral. But there was an additional bit of coverage Ford City wasn't accustomed to – television.

Few people in 1948 received television outside New York City, Philadelphia and Schenectady, N.Y., so Ford City was really unfamiliar with the new contraption.

In the state title game, Ford City led, 18-16, after three quarters, but Norristown caught fire in the fourth quarter and froze the ball toward the end of the game to garner a 30-23 victory.

Despite the loss, the townspeople welcomed the 23-5 Glassers back home with a giant parade the night after the game. The late Dave Miller wrote brilliantly about that season in a piece called 2500 Miles, written as part of the book Ford City Basketball History, 1909-1971.

The incredible run of 25 consecutive winning seasons would end the following year. The dynasty consisted of 18 section titles and two other first place ties. In 16 of the 25 seasons, Ford City won at least 15 games.

The record of the quarter century of excellence was 404-160, a winning percentage of .716.

After an 8-12 campaign in 1948-49, Ford City got on another roll with four straight section titles, from 1950-53. That led to three more WPIAL semifinal appearances and a title game loss to Sharon in 1953. Rupert would win five more section titles before turning over the reins to Jack Christy in 1966.

Rupert finished with an all-time record of 333-151 for a winning percentage of .688. But more than a glittering record, Rupert earned the unyielding devotion of his players, many of whom kept in touch with him as the years went on.

Every Aug. 22, former players would meet up with Rupert for a birthday celebration. Rupert died on Dec. 26, 2006 at 96.

Two More Runs

After Rupert retired, high school basketball began to change. Ford City, by then known as the Sabers, routinely was the smallest school in the section. But mergers came along creating larger high schools such as Valley, Highlands and Kiski Area.

But before dropping in classification, Ford City had one more section title run in 1971. The Sabers became the giant slayers, clinching the school's 30th section title in the penultimate game of the season, a 55-46 victory on Feb. 19 over Highlands before an overflow crowd.

"I can remember taking a shot near the corner and falling backwards into a sea of people," Dinga said.

Sophomore Dinga led the Sabers with 17 that night.

Coach Mark Fruehan's team lost to Sto-Rox in the opening round of the 1971 WPIAL playoffs at the Pittsburgh Civic Arena. After qualifying for the playoffs in 1978 as a Class AA school, Ford City put together a remarkable season, going 28-4 overall, 22-2 in the regular season and finished as the runner-up in both the WPIAL and PIAA tournaments.

A rugged nonsection schedule included a loss to eventual Class AAA state champion Valley. The Sabers pulled out a thrilling over-time victory against Punxsutawney. The Chucks were coached by former Shannock Valley standout Les Shoop and included point guard John Mizerock, later a catcher with the Houston Astros. Ford City rolled through the Section 13-AA campaign. On Feb. 2, 1979, Springdale entered the night just 1-1/2 games behind the Sabers. But Fruehan's team put on a defensive clinic, holding the Dynamos to 7-of-38 shooting from the field in the second half to come away with a convincing, 82-43 victory.

After defeating Clairton and Riverside in the playoffs, Ford City experienced one of the most disappointing defeats imaginable, leading Midland, 47-46, with 8 seconds left. After a time out, Midland's Roosevelt Kirby tossed an off-balanced shot fading away toward the sideline near midcourt. That shot somehow hit the banking board and sailed through the net as disbelieving Ford City players fell to the floor in despair.

The Sabers rebounded to defeat PIAA opponents Sharpsville, Redbank Valley, Girard and Bishop Boyle to earn a spot in the state finals for the first time since 1948. But the Sabers never got un-tracked against York Catholic at the Civic Arena and dropped a 69-48 decision.

Credit: William Englert

Ford City coach Hube Rupert poses with key members of the 1948 WPIAL chanpions and PIAA runner-up.

Credit: William Englert

The Ford City team gets ready to board the bus to Philadelphia and the 1948 PIAA title game at the Penn Palestra. Front row from left: John Portasik (with bus driver's cap), John Gurski, Joe Krucar, Ed Halas, Bob Stivason, Howard Zerich, Gerry Slagle, Val Wojton, Bill Englert. Rear: Bill Jansen, John Skukalek, Don Wolfe, Rich Asay.

Credit: William Englert

Ford City (dark jerseys) takes on Wilkinsburg in the 1948 WPIAL semifinals at the Pitt Pavilion. Wearing No. 9 in white is Alexander Jaffurs, who later became mayor of Wilkinsburg and general counsel for the state Liquor Control Board.

Credit: Thomas Dinga

Ford City gets ready for updcoming season. From left, coach Mark Fruehan, Chuck Nelson, Tom Dinga, Don Tylinski, Marvin Russell and Steve Heffner.

chapter 3

DEFENSE RULES THE DAY

An old sports cliché says defense wins championships.

That was never more the case than in 1986 when the Burrell Bucs blanked three consecutive playoff opponents to win the WPIAL Class AA title, becoming the first school to pull off that remarkable feat.

Burrell opened the postseason with a 19-0 shocker over favored New Brighton. Defensive back Tom Hornack tied a state record with five pass interceptions.

A 14-0 whitewash over South Allegheny preceded a 3-0 victory in the championship game over Beth-Center at Three Rivers Stadium.

Burrell had a number of obstacles to overcome en route to the title.

Starting tailback Rob Hrivnak was injured before the season, forcing coach Al Mauro and his staff to elevate sophomore David Beal to the key position. Beal responded with 1,140 rushing yards and 15 TDs.

Nick Como, though undersized, ignited the offense to take some pressure off Beal. Como was adept at rolling out or dropping back with play action passes. He completed 60 of 110 passes for 1,010 yards and nine touchdowns.

The Bucs had a couple of close calls during the regular season, particularly a 12-6 win over Leechburg and a 7-0 escape at Jeannette. But as the regular season ended against Valley, Burrell could clinch the Allegheny Conference with a victory over their arch-rivals. The largest crowd in Buccaneers Stadium history – 6,512 – watched the Bucs handle Valley, 36-21.

But Matt Pletcher, John Motosicky and Chuck Johnston sustained injuries and tackle Jimmy Brown also missed time. Scott Miller was ill as the playoffs loomed.

However, Scott Johnson and Tim DeSantes filled in admirably and Brown eventually returned.

New Brighton rolled into Burrell with confidence, anywhere from a 10- to 15-point favorite.

But the Lions couldn't get untracked as Burrell picked off nine Dave DeMarco passes, including Hornack's five. Burrell's linebacking corps of Mark Shemanski, Tony Sharkins, Bryn Marelli and Mike Kennedy were superb, along with the secondary of Hornack, Dave Bellinotti and Ken Mazzei.

As a footnote to the game, Hornack and DeMarco later became teammates at Geneva College.

In the semifinals, South Allegheny dressed just 28 players. But the Gladiators were riding high, coming off a victory over Burgettstown in the playoff opener and hoping for their first trip to the finals in nine years.

The game was close until Mazzei returned a fumble for a touchdown, securing the win at Jeannette's McKee Stadium.

Interest was high as the WPIAL scheduled all four finals for Three Rivers for the first time. Burrell fans arrived at the stadium early, tailgating before the team arrived.

Once inside, it was all business at Beth-Center provided solid opposition. All the Bucs could manage was a 30-yard field goal by Rich Marriott. It was enough, though, as Burrell held on for a 3-0 victory.

The Bucs finished the season at 13-0.

The day turned into a veritable festival of high school football. A number of Kiski Area fans arrived early and rooted for Burrell, while some Bucs fans stayed after the trophy presentation and cheered for the neighboring Kiski Area Cavaliers against Mount Pleasant.

Most of the crowd of 34,454 was there for the Class AAAA matchup later in the evening as Gateway edged North Hills, 7-6.

The crowd would be the largest to witness WPIAL football until 2001 when more than 38,000 poured into Heinz Field to watch the football extravaganza.

It would be Mauro's second WPIAL title, coupled with the one he guided Plum to three years earlier. The championship came two years before the PIAA state football playoffs were instituted. Many Burrell fans have wondered for years how the Bucs could have fared against opponents from elsewhere in the state.

Awards came quickly after the season ended. Hornack was named WPIAL Class AA player of the year and second team all-state defensive back by the Associated Press.

Burrell returned the following season going undefeated in the regular season until losing to Valley, 27-7, in the regular season finale. That ended the Burrell winning streak at 24 games.

Burrell's Tom Hornack watches time expire on Nov. 8, 1986 as the Bucs upset New Brighton, 19-0, in the opening round of the WPIAL playoffs. Hornack's five interceptions in that game tied a state record.

Burrell players and cheerleaders celebrate winning the WPIAL title in a rally at Hillcrest Shopping Center, Lower Burrell, on Nov. 25, 1986.

chapter 4

THE NIGHT THE FOG CAME

It can be argued that the strangest sporting event in Alle-Kiski Valley history took place in New Kensington on Jan. 21, 1938. Ken High was playing host to Arnold in a basketball game at the old Ridge Avenue gym.

The buildup to that Friday game was substantial. Advance tickets were sold at Turner's Book Store in downtown New Kensington, and all 1,800 tickets were sold two days before the game. New Kensington school officials asked that anyone not holding a game ticket to stay home and avoid congestion around the school, located in a residential section of the city.

The gym's windows were opened so fans in the capacity crowd could feed a play-by-play to those non-seat holders who didn't heed the request to stay home. An unseasonably warm layer of air was sealed by a flow of cold air in the upper atmosphere, causing a fog to envelop the town. Condensation resulting from the fog seeped into the gym towards the floor, which was constructed of rubberized cork. By the end of the first half, the floor was extremely slippery. New Kensington school officials scattered some resin on the floor at halftime and ordered the windows closed.

Now the fog was trapped inside the gym and the damage was done. Players had trouble keeping their footing in the third period. At the quarter break, coach Carl 'Dutch' Glock conferred with game officials and, after a 10-minute huddle, decided to call the game with Ken High leading, 22-18. Arnold was on a hot pace before the game was called, and with one Ken High players fouled out and two more starters playing with three fouls – players fouled out with four personals then. – The reporter covering the game thought New Ken got a break when the game was called.

In that era, a game interrupted would have to be replayed in its entirety.

Administrators from both schools declared the game would be replayed only if it would help determine the outcome of the section championship.

Har-Brack won the section by two games and the game was never replayed.

Credit: Ken High yearbook

This is a look at the New Kensington High School gym along Ridge Avenue, site of the great 'fog-out' in 1938. This 1951 view shows how close the fans were to the action. The policeman with his foot on the bleachers is Barnet 'Barney' Sakulsky, who later became a Justice of the Peace.

chapter 5

THE MIRACLE AT THE PARK

Even in mid-autumn, the idyllic setting of Oakmont's Riverside Park remains one of the great venues for high school football. Besides the great setting, local fans highly anticipated the Nov. 12, 1994 playoff clash between the Riverview Raiders and the Jefferson-Morgan Rockets in the opening round of the WPIAL Class A tournament. After all, Riverview was undefeated and seeded No. 1 in the tourney. The Raiders had won just one of five previous WPIAL playoffs games, and the players were anxious to make up for past shortcomings.

What was close to the largest crowd in Riverside Park history filed in early. Fans who couldn't get seated in the bleachers stood, ringing the gridiron. The stadium press box was filled beyond capacity.

There was plenty of media interest in the game. At least two broadcast crews and representatives from at least 5 newspapers were ready to report on the game. In fact, the press box was so crowded that when a Riverview school official motioned to Allegheny County fire marshal and Oakmont resident, the late John Kaus, to come up and visit, some media members frantically asked the official to rescind the invitation for fear that Kaus would clean out the packed facility.

No one present could have predicted the amazing turn of events, late in the game, that has come to be known as The Miracle at the Park.

A desperation TD pass of 94 yards in the final minute of regulation play and another subsequent pass in the overtime period gave Riverview a 34-28 victory.

It was apparent early on that Jefferson-Morgan came to play. The Rockets took the opening kickoff and drove to the Riverview 1, picking up and first-and-goal. Jefferson-Morgan's three tries to break through came up short. Following third down, a delay of game penalty moved the ball back to the 8.

On fourth down, a screen pass to Nathan Hassett looked like a sure touchdown, but Orlando Bellisario knocked Hassett out of bounds inside the 1.

Mike McCort put Jefferson-Morgan on the scoreboard with a 36-yard TD run late in the first period. Scott Whetsell's 60-yard pass to Hassett late in the half gave the Rockets a 14-0 advantage.

Riverview finally got a break when an 8-yard punt by Matthew Dick gave the Raiders possession at the Jeff-Morgan 43. Quarterback Jeff Cappa broke the scoring ice for Riverview on a 5-yard run, but Jefferson-Morgan answered less than two minutes later with a 72-yard scoring run by Xavier Lockette to lead, 21-7, after three quarters.

With 8:19 left in the fourth quarter, Jason Cappa tossed a 10-yard scoring pass to twin brother, Jeff. Justin Graham's 2-point conversion run brought Riverview to within 21-15.

But Whetsell hit McCort with a 27-yard touchdown pass with 4:06 remaining, giving the Rockets a 28-15 lead.

Riverview wasn't through yet, however. The Raiders drove to the Jefferson-Morgan 34, and on a fourth down conversion attempt, Ben Erdeljac caught a 34-yard pass from Jason Cappa to make it 28-22 following Bellisario's extra point.

With no Riverview time outs remaining, the Rockets looked ready to put the game away after McCort got loose for a 46-yard run to the Riverview 5. All that was needed was for Whetsell to take a knee and run out the clock. Instead, Whetsell prepared to hand off to McCort. But Whetsell put the ball on McCort's hip, fumbling the exchange.

Riverview tackle Justin Pappa pounced on the football at the 6, allowing the Raiders a final gasp. It was the first time in 181 carries that McCort had fumbled the ball.

Andy Flaherty, the center, came running over to a stunned Raiders head coach Jake Cappa after the fortuitous change of possession.

"Coach, we need a play," Flaherty said. "Run a one-man fly," coach Cappa replied. That meant for one receiver, speedy sophomore Ben Erdeljac, to take off down field.

Cappa hit Erdeljac in stride at midfield and Erdeljac raced to the end zone for a 94-yard touchdown play.

The funniest part of the miraculous turn of events was seen

Credit: Riverview High School Library

Riverview head coach Jake Cappa talks with the media moments after the Raiders defeated Fort Cherry, 19-14, in the 1997 WPIAL Class A title game at Three Rivers Stadium. Cappa was the maestro of Riverview's log of 85 games won during the decade of the 1990s.

from the press box level. Much of the crowd, sensing the game was over, began to head for the exit. When they heard the roar of the crowd, fans tried to re-enter, only to meet up with fans also trying to leave, forming a glob of humanity at the gate. A couple of motorists on Third Avenue even abandoned their vehicles and ran in to see what all the excitement was about.

Riverview was called for a celebration penalty, sending the extra point attempt back 15 yards. Bellisario missed the point after setting up the overtime and more thrills.

The Rockets had first possession. On fourth down, Jeremy Dudczak broke through, grabbing Whetsell by his shoulder pad and throwing him down for an 8-yard loss.

It was then Riverview's turn. On the third play, Jeff Cappa threw a pass to Jason Cappa, who was heading for the right side of the end zone to end the game and give Riverview a 34-28 victory. The final play was "58 fade on 2." Later, son and assistant coach Johnny Cappa bought a dog and named him "On 2."

And Coach Cappa bought a boat and dubbed her "58 fade."

The Raiders followed with a semifinal victory the following week against Rochester before losing in the finals to Western Beaver at Three Rivers Stadium.

The Raiders finally broke through in 1997, defeating Fort Cherry, 19-14, on a 52-yard pass from Justin Dudczak to Chad Beynon, giving the school its first WPIAL football title.

The Miracle at the Park

Score by quarters: Jefferson-Morgan   7   7   7   7   0 - 28

Riverview   0   0   7   21   6 - 34

How they scored: J-M: Mike McCort 36 run (Mike Kubik kick), 0:10 1st
J-M: Nathan Hassett 60 pass from Scott Whetsell (Kubik kick), 2:38 2nd
Riv: Jeff Cappa 5 run (Orlando Bellisario kick), 1:54 3rd
J-M: Xavier Lockette 72 run (Kubik kick), 0:23 3rd
Riv: Jason Cappa 10 pass from Jeff Cappa (Justin Graham run) 8:19 4th
J-M: McCort 27 pass from Whetsell (Kubik kick), 4:06 4th
Riv: Ben Erdeljac 34 pass from Jeff Cappa (Bellisario kick), 1:49 4th
Riv: Erdeljac 94 pass from Jeff Cappa, kick failed, 0:36 4th
Riv: Jason Cappa 10 pass from Jeff Cappa OT

chapter 6

OUR PRECIOUS GEM

Pittsburgh industrialist Henry Clay Fownes designed only one golf course.

But that one is among the greatest golf courses in the world – Oakmont Country Club.

No matter whose rating system you use, Golf Digest Magazine, Golf Atlas, or, any number of websites devoted to evaluating golf courses, Oakmont always has an incredibly high ranking.

Late entertainer and golf enthusiast Bob Hope listed it among his favorite 18 courses, adding a blazer to his wardobe with a shade described as Oakmont Olive.

As for Fownes, it's like Leonardo da Vinci started off with the Mona Lisa and stopped right there. Fownes, 43 at the time, designed the course to challenge golfers with tight fairways, some 210 deep bunkers – including the famous Church Pews – and hard greens that slope away from the player.

The course is nestled in the beautiful rolling hills north of Pittsburgh, straddling the boroughs of Oakmont and Plum. Fownes obtained 221 acres of flat farmland, a tract difficult to find in western Pennsylvania. Oakmont Country Club conforms, in an odd way, to a bend in the Allegheny River below.

It's tantamount to a precious gem in the Alle-Kiski Valley.

Fownes founded the Oakmont Country Club in 1903 and the signature structure is the early 20th Century, gabled clubhouse. In that era, it served as a weekend retreat for about 100 prosperous Pittsburgh businessmen. It wasn't easy getting the course constructed. Fownes had to transport building materials and supplies up Hulton Road from the flats of Oakmont using 100 workmen and 25 teams of mules, as the automobile industry was in its infancy.

It didn't take long for the golfing community to fall in love with its setup, and Fownes (pronounced 'phones') remained the as president of the course's founders group until 1935. The course today is close to its original state. Trees were eventually planted, but 4,000 of them were removed prior to the 2007 U.S. Open.

The only other major change was the Pennsylvania Turnpike slicing through the course, starting in the late 1940s. The 8th hole was moved a few yards to the left to accommodate turnpike construction.

It didn't take long for the parade of national tournaments to begin making their way to Oakmont, starting with the U.S. Amateur in 1919. Oakmont has hosted 18 major championships, with the U.S. Women's Open arriving in 2010.

Many historic events have taken place at Oakmont, such as the performance by Johnny Miller at the 1973 U.S. Open where he shot an 8-under par 63 in what some call the greatest round of golf in the sport's history. Another memorable weekend at Oakmont was the 1978 PGA where John Mahaffey made up seven strokes in the final 14 holes and won a three-man playoff on the second hole of sudden death.

But any conversation about the great events held at Oakmont should begin with the 1962 U.S. Open. A week that ended up lasting eight days.

In the years leading up to the 62nd Open, Arnold Palmer was undoubtedly the king of golf. He not only won with regularity, but he was bringing golf to the masses. Steelworkers from the Pittsburgh area began following Arnie. He was easy to like, matinee-idol looks, a rather humble tone during interviews, and the ability to excite fans with come-from-behind efforts – even the ones that fell short.

Palmer's popularity, coupled with golf becoming a staple of network television, brought significantly larger purses to the players.

Also emerging that famous weekend was a 22-year old golfer fresh out of Ohio State University, Jack Nicklaus. Compared to Palmer's virile charm, Nicklaus was chubby and often-scowling. Nicklaus was a rookie on the pro tour – still looking for his first victory. Jack has finished in the money, however, in every tournament that season and had already set the rookie record with $30,000 in winnings.

Nicklaus finished second in the Thunderbird Open the previous week and was yearning for that breakthrough victory. It's been said that champions are made while nobody is watching, and with the events of Tuesday evening, June 12, 1962, that might be true. Nicklaus had just completed eight hours of practice on the famed course. It was 7:30, and Jack was finishing dinner. He looked out onto the course and decided he could get in a few more holes, according to a *Sports Illustrated* article by Dan Jenkins in 1973. Nicklaus and his caddie went back out onto the course and played seven holes before nightfall. Palmer didn't go back out, but was impressed with Jack's desire.

The next day's practice round was rained out, and Palmer and Nicklaus would be paired in the same group throughout the tournament, which began, as tradition dictates, on a Thursday.

Palmer, the pre-tournament favorite, appeared poised to take control by the 18th hole on Saturday, a round that was witnessed by a then-record crowd of 24,492. Arnie's drive and approach was wildly cheered by fans who sensed he was about to take a 2-stroke lead going in to the tournament's final day. But disaster struck. Palmer missed a 5-foot putt and a subsequent 2-footer. Nicklaus, meanwhile, had rather quietly played a 72 to come within two strokes of the lead.

The final portion of Sunday's round was similar, with Palmer missing putts on Nos. 17 and 18 as Nicklaus seized the momentum to tie Arnie at 283 after 72 holes.

In the 18-hole Monday playoff, Nicklaus had a 4-stroke lead after 6 holes, but Palmer had cut the lead to one after 12 holes. But Arnie three-putted the 13th, and Nicklaus seemingly never looked back that day, or for years afterwards.

Nicklaus won $17,500 of an $81,600 purse.

Besides the '62 Open, here's a look at the tournaments that made Oakmont famous:

U.S. Open Championships

1927
Won by Tommy Armour, who defeated Harry Cooper in a playoff. Prize money was $800.

1935
A shocking upset by South Hills CC pro Sam Parks Jr. at 11 strokes. Total prize money was $5,000.

1953
Ben Hogan won his second of three straight majors by coming in at 5-under par. The prize money totaled $14,900.

1973
Johnny Miller shot a final round 63 (8 under par) for a record low score at a U.S. Open. He won by just one stroke. Miller entered the final day in 12th place and took advantage of an overnight rainfall that softened the course. He bogeyed just one hole –the 8th– en route to a score that has never been equaled in a Major.

1983
Larry Nelson shot 65-67 over the final two rounds, breaking the previous Open record by four shots. Nelson earned $72,000 of a $506,184 purse.

1994
Ernie Els outlasted Loren Roberts and Colin Montgomerie in a Monday playoff as temperatures approached 100 degrees. Els earned $320,000 of a $1.75 million purse.

2007
Argentine Angel Cabrera defeated Tiger Woods with a 5-over par 285. Cabrera earned $1.26 million of a $7.0 million purse.

PGA Tournaments

1922
Gene Sarazen, just 20 years old, defeated Emmett French, 4 & 3, in the finals of a match play event.

1951
Slammin' Sammy Snead defeated Walter Burkemo, 7 & 6, in match play. The following year, and continuing up to 1970, 19 different golfers won the PGA Tournament.

1978

In the greatest come-from-behind effort in tournament stroke-play history, John Mahaffey trailed Tom Watson by 7 strokes going into the final day of play. Mahaffey carded a 66 while Watson staggered to a 73. Mahaffey then sank a 12-foot birdie on the second playoff hole to win. His opening day 75 put him in 47th place overall.

U.S. Women's Open

1994

Less than five years after she lost her home and personal possessions in the San Francisco earthquake, Pattty Sheehan birdied the final two holes to tie Juli Inkster forcing an 18-hole playoff, where she won by two strokes.

2010

? ? ?

U.S. Amateur

1919

S. Davidson Herron defeated Bobby Jones in match play 5 & 4.

1925

Jones returned to Oakmont and defeated Watts Gun 8 & 7.

1938

William Turnesa defeated B. Patrick Abbott 8 & 7

1969

Steve Melnyk bested Vinnie Giles 280 to 291.

2003

Australian Nick Flanagan became the first non-American to win Amateur since 1971.

Credit: Courtesy Oakmont Country Club historical dept.

This is a 2007 panoramic view of the historic clubhouse at the Oakmont Country Club. On June 17, 2009, it was announced that the club will host the 2016 U.S. Open.

Credit: Courtesy Oakmont Country Club historical dept.

The crowd crosses the Pennsylvania Turnpike during the 1962 U.S. Open. The narrow bridge was replaced in 2006.

Credit: Courtesy Oakmont Country Club historical dept.

This is the most famous picture in Oakmont Country Club history. Veteran Arnold Palmer congratulates rookie Jack Nicklaus on June 18, 1962 after Nicklaus won an 18-hole playoff.

chapter 7

THIRD SHALL BE THE BEST

Sometimes, the third choice turns out to be the best. That's what the Kiski Area School District found out when it was searching for the person to run its football program when the high school first opened its doors in 1962.

The new school district, a consolidation of Vandergrift and Bell-Avon high schools, first settled on Ray Fiorini, the coach who led Avella to the WPIAL Class B title in 1961.

But, at the same time, that school district elevated Fiorini to the principal's job.

Kiski Area then turned its attention to Ronald Corrigan, coach of Tyrone High School. But the superintendent there would not release Corrigan from his contract and gave him a substantial pay raise, leaving the fledgling school district in a lurch.

With the season just around the corner, assistant coach Frank Morea, a holdover from the Vandergrift staff, told Kiski Area officials to contact his buddy from their playing days at Slippery Rock College, Dick Dilts.

Dilts was coaching Richland High School at the time, but he agreed to come on board and Kiski Area finally had a coach for its lidlifter on Sept. 7, 1962 against Greensburg. Though Dilts was the third choice, he quickly established the Cavaliers as one of the top programs in the WPIAL, eventually attracting national attention. Kiski Area went undefeated in 1964, its third season. The Cavaliers once won 45 straight Foothills Conference football games, then a WPIAL record. Kiski Area made the WPIAL title game in 1968, '70, '71 and '86, bringing home the championship in 1971. It took the Cavaliers less than 14 seasons to win 100 games; less than 29 seasons to win 200 games. The school won 13 conference titles under Dilts.

But it was tough at the start.

Just a few minutes into the first game ever against Greensburg, Golden Lions tackle Don Bailey picked up a fumble, one of nine on the night for the Kiski Area backfield, and things went downhill from there. Greensburg won, 47-0, and Bailey later became a U.S. Congressman and Pennsylvania's auditor general.

Kiski Area would win just one game that first season, a 13-12 decision over Latrobe. Things got better the second season, as the Cavaliers posted a 4-6 mark. But 1964 proved to be Kiski Area's breakout season. The Cavaliers went 10-0, with the closest game being a 14-7 victory over Hempfield in Week Four.

Kiski Area outscored the opposition 393-76 and had the state's leading scorer, Phil 'Jo-Jo' Booker, who tallied 24 touchdowns and was named second-team all-state by the UPI.

Kiski Area won the Foothills Conference title, but the team couldn't accumulate enough Gardner Points to qualify for the WPIAL title game. Instead, Aliquippa defeated Monongahela, 7-0. Many felt the Cavaliers could have beaten either team that afternoon at Pitt Stadium.

But off the field, all the success brought together the diverse factions of the new school district, a conglomeration of nine municipalities that included the boroughs of Vandergrift, East Vandergrift, Avonmore, Hyde Park, Parks Township, Allegheny Township and Bell Township.

By 1965, Washington Township and Oklahoma Borough had come on board. Dilts and his staff had successfully melded the kids from the urbanized neighborhoods with the kids from the more rural sections of the school district. The next two seasons brought respectable records of 5-4-1 in 1965 and 6-4 in 1966.

But those marks paled in comparison to what was just around the corner.

The Big K Dynasty

From 1967 through 1972, Kiski Area put together a remarkable run of 57 wins and only 6 losses. Few schools ever approached that rate of success, a .904 winning percentage.

There were great players during that run, such as 19 different players named to all-state teams selected by the AP and the UPI

But the real secret to the Cavaliers' success took place off the field while nobody was watching.

Credit: Kiski Area Sports Hall of Fame

Here is the first undefeated Kiski Area football team from 1964: Front row, from left, Assistant Tony Nicholas, Jerry Minik, James Lewis, Larry Orvosh, Charles Lutz, Phil 'Jo-Jo' Booker, Danny Fassio, Mike Olinger, Dan Reilly, Richard Price, Joe Kotts, assistant Frank Morea. Row two: Head coach Dick Dilts, Ralph Antenucci, Lewis Lawhorn, Chester Jastrzemski, James Bolcar, Rich Helhowski, John Gaydeski, Walt Poleski, Ivan White, James Woods. Back row: George Miller, Dennis Morabito, Harry Cleveland, Mike Meighan, Alam Smetanick, Frank Poleski, William Donaldson, Joe McCain, Anthony Nicholas, Ken Donaldson.

Credit: Valley News Dispatch

The famous Forbes Field scoreboard is in the background on Nov. 15, 1968 as Latrobe's Jim Siko tries an extra point against Kiski Area.

Dilts and his staff created a weight training and nutrition program that seemed light years ahead of other high school programs. Even the players who weren't large in stature were in shape and their bodies were configured for master efficiency. Dilts also was big on nutrition. Players would eat foods tailored to weather conditions. For hot days early in the season, Dilts had his players eat certain foods and change the menu later in the season for chilly nights.

Another ingredient was the old adage that you get quality from quantity. At Kiski Area, there would often be around 100 athletes out for football. There were a number of years where Kiski Area fielded a varsity team, a junior varsity team, a 10th grade team and a freshman team. Many players didn't have a chance to start until their senior season.

In 1967, the Cavaliers appeared ready for another run at an undefeated season. But in the penultimate game of the season, Wilkinsburg knocked Kiski Area from the WPIAL title race, 14-0, in a Foothills Conference game.

That would be the last conference loss as the following week against Connellsville, the Cavaliers embarked on a 45-game conference winning streak with a 14-0 victory. Kiski Area wouldn't lose another regular season conference game until Sept. 21, 1973.

Kiski Area got off to another flying start in 1968, this time resulting in its first WPIAL title-game appearance. The Cavaliers lost to Latrobe, 19-7 on the muddy outfield grass at Forbes Field, following two days of torrential rains.

Kiski Area's stellar defense had yielded just 727 rushing yards overall in 10 regular season games, but gave up 208 vs. Latrobe.

It turned out to be the final WPIAL title game at Forbes Field.

While another conference title was collected in '69, the Cavaliers were eliminated from the WPIAL title race on the second week of the regular season, losing a non-conference shocker to Highlands, 16-14.

In 1970, Kiski Area didn't take any chances, rolling through 10 regular season games, winning by an average margin of 29.7 points per game. The defense again was spectacular, shutting out six of the 10 opponents.

As old Forbes Field met the wrecking ball, the Three Rivers

Stadium era was ushered in and the Cavaliers were matched up against Mt. Lebanon. The Blue Devils won convincingly, 35-12. After the game in the Kiski Area locker room, Dilts told the underclassmen "to take a good look at the place, because they won't see it again."

Dilts made the statement because only two starters would return for the 1971 season. But the players heard their coach's words and wanted to prove him wrong.

Did they ever.

With 20 new starters on the field, Kiski Area traveled to Norwin and pounded the Knights, 48-20. The Cavaliers were relentless, scoring an average of 38.3 points per game over their first six outings, setting up a showdown with similarly undefeated Hempfield.

On Oct. 22, 1971 before what is widely believed to be the largest crowd in Davis Field history, some 9,500 fans watched Kiski Area get by the Spartans, 13-8. Victories over Wilkinsburg and Greensburg Salem rounded out the conference schedule. In the regular season finale, the Cavaliers traveled to Highlands and made sure the upset that occurred in Natrona Heights two years earlier wasn't repeated as Kiski Area racked up a school record for points in a game by battering the Golden Rams, 56-7.

The Cavaliers were the beneficiary of a major change in WPIAL policy. For the first time, all undefeated and untied teams in a classification would engage in a playoff tournament. In Class AA, then the largest classification, there were three undefeated teams – Kiski Area, Penn Hills and Thomas Jefferson.

TJ would sit out while Kiski Area and Penn Hills would decide the Jaguars' opponent.

In the first-ever, sub-championship playoff game, the Cavaliers and the Indians were tied, 6-6, late in the contest. Since somebody would have to advance, the WPIAL said the winner of a tie game would be determined by overall offensive yardage.

The Cavaliers started a late drive at their 33, knowing that they couldn't possibly catch Penn Hills in yardage. With the ball on the Penn Hills 8 and 37 seconds left in the game, Joe Stone kicked a 25-yard field goal to give Kiski Area the win, 9-6.

Remember the Cavs

Dilts turned out to be technically correct with the statement he made after the 1970 title game loss: The Cavaliers wouldn't see the inside of Three Rivers Stadium. That's because the finals were scheduled for Pitt Stadium.

An early touchdown by Steve Kanas and an extra point and a field goal by Stone put the Cavaliers ahead, 10-0. But Thomas Jefferson shook off three weeks of idleness and came back to make it 10-8. A potential game-winning field goal with 3:08 to play misfired. Kiski Area, however, scored an insurance touchdown on quarterback Tom Giotto's 45-yard run with 1:08 remaining for a 16-8 victory.

The accolades kept coming for the Cavaliers. Soon after the game, Kiski Area (12-0) was rated the No. 1 team in the state according to the ranking system devised by PIAA historian Dr. Roger B. Saylor.

In a poll sponsored by the St. Paul Pioneer Press, the Kiski Area finished fifth in the country. The No.3 team that season was E.C. Williams High School in Alexandria, Va., the team immortalized in the movie *Remember the Titans*.

Kiski Area marched on in 1972, setting a school record by yielding just 25 points in the regular season. But in a playoff game at Three Rivers, Gateway took the measure of the Cavaliers, 22-13.

In 1973, Kiski Area showed no sign of letting up, starting the campaign with a 7-0 win at Derry Area and a 14-7 decision over Latrobe for the 45th straight Foothills Conference victory.

Streak-stopper

The Cavaliers rolled into New Kensington to play the Valley Vikings, who were 2-0 for the first time. In fact, it was the first time Valley had ever won 2 in a row since coming on the scene in 1967.

But Kiski Area was confident. After all, it had outscored Valley, 279-15 in the six previous games between the two schools, and 158-8 the past three years.

More than 9,000 had crammed into 8,000-seat Valley Memorial Stadium, the most for a regular season game since the championship runs of the late 1940s. The pre-game atmosphere was incredible.

In the opening drive, Valley drove from its own 24-yard line to the Kiski Area 35 on eight straight rushing plays. Then Vikings coach Tim Thyreen called for a play-action pass. Quarterback Frank Milito spotted tight end Paul Collodi open for a touchdown. Later in the first quarter, John Martin weaved 44 yards for a touchdown to make it 14-0.

Valley outgained Kiski Area, 165-45, in the first half.

But the second half was different, as the Cavaliers dominated. Vince Woody's 2-yard burst and a 2-point conversion made it 14-8 Valley. Kiski Area smelled a comeback, regaining possession in the fourth quarter. The Cavaliers drove to the Valley 32, but Paul Collodi recovered a fumble for the Vikings. After a lengthy delay while the officials tried to determine possession, Collodi finally emerged with the football and Valley, despite being outgained by Kiski Area in the second half 123 yards to minus-18, held on to the victory, ending Kiski Area's 45-game Foothills Conference winning streak.

The Cavaliers would finish the campaign 6-3, followed by a 6-2-1 mark in 1974.

Sharing the Wealth

Following what, for Kiski Area, were subpar seasons, Dilts and the Cavaliers staff realized why the rest of the Foothills Conference was catching up to them: Kiski Area's generosity was backfiring.

The weight and nutrition training the Cavaliers were using was so effective that Dilts and his staff traveled to other schools to demonstrate the secret of Kiski Area's success. Now, those same schools were beating the Cavaliers.

By the time the 1975 season arrived, the WPIAL had taken over conference alignments. Before then, schools were on their own in formulating conferences and conference schedules. The All-West Conference was broken up as Penn Hills and Johnstown were shifted to the Foothills Conference, while Wilkinsburg, facing a severe population decline, left to join the Class AA ranks.

Kiski Area was back on top, winning the Foothills in '75. The biggest victory of the season was a hard-fought 18-13 win at Penn Hills. It was also the 100th victory in school history as the boosters club treated the players at Johnny Garneau's Restaurant in Monroeville, a top-notch dining facility in its day.

In the 1975 Class AAA playoff opener, Kiski Area lost to North Allegheny, 13-10, in the first overtime game in WPIAL history. It was the initial game using the National Federation rules where each team would have an opportunity to score from the 10-yard line.

The road to the 1979 Foothills title was a strange one. Kiski Area's only conference loss was to Penn Hills, 14-0, as the Indians appeared head toward a fourth consecutive WPIAL title. But it was discovered late in the season that Penn Hills used an ineligible player in three games and had to forfeit those wins. Those reversals made Kiski Area the conference winner. But Penn Hills took legal action and won a stay of the WPIAL's ruling, essentially allowing the Indians to enter the WPIAL playoffs. After a delay of a week to the start of the playoffs, Penn Hills won the title on a snowy night over neighboring Gateway, 3-0.

The WPIAL eventually prevailed in court, long after the playoffs. As a result, Kiski Area stayed home from the 1979 postseason, though it was the Foothills Conference champion.

Dilts would have one more championship-game run, coming in 1986 when the Cavaliers faced former Foothills Conference rival Mount Pleasant at Three Rivers Stadium. In one of the most exciting finishes in WPIAL history, the Cavaliers trailed Mount Pleasant, 13-7, with the ball at their 33 and 1:02 showing on the clock. On the fourth play of the drive from the Mount Pleasant 31, quarterback Tim Joyner found tight end Dean Yanacci in the end zone with eight seconds remaining.

The moment Yanacci scored, Dilts spun around to the press box and held two fingers in the air, signally the decision to go for a two-point conversion and win the game. The Cavaliers lined up in the Power-I and halfback John Vida got the call. Vida got through the initial resistance, but couldn't get past the second wave of Vikings tacklers, and Mount Pleasant took home a 14-13 victory.

The final conference title of Dilts' career came in 1990 as the Cavaliers won the Quad East Conference and lost in the semifinals to North Allegheny.

Dilts retired after the 1992 season with 234 victories, 90 losses and seven ties. He ranks ninth on the WPIAL list for coaching victories.

Credit: Kiski Area Sports Hall of Fame

Davis Field was the place to be, particularly during Kiski Area's 45-game conference winning streak from 1967-73. The program's motto was 'We Believe.' Judging by the big crowds, there were a lot of believers.

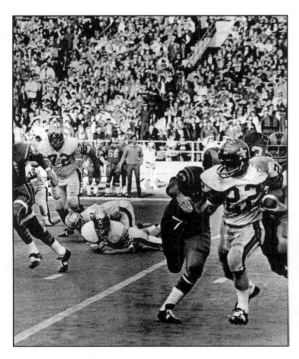

Credit: Kiski Area Sports Hall of Fame

Kiski Area's Jim Minik looks to turn the corner at Three Rivers Stadium in 1970 against Mt. Lebanon. Minik had one of the area's best seasons as a special teams member, returning 10 punts and kickoffs for TD's.

Credit: Valley News Dispatch archives

Kiski Area halfback Larry Wilson (40) looks for some running room on Nov. 19, 1971 as the Cavaliers battled Penn Hills at Latrobe in the WPIAL semifinals. Kiski Area advanced with a 9-6 victory.

Credit: Kiski Area Sports Hall of Fame

The Kiski Area braintrust for many years included assistant Tony Nicholas (left), head coach Dick Dilts and assistant Frank Morea.

Credit: Kiski Area Sports Hall of Fame

Tom Giotto (15) takes the snap for Kiski Area at Pitt Stadium on Nov. 27, 1971 as the Cavaliers defeated Thomas Jefferson. 16-8, in the WPIAL title game.

Credit: Kiski Area Sports Hall of Fame

1971 WPIAL Champions

First row, from left: Paul Ross, Doug Sober, Joe Pierret, Steve Kanas, Tom Giotto, Joe Lynch, Dave Soltis, Marty Carricato, Mike Milito, Joe Carpentiere, Tom King, Dan Bufalini. Second row: John Jackson, Don Cocco, Jim Scalzott, Bob Silva, Dave Greenlee, Frank DeCarlo, John Varhola, Barry Lekavich, Gary Mazanek, John Urik, Joe Weaver, Larry Wilson, Sam Anderson, Neil Capretto.

Third row: Craig Phillips, Keith Weaver, Joe Jackson, Mike Hansen, Dave Uskuraitis, Ulers Tutchstone, Casimer Maszgay, Bill Marhefka, Bob Hrobak, Tom Booker, Rich Rearigh, Don Miller, Clyde Shutt, Martin Feroce, Roger Grimm, Randy Milliron. Last row: Dan Lace, John Stancik, Tom Lekavich, Larry Gibson, Eugene Jankowski, Steve Earley, Joe Stone, Jim Henderson, Joe Bushovsky, Ray Newell, Paul Noble, Jim Bracy, Russ Clark, Dave Hildebrand.

Credit: Kiski Area Sports Hall of Fame

Pitt officials cleared the field of snow in time for Kiski Area's game against Thomas Jefferson on Nov. 27, 1971.

chapter 8

The Hoops Master

In 1947, Springdale High School teacher Chuck DeVenzio took the basketball head coaching job as a way to supplement his income after a one-year stint in North Lima, Ohio.

One couldn't blame him; teachers were only making a salary of about $1,600 then. That's $1,600 - per year. These days, for a teacher with a Masters degree and over 30 years of experience, $1,600 is an ordinary week.

But that bid for a little more income ultimately resulted in a legendary coaching career. DeVenzio, or simply 'DV' as many called him, won 659 games, 2 WPIAL championships, 2 state championships (one in Pennsylvania, the other in North Carolina) and gained entry into numerous halls of fame.

While DeVenzio is credited with guiding Ambridge High School to the WPIAL and PIAA titles in 1967 with what many call the greatest team in Western Pennsylvania history, his career basically began and ended in the same place – Springdale.

There was always something about Springdale that kept him coming back. His first stint at Springdale lasted 20 years before he moved on to Ambridge. When the Dynamos had a coaching vacancy in 1977, he came back for just one year, but he helped lay the foundation for another stellar Springdale run of success.

During the 1980's when the call went out for a girls coach, DeVenzio rode to the rescue, even though he had never been a girls coach. After Harry Orbin left the head coaching ranks to concentrate on administrative work in 1988, the legendary coach returned for a final, three-year stint that put the finishing touch on an incredible career.

While DeVenzio's teams included some immensely-talented players, many of those 659 victories came while working with players of average talent.

The Secret of Success

DeVenzio's secret? Defense. He employed a devastating match-up zone defense that zeroed in on the other team's strengths. Often, the defenses would switch during games, further befuddling opponents. By the time the fourth quarter would roll around, teams would simply be worn down.

Watching DeVenzio coach was sometimes the highlight of a game for fans and the media. Coaches were not allowed to stand during play throughout much of his career, but his antics from a seated position were memorable. When he did stand during a time out, he would hold the palm of his hand a few inches from his mouth, hollering at a referee. The puzzled official really couldn't call a technical foul because he couldn't see DeVenzio's lips move.

While many basketball programs employ a sophisticated style of scouting opponents and breaking down the opposition on tape or by live charting, DeVenzio didn't believe in scouting.

Once a game got underway and he recognized what the opposition was doing, he'd simply call time and make the proper adjustments. DeVenzio also displayed a fierce passion for the fundamentals of the game.

When the PIAA tried to limit the time coaches could spend with their teams during the off-season, DeVenzio had a simple solution: An alley ran beside the rear of his home in Springdale. He put up a hoop, painted regulation boundary lines, and had his players come over and play in the alley while he sat on the porch and watched.

DeVenzio, in no uncertain terms, put Springdale on the basketball map. On Jan. 29, 1960, DeVenzio brought the Dynamos to Farrell High School to face the defending state champs who were nearly invincible at home. The Steelers had won their last 16 games and hadn't lost at home in more than a year. Nearly 3,000 fans packed the gym, expecting to see a routine Farrell victory.

Springdale and Farrell were neck-and-neck, heading toward the final seconds. Curt Carson hit two free throws to make it 44-43, Springdale. But All-American Willie Somerset's jumper gave Farrell a 45-44 advantage. Carson drove toward the hoop but was fouled just before the buzzer sounded.

The Farrell fans seated in the balcony above the Springdale hoop were so raucous they caused the banking board to shake. The moving target didn't bother Carson, who calmly sank both foul shots for a 46-45 Springdale win.

The reaction was sudden and swift.

"I got all sorts of calls the next day asking 'what are you called, Springfield, Springdale, or what?'" DeVenzio said.

Jack Derlink, a junior on the team who later coached at Kiski Area and Burrell high schools recalled a Farrell-area radio station wondering "who was that hick town that beat Farrell?"

It was a signature win in DeVenzio's career.

In his final years of his first go-around at Springdale, DeVenzio's teams played in the largest enrollment classification and constantly defeated schools 2 or 3 times its size such as Penn Hills, Churchill and Gateway. The 1966 regular season ended in a tie with Fox Chapel, as Springdale again won a series of games it had no business winning. The Foxes won the tiebreaker game, and, soon after, DeVenzio answered the call to go to Ambridge and be part of history.

Over and Back

DeVenzio, along with his son, Dick, one of the top high school players in the country, led Ambridge to a 27-0 record. Dick De-Venzio, whose devastatingly-long jump shots could tear the heart out of an opponent, went to Duke University. Teammate Denny Wuysick also earned All-America status and went to North Carolina. Both players had their jersey numbers retired by the Ambridge Area School District. The tiny Ambridge gym could only seat about 210 fans at the time, but interest in Ambridge basketball was so huge that a closed-circuit TV system was set up in the cafeteria, allowing more fans to watch the Bridgers.

Observers recall the fans in the gym cheering a great Ambridge play, then, a second later, hearing cheers from the cafeteria as fans watched on a slight delay.

Ambridge put the icing on a memorable cake by dismantling a previously-undefeated Chester team by 32 points in the state title game.

Ten years after the Ambridge team became an instant legend,

DeVenzio returned to Springdale and finished the regular season tied with Mars, necessitating a playoff for second place. Mars led Springdale by 14 points early in the fourth quarter. DeVenzio called one of his famous time outs at the right time, igniting a furious Dynamos rally that tied the game. Mars eventually eked out a 58-54 victory, but DeVenzio had made his mark again. He came back to Springdale in 1987 to guide the girls team, though he had never coached females before.

In an interview where the question of how he adjusted to coaching girls basketball arose, DeVenzio said: "At least they smell better than the boys."

But it was soon time to switch back to the boys. At 67, he returned to the boys program once again, leading the Dynamos to the 1989 WPIAL Class AA title, the first in the glorious Springdale basketball history.

From the first weekend of the1988-89 season, it quickly became apparent that the campaign would evolve into a DeVenzio nostalgia tour. The Dynamos won the A.E. O'Block Tip-Off Tournament at Plum by defeating Hampton and Penn-Trafford, much larger schools than Springdale. Four nights later, scouts from five upcoming Springdale opponents were in the stands watching the Dynamos dismantle Freeport and see DeVenzio's matchup defense in the flesh.

In Game 7 against Mars on Dec. 22, 1988, DeVenzio reached a milestone, winning the 600th game of his illustrious career as the Dynamos hammered the Planets, 62-41.

The only game Springdale would lose in the regular season would be to Monessen in a Christmas Tournament. The Dynamos finished the regular season at 23-1 and drew a first round bye in the WPIAL Class AA playoffs. In the playoff opener against Wilkinsburg, it looked as if the Dynamos would be making a quick exit from the postseason, trailing Wilkinsburg, 59-49, with 5 minutes to go. But Springdale, supported by a huge fan following, went on a 19-4 tear to finish the game and emerge a 68-63 winner.

After an 83-80 semifinal win against Rochester, Springdale headed to Pitt's Fitzgerald Field House for the WPIAL title game. Brentwood was the favorite, but Springdale was undaunted, building up a 15-point lead before Brentwood came back. Springdale's late spurt earned a 76-74 victory behind Jeff Clark's 28 points.

Springdale would lose to Brentwood in the PIAA semifinals to finish at 29-2.

DeVenzio, with no starters returning, led the Dynamos to another playoff berth the following season, finishing at 15-10.

It became apparent that the 1990-91 season would be DeVenzio's last, and the Dynamos wanted to send him out a winner. In the WPIAL semifinal, however, at Duquesne University's Palumbo Center, Springdale and Clairton came down to the final seconds when point guard Brian Guerrieri severely sprained an ankle.

Without their floor leader, the Dynamos couldn't escape Clairton, but defeated Sharpsville in the PIAA opener. Two nights later on March 14, 1991, Conemaugh Township defeated Springdale, 68-47, and DeVenzio's career ended with 659 victories. DeVenzio died on Nov. 12, 2006.

Credit: A-K Valley Sports Hall of Fame

Springdale graduate Denny Ferguson guards an opponent while playing for Duke at Cameron Indoor Stadium. Ferguson helped lead the Dynamos to the 1961 section title and an undefeated regular season

Credit: Valley News Dispatch

Ambridge's Dick DeVenzio (11) gets ready for a shot against Fox Chapel at the Civic Arena on March 3, 1967.

Credit: Valley News Dispatch

Springdale coach Chuck De-Venzio confers with his team during a time out on Dec. 22, 1988 at Mars High School where Springdale defeated the Planets, 62-41, for De-Venzio's 600th career victory.

Credit: Valley News Dispatch

Springdale coach Chuck DeVenzio shouts instructions from the bench at the Pitt Field House on March 10,1989 at the WPIAL Class AA championship game.

Credit: Valley News Dispatch

The Springdale Dynamos celebrate their 1989 WPIAL championship game victory over Brentwood.

chapter 9

A CATCH FOR THE AGES

College football celebrated its 140th anniversary in 2009.

And in the 14 decades since Princeton and Rutgers locked horns to begin intercollegiate football in 1869, one of the most memorable plays involves an area athlete.

Burrell graduate John Brown's touchdown on a 33-yard pass play from quarterback Dan Marino gave Pitt a 24-20 victory over Georgia in the Sugar Bowl on Jan. 1, 1982.

Following a season that ended with a No. 2 national ranking, Pitt was undefeated before losing to Penn State in the 1981 regular season finale at Pitt Stadium. Georgia, with sophomore running back Herschel Walker, was the defending national champion, looking for another undefeated season that night in the Louisiana Superdome.

Georgia had a 20-17 lead late in the game. Pitt took over and had time for a final scoring drive.

Marino surprised everybody with an 8-yard, fourth-down quarterback keeper for a first down and wide receiver Dwight Collins recovered a fumble to keep the drive alive.

Pitt finally made it to the Georgia 33 but faced another fourth down situation and called a time out.

A field goal would have tied the game and the Bulldogs would have finished 11-0-1 and probably won the national title. But Marino sold coach Jackie Sherrill on the idea of going for the victory.

Pitt broadcaster Bill Hillgrove was on the sidelines that game because the Mutual Broadcasting Company had the radio rights to game. Hillgrove recalled assistant coach Sal Sunseri pleading with Sherrill to kick a field goal.

But Marino said:"We didn't come down here to play for a tie, let's try to win. Give me the ball and I'll win the game."

Assistant coach Joe Daniels made the final call from the booth. It was a "check with me" play where Marino would read the defense at the line and make the call.

Indeed, Marino saw the strong safety coming up to blitz and called "69," which meant the backs would stay in and block. Brown then moved into a slot.

A tight end, Brown came to Pitt as a wide receiver, but was switched to tight end in 1981 after Benji Pryor graduated. So, at 6-foot-4, 218 pounds, he had receiver's speed and he needed it to get inside of the coverage man.

Marino dropped back 13 or 14 yards, as opposed to the five or six yards he normally set up from, fired a perfect pass to Brown who jammed the ball underneath his chin guard and took a hit from a defender.

Georgia took the ensuing kickoff and began a late drive, but Panthers safety Troy Hill, who would later go on to coach Valley High School, intercepted a pass to seal the victory.

Clemson was named the No. 1 team in the country the following day as Georgia fans silently headed back to the Peach State after seeing a second consecutive national championship slip through their hands.

Bulldogs fans were really floored when it they discovered that Brown grew up on Georgia Avenue in Lower Burrell.

Brown has never liked the notoriety for a single play, and he has a point. He finished the season with 43 catches for 530 yards, But like it or not, he will always be associated with that magical moment.

Brown and Marino reenacted the play in 2000, the last year of Three Rivers Stadium. By then, both players' knees had shown the effects of football, but the fans got to see to see the two hook up for one more time.

Credit: A–K Valley Sports Hall of Fame

Burrell graduate John Brown played tight end for Pitt from 1979-82.

Credit: University of Pittsburgh athletics

John Brown and Dan Marino triumphantly leave the field after the two hooked up for one of the most memorable plays in college football bowl history on Jan. 1, 1982.

chapter 10

BE A GIANT

When Willie Thrower was asked to give a young person advice, he made it very simple:"In everything you do – be a giant." But it was Thrower who made gigantic contributions to the game of football. From his passing ability in helping New Kensington High School to back-to-back WPIAL football titles to his trailblazing efforts as the first black Big 10 quarterback at Michigan State to the first black quarterback in the NFL, Thrower had to navigate his way through racial barriers that were difficult to overcome.

Legendary coach Don Fletcher saw Thrower's talent early, inserting him as a freshman halfback in 1945 on team that would eventually become known nationwide. Thrower always seemed to be a giant in the biggest games, even as a ninth grader.

In the 1945 regular season finale, the Red Raiders needed a win over Redstone High School of Fayette County to clinch a berth in the WPIAL championship game. Ken High fell behind early, but the Red Raiders switched to a passing attack out of the single wing offense, where Thrower thrived. Thrower's passing led to a second half comeback that resulted in a 26-20 victory.

After losing the WPIAL title game to powerful Donora, 38-6, the Red Raiders would not drop another football game until the penultimate game of Thrower's senior season in 1948.

The 1946 season saw many key members return to pick up where they left off. Ken High rolled over eight opponents by an average of 26 points per game. The closest game was a 19-6 victory over Har-Brack in Week Four.

It became apparent that New Kensington and Vandergrift would be the only undefeated, untied teams in the WPIAL Class AA ranks. So when the clash between the two teams took place, the game had to be moved to Forbes Field.

Ken High won that one, 21-0, completing the regular season by never yielding more than one touchdown a game. The Red Raiders outscored the opposition, 232-25.

The WPIAL declared Ken High the WPIAL champion, since

it was the only undefeated and untied team.

But the season didn't exactly have a happy ending. Promoters of the Peanut Bowl in Miami invited Ken High to the Sunshine State with one stipulation – the team would have to leave the black players, Thrower and Flint Greene, behind because the Jim Crow Laws prevented integrated athletic events. Fletcher and the team agreed that if everybody doesn't go, then nobody goes. McKeesport went in Ken High's place.

Thrower and backfield mates George 'Cubby' France, Vince Pisano and Harold 'Hawk' Vestrand all returned for the 1947 season. Not only was Ken High the defending WPIAL champs, but Memorial Stadium swung open its doors for the first time on Sept. 6, 1947. "It was the Cadillac of stadiums at the time," France said.

The Red Raiders christened its new ballpark with a 26-0 victory over Central Catholic. After a scary, 7-6 defeat of Beaver Falls the following week, Ken High continued to roll through the remainder of the season. This time, however, the Red Raiders would face neighboring Har-Brack for WPIAL honors.

More than 15,000 fans braved 17-degree weather on Thanksgiving Day as Ken High blanked the Tigers, 28-0. Thrower came up big, completing 12-of-19 passes for two touchdowns, both to Pisano. Thrower scored a touchdown himself and intercepted a pair of passes for its second straight WPIAL championship.

Thrower and the Red Raiders picked up where they left off in 1948, Willie's senior season. Ken High won its first five games before playing Allentown's William Allen High School to a 7-7 deadlock. Since Allen was not a WPIAL school, the Red Raiders were still eligible for a third consecutive title.

But a big game at Ambridge loomed. The game was so big that the old Pittsburgh Sun-Telegraph published a commemorative, souvenir issue.

The game was as hard-hitting as anticipated. A 97-yard run by Joe Giordano put Ken High in the driver's seat as the Red Raiders posted a 25-19 victory marred by cheap shots from the Ambridge players. The referees basically put away their whistles, encouraging the Ambridge players to further dirty play. Much to the dismay of New Kensington school officials in the stands. It wasn't the first time a team encountered problems at Ambridge.

Earlier, a special "fan train" that carried Rochester followers to Ambridge was stoned after a Bridgers loss.

Ambridge and Ken High never played again.

The real effect of the Ambridge fiasco didn't manifest itself until the following week. Some players who were injured in the Ambridge game were out of the lineup while others were hobbled and couldn't perform at their accustomed levels.

The time was ripe for a major upset as 2-6 Vandergrift came to town and pulled off a 20-14 shocker that knocked New Ken out of the WPIAL title race..

But postseason accolades soon came Thrower's way. He was named to the all-WPIAL team and to the AP all-state first team as a back. To top it off, he was named to the Wigwam Wiseman All-American team, perhaps the honor that Willie was most proud of.

But Thrower suffered another racially-motivated snub when he was named as a captain to a national all-star game in Corpus Christi, Tex. But when game officials found out he was black, they told Willie he couldn't play in the game.

Even so, it was on to Michigan State for Thrower and nine others from the great Ken High teams. In 1952, Willie became the first black quarterback in Big 10 Conference history, helping lead the Spartans to a national championship. He passed for 400 yards, completing 29 passes in 48 attempts, backing up quarterback Al Yewcic.

NFL History

Thrower, undrafted by the NFL, signed with the Chicago Bears where he roomed with another Westmoreland County athlete, first-string quarterback George Blanda, a Youngwood native. On Oct. 18, 1953, Thrower made NFL history when he became the league's first black quarterback, completing three passes in eight attempts. He so impressed the usually jaundiced crowd at Wrigley Field that the fans began to chant "Willie, Willie," wanting to see more of Thrower's strong throwing arm.

But Blanda was re-inserted later in the game as the Bears lost a 35-28 decision to the San Francisco 49ers. Thrower would make one more appearance that season for Chicago.

In 1954, the Bears signed backup quarterback Zeke Bratkowski for the 1954 campaign. Thrower played for several teams in Canada before a separated shoulder ended his playing career in 1957 with what amounted to a Canadian Football League farm team.

However historical, there wasn't much of a media splash surrounding Thrower's NFL debut. The NFL received nothing near the coverage it enjoys today. Also in 1953, George Taliaferro started two games for the Baltimore Colts and Charles Brackins played in seven games for Green Bay in 1955.

It wouldn't be until 1968 that another black quarterback, Denver's Marlin Briscoe, would take snaps in a pro game.

In 1975, James Harris started late-season games for the Los Angeles Rams.

As for Thrower, he entered social work after his playing days were over. He was employed in the 1960s as a child care counselor at the Hawthorne Cedar Knolls, a residential treatment center in Westchester County, New York, just north of New York City.

Thrower returned to New Kensington in 1969, owning two taverns and working in construction, fading into quiet obscurity. He declined to boast about his history-making efforts, but when he did mention it, some of his neighbors, particularly young people, didn't believe him.

That gnawed at Willie, saying as much in a *New York Times* interview.

It wasn't until an ABC-TV production assistant called the *Valley News Dispatch* in late 2000, inquiring about Thrower's career as part of a special for Black History Month in Feb., 2001 that Willie finally received national exposure.

Willie Lawrence Thrower died of a heart attack on Feb. 20, 2002 at 71. A number of community members stepped forward to make sure Thrower wasn't forgotten again. New Kensington resident Will Varner spearheaded an effort to raise money for a statue in Willie's honor that was unveiled at Valley High School on Sept. 28, 2006. The statue was placed inside Memorial Stadium where the Valley Vikings still play.

An historical marker also was erected by the Pennsylvania Historical Society at the Valley High School entrance. Several years after his death, Thrower was inducted into the African-American Hall of Fame in Harlem.

Credit: George France family

Willie Thrower looks for some running room in a 1947 game.

Willie Thrower's family gathers around his statue at Valley High Memorial Stadium on July 27, 2009. From left, son Jason, son Melvin, his wife Mrs. Mary Thrower and son Willie, Jr.

chapter 11

FORD CITY'S BASKETBALL AMBASSADOR

It all started by going to the movies and missing curfew. Young Zigmund 'Red' Mihalik and a friend hitchhiked from Ford City to Kittanning one night to see a movie and made it home too late and missed curfew.

Missing curfew wasn't a good idea under the reign of Ford City coach Cornelius 'Neenie" Campbell. Besides a brief suspension, part of Mihalik's punishment was to officiate junior high games. That 'punishment' turned out to be the start of a trip to the Basketball Hall of Fame in Springfield, Mass.

Mihalik took to the floor and discovered he enjoyed officiating, and a legendary career was born. From that winter night in Ford City, Mihalik went on to a remarkable, whistle-tooting career that included six NCAA Final Fours, an Olympic trials and two Olympic Games.

His career included a stint in the NBA, where Mihalik decided the collegiate and amateur games were his cup of tea.

Red was born in Ford City on Sept. 22, 1916 to Polish immigrant parents who settled in Western Pennsylvania. He became a stellar athlete, along with his brothers Clem and Karl. But tragedy struck and Red's father died, and Red had to forget about playing college sports and entered the work-a-day world.

Despite full-time employment responsibilities, Mihalik still found time to officiate basketball. When World War II began, Mihalik served in the Army Air Force where he continued to play and officiate basketball. When the war ended, he found himself in great demand around the country. Mihalik had a way of keeping control of the game, but never making a spectacle of himself.

In 1951, Dell Publications named Mihalik the best official in the country. Coaches like Pete Newell, who piloted California to the NCAA basketball title in 1959 praised Mihalik's officiating, comparing it to athletic prowess.

Mihalik would seem to some to be in at least two places at once. Legendary football coach Chuck Klausing recalled seeing him in a parking lot near Turtle Creek once. Mihalik was drinking from a thermos of soup his wife had prepared for him as he had a few minutes to spare between doing a junior high game and a varsity game in a nearby community one Friday.

After the varsity game, Mihalik headed to Morgantown to call a West Virginia University game the following night, and then got little sleep as he made his way to Raleigh, N.C., on a Sunday night to call an Atlantic Coast Conference game.

Mihalik called numerous NCAA games, including Big 10 Conference battles. In 1964, he got the call to go to Tokyo for the Summer Olympics and returned to the floor for the 1968 Mexico City Games. By the time 1972 rolled around, Mihalik suggested the International Olympic Committee find someone else.

He continued to call high school games and, when he got older, junior high games. Mihalik worked nine WPIAL finals and five PIAA finals. In 1986, he received basketball's ultimate honor, enshrinement in the Naismith Memorial Hall of Fame in Springfield. That same year, he called his last game, a junior high encounter at Kittanning when he was 69 on February 19.

Shortly before his death, he was named to the National Polish-American Sports Hall of Fame in Hamtramck, Mich. The Ford City gym where it all started now bears his name.

Credit: A-K Valley Sports Hall of Fame

Red Mihalik was one of basketball's most well-respected officials.

chapter 12

INTER-GENERATIONAL LOVE

Baseball and Vandergrift have shared a love affair that has spanned several generations.

Start with the old merchant leagues of the 1920s and '30s, where businesses would sponsor teams of adults that would provide keen competition to the success of the Vandergrift Blue Lancers on the high school level, to the professional Minor League Pioneers from 1947-50 to the creation of the Vandergrift Little League in 1952 – and don't forget the annual Pittsburgh Pirate Days celebration.

Even when Kiski Area High School came along, baseball continued to thrive. The Cavaliers won the 1966 WPIAL baseball title in just the fourth year of the school's existence. Kiski Area was site of numerous WPIAL playoff games over the years, particularly with Vandergrift's William K. Miller serving as WPIAL Baseball Steering Committee chairman.

The 2004 Cavaliers made it to the PIAA state semifinals under Vandergrift-bred head coach Jack Jewart.

Professional Ball Arrives

Vandergrift was awarded a franchise in the Class A Mid-Atlantic League for 1947. The league, which started in 1929, had shut down during World War II.

The league was reborn after the war, and lights were added to Davis Field during October of the 1946 high school football season.

As the '47 campaign approached, the Vandergrift Pioneers were set to be part of the league that included the Butler Yankees, the Johnstown Johnnies, the Oil City Refiners, the Uniontown Coal Barons, the Youngstown Colts, the Niagara Falls Frontiers and the Erie Sailors.

Vandergrift was an affiliate of the Philadelphia Phillies. Players stayed at a boarding house in Apollo. Leechburg's Joe Verer won a name-the-team contest with his entry of "Pioneers." Minor league baseball proved to be an immediate hit in Vandergrift, as the Pioneers won the league championship. The team also won the hearts of local citizens, drawing 87,000 fans, about 1,450 per game.

Vandergrift was unstoppable in the 1947 playoffs, defeating Erie 3 games to none and Butler, 4 games to none. The team included Mike Goliat of Yatesboro, Armstrong County, who would go on to be part of the 1950 Whiz Kids that brought a rare National League pennant to Philadelphia.

The 1948 season featured another first place finish, as the Pioneers posted an 86-39 record, a .688 winning percentage. The team had Alex Garbowski, who led the league in hitting with a .396 average, and league-leading pitcher George Heller, with 20 wins and 161 strikeouts. Eric Littenberger led the Mid-Atlantic with 26 home runs and Rocky Tedesco had 176 hits.

In the playoffs, however, a 3 games to 1 win in the series over Uniontown was followed by Erie winning the league title, 4 games to 1 over Vandergrift. The Pioneers drew 51,367 fans and about only people not on board were those affiliated with the Vandergrift High football team. Because of the length of the baseball season, the Blue Lancers couldn't play any home games until late September. Head coach Johnny Karrs, in fact, was so angry that he left Vandergrift to coach at nearby Freeport.

In 1949, the Pioneers slipped to sixth place with a 63-72 record. The manager was George Savino who, in his playing days, was traded during the season for a manager. On May 20, 1937, Savino was sent from Baltimore of the International League to Buffalo for Buck Crouse, who was immediately named Baltimore manager.

The 1949 team included Joe Lonnett of New Brighton, who would later coach third base for the Pirates under manager Chuck Tanner from 1977-85.

Attendance dipped to 40,423, about half of what it was two years earlier. It would foretell what was to come.

Not all love affairs have a happy ending. By the time the middle of the 1950 season rolled around, the team was broke. The Vandergrift Athletic Association, whose members operated the team, took money out of their own pockets for a while, but low attendance forced the issue.

Vandergrift and the surrounding area proved to be too small to sustain a professional sports team. Plus, television antennas began to spring up everywhere, as people began to stay indoors for entertainment. Dozens of minor league franchises, and entire leagues themselves, folded.

On July 20, 1950, the Vandergrift Pioneers played their final game, an 11-10 victory over Butler in 10 innings before just 247 fans. After winning pitcher Art Smith drove in Bill Blanchard with the winning run with one out in the 10th, VAA president Joseph Bucci announced over the p.a. system: "Thanks to all you players and loyal fans. We are sorry we have to fold up."

Philadelphia then disbursed the players elsewhere in its farm system. Following the 1951 season, the entire league disbanded.

Love those (Blue) Lancers

After more than 20 years without fielding a baseball team, Vandergrift High School returned to the diamond in a big way. Vandergrift won the WPIAL championship in 1948 and repeated the feat in '49.

Pitching is the name of the game – even in the scholastic ranks. Rudy Minarcin, who would later pitch in the major leagues with the Reds and the Red Sox, led Vandergrift to the 1948 title, while Stan Szymanski pitched in three of the five 1949 postseason victories.

After learning the game playing on "town teams" as youngsters, the Blue Lancers made their varsity debut in 1948 with a 5-4 victory over Ken High, a well-established program. Vandergrift went on to win the Section 18 title to enter the WPIAL playoffs. Only section winners were admitted to the tournament and there were no classifications.

The Blue Lancers beat Ken High in a rematch to start the playoffs. After victories over McKeesport and Carmichaels, Vandergrift defeated Crafton, 7-5, to take WPIAL honors at Munhall's West Field. Pirates slugger Ralph Kiner was at the game, even calling a couple of innings on the radio in a preview of what would be a 45-year+ broadcasting career with the New York Mets. In 1949, Rudy's brother, John Minarcin, slugged a three-run homer in the seventh inning at Shannock Valley High School to lift Vandergrift to a 5-4 victory en route to the section title. The Blue Lancers finished the section campaign undefeated behind Don Virostek's pitching in a 5-4 win over Kittanning to end the regular season.

There's nothing like opening the playoffs at home, and Szymanski responded with a one-hitter over Elders Ridge at Davis Field. Szymanksi fanned 11 Rams.

The Blue Lancers edged Arnold, 10-9, in the second round before Minarcin slammed a two-run homer to defeat Mount Pleasant Hurst in the quarterfinals at Herr Stadium, New Kensington.

In the semifinals at West Field, Vandergrift eliminated California Area, 5-4, as Tony Donghia doubled and scored on Eddie Halas' single. At the same time, West Deer defeated Clark, a forerunner of Chartiers Valley High School, 2-1, to set up an all-A-K final.

Vandergrift used two-run homers by Minarcin and Ronnie Bills and rode the pitching of Szymanski to win a 5-3 decision and bring another WPIAL trophy back to Vandergrift.

The Majestic Minarcins

Nothing said Vandergrift baseball like the Minarcin brothers – Rudy and John.

Both excelled at football, but baseball was their mainstay.

Each had a hand in the back-to-back Vandergrift WPIAL baseball titles and each played in the pros.

Rudy played for the Vandergrift Pioneers immediately out of high school and eventually made his way to Cincinnati via Utica, Tulsa and Buffalo. On his return to Pittsburgh in 1955, Minarcin pitched a one-hitter against the Pirates at Forbes Field.

After being with Boston for a third major league season, Minarcin spent time with the Class AAA Havana Sugar Kings and the Toronto baseball Maple Leafs, posting an 11-2 record. He finished his career with Toronto in 1959.

After leading the Blue Lancers to their second straight WPIAL title, John Minarcin played in the pros with various Boston Red Sox affiliates, climbing from Class D to AA in just two years.

John Minarcin made it to the Class AA ranks with Birmingham. He served in the military in 1953-54, coming back to play in a final season in 1955, before making Oneonta, N.Y. his permanent home, where he became a firefighter.

John Minarcin played 460 games with 1544 at bats and a .280 batting average.

John earned praise from his older brother, Rudy:

"I played against Willie Mays and Jimmy Piersall, but my brother was one of the three best centerfielders I ever saw."

Credit: Victorian Vandergrift Museum

This is an aerial view of Davis Field just before the Vandergrift Pioneers opened the 1947 baseball season.

Credit: Victorian Vandergrift Museum

Fans enjoy baseball action with the Vandergrift Pioneers at Davis Field in Vandergrift.

Yatesboro native and second baseman Mike Goliat played for Vandergrift in 1947 and for the Phillies in the 1950 World Series.

Catcher Herman Kiel hit .393 for the Pioneers in 1947.

Stan Covelewski batted .263 for the 1947 champion Pioneers.

Credit: A–K Valley Sports Hall of Fame

Vandergrift's Rudy Minarcin, center, celebrates the aftermath of a 4-hitter against the Brooklyn Dodgers at Cincinnati's Crosley Field on June 15, 1955. Minarcin threw a complete game, 5-2 victory. Redlegs 3B Bobby Adams, left, and CF Gus Bell drove in all five runs.

Credit: Minarcin family

North Vandergrift's Rudy Minarcin poses with his parents, Mary and Martin at Forbes Field as he was given luggage on Rudy Minarcin Night in 1955.

Credit: Minarcin family

Johnny Minarcin (32) poses with fellow Vandergrift football teammate Don Earley. Minarcin helped lead Vandergrift to the 1949 WPIAL baseball title and later played in the pros. He died on June 23, 2009 at age 77.

Credit: Valley News Dispatch

The annual Pirate Days were big in Vandergrift. On July 28, 1969, Richie Hebner, Freddie Patek, and Bill Mazeroski sign autographs.

Credit: Courtesy Victorian Vandergrift Museum

Pitcher Nellie Briles and broadcaster Bob Prince say hello to Buccos fan Lena Crissman, 92, during the annual Pirates Days in Vandergrift on Aug. 9, 1971.

chapter 13

FOOTBALLTOWN, USA

Freeport is the quintessential Western Pennsylvania riverfront town.

It's a great place to live, work, worship and, even in the 21st Century, a place where you don't have to worry if you forget to lock your doors.

Freeport is also a great place to watch football.

And the fans in Freeport have watched some great football over the years. Their Yellowjackets are on the verge of becoming the first Alle-Kiski Valley school to win 500 football games. Freeport has made the WPIAL playoffs 21 times, the most in local history.

The school once had 21 consecutive winning seasons. If the current WPIAL playoff format was in existence in an earlier era, Freeport would have made the playoffs 20 consecutive seasons. In one 34-year stretch beginning in 1952, the Yellowjackets posted 30 winning seasons.

Surely, the school has fielded some outstanding basketball teams, the baseball program has brought home three WPIAL titles and the track program annually attracts over 100 athletes. During the decade of the 1970s, Freeport won 77 football games.

But football has been a community mainstay since 1922, even though the political and financial power has switched from Freeport Borough to nearby Buffalo Township. Even though the school has come up short 7 times in WPIAL title games, there nothing like the atmosphere of a fall Friday night in Freeport.

Attendance has slipped somewhat, but the Yellowjackets, because of classification changes over the years, no longer play long-time rivals like Knoch, Leechburg, Springdale and Pine-Richland. One-time rivals like Tarentum and Arnold have faded into history.

Still, the sight of an endless stream of headlights coming from the bridge onto a ramp leading to the old stadium is etched in one's memory forever.

The First Unbeaten Team

Following an 8-3 season in 1929 and a 7-3 campaign in 1930, Freeport posted an 8-0-0 record in 1931. In that season, the WPIAL selected the football champion without a playoff and Mount Pleasant Hurst was designated as the top team. When the current stadium opened in 1940, the Yellowjackets could only muster a lone win, 7-6, over Springdale. By 1943, however, the program rebounded with an 8-1 mark, with the lone loss coming to Aspinwall, 27-0. Losing to Aspinwall in shutout fashion that season was no great sin. After all, Aspinwall finished the season at 10-0 and was undefeated, untied – and unscored upon.

Freeport played its first night game at home on Oct. 4, 1947. Bud Carson was the quarterback that night in the single-wing offense.

"It was such a big deal for a small town like Freeport to get lights," Carson said in a 1995 interview with the *Valley News Dispatch*.

Temporary bleachers had to be installed for the huge Saturday night crowd watching the game under state-of-the-art lighting. The Yellowjackets responded with a 30-0 victory over Washington Township.

Two weeks later, some 5,000 fans jammed the borough field to watch the battle of two undefeated teams as Freeport blanked Apollo, 9-0. Carson held for Chuck Lesneski's field goal and passed to George Williams for the game's only touchdown.

In 1948, Freeport went 8-0-1, with the tie coming against Leechburg, 13-13, keeping the Yellowjackets out of WPIAL title consideration.

In 1955, Freeport posted an 8-0-2 record, winning the old Allegheny Valley Football Conference (AVFC). A conference title was repeated in 1956, as the Yellowjackets went 8-1.

The First Title Trip

After compiling a 7-1-1 record in 1962, including five victories in a row to close the season, expectations were high for Freeport in 1963.

Freeport met those expectations by rolling through the nine-week regular season schedule with nine wins, including a narrow,

13-7, win over Arnold at home in Week Three.

The Yellowjackets clinched the title game berth with a 21-7 victory over Leechburg.

The team was coached by Bob King and led on the field by Charles 'Chip' Young, a second-team, AP all-state running back.

But in the championship game, Montour, led by future NFL great Ted Kwalick, hammered Freeport, 34-12.

The Earley Era

In 1967, Freeport pulled off a coaching coup. Don Earley had been a highly-successful coach at nearby Washington Township, winning the WPIAL title in 1960 and finishing as the runner-up in 1961.

But Washington Township was absorbed into the Kiski Area system in 1965, leaving Earley available. Freeport gobbled up Earley quickly. What resulted was 19 consecutive winning seasons for the Yellowjackets, including 10 playoff trips and five WPIAL title game appearances.

In all of Earley's 19 seasons at Freeport, the Yellowjackets went into at least the next-to-the-last week of the regular season with a mathematical shot at postseason play – either in the WPIAL playoffs or the old AIC Bowl.

Earley was a lineman on some great Vandergrift football teams of the late 1940s. He attended South Carolina and played offensive guard for the Gamecocks. Earley was taken by the Steelers in the 21st round of the 1953 NFL draft.

But he cast his lot in high school coaching, taking over the Washington Township program in 1959 and compiling a 3-3-3 record. Washington Township never had a home field, instead sharing Owens Field with Apollo. The first order of business for Earley was to switch the Washington Township home games from Thursday to Saturday nights.

But in his second season, Washington Township would win the WPIAL Class B championship, defeating Perryopolis, 26-0. The Red Raiders gave up just two touchdowns in the last 20 quarters of the 1960 season.

Earley took Washington Township to the WPIAL title game again in 1961, recording five consecutive shutouts in one stretch.

This time, however, Avella prevailed in the championship game, 13-0.

By the time Earley arrived in Freeport, his coaching credentials were well-established.

It took Earley two seasons to get Washington Township to the WPIAL title game. But at Freeport, the Yellowjackets made it in each of his first two seasons. Freeport lost both the 1967 and 1968 Class A title games to Burrell.

Both games were lost by a 6-0 margin, both games were played at Memorial Stadium in New Kensington, both games were decided by a touchdown in the end zone closest to Little Pucketa Creek.

Freeport ended the 1969 campaign with a postseason victory, a 28-7 decision over Kittanning in the AIC Bowl.

Another run to the WPIAL title game took place in 1972, with the Yellowjackets blanking six of their first 10 opponents before losing the championship game to Beaver Area, 20-14.

The Yellowjackets appeared headed for another trip the title game in 1973, shutting out six of their first seven foes. But in Week Eight, the Springdale Dynamos unexpectedly overwhelmed Freeport, 35-6, before a huge throng at Tarentum's Dreshar Stadium, Springdale's temporary home.

But Freeport rebounded and won the AIC in 1974 and defeated Rochester, 14-6, in the WPIAL semifinals on a sub-freezing night at Geneva College. But Freeport would come up short in the finals again, this time by a 41-13 margin to Albert Gallatin.

Freeport played the bridesmaid in each of the next four seasons, finishing in second place in the AIC. In 1978, Freeport and Leechburg clashed in the Game of the Decade at Leechburg Veterans Memorial Stadium. Both teams came into the game with 8-0 records. The line for tickets circled the block as fans jammed the stadium for the big showdown, where Leechburg secured a 14-6 victory.

Freeport, however, would make the WPIAL playoffs six of the next seven seasons, starting with winning the AIC North crown in 1979. The Yellowjackets were eliminated quickly, 10-0, by neighboring Knoch before the third-largest crowd ever at Staresenic Stadium in Natrona Heights.

Freeport made the playoffs from 1981-85, taking another shot at the WPIAL Class AA crown in 1981, losing to Jeannette, 26-7. Earley did, perhaps, his best coaching job in 1982. After losing 20 of 22 starters from the 1981 team, Freeport went back to work and finished second in the Allegheny Conference. The Yellowjackets surprised Northgate in the first round of the WPIAL playoffs before losing to Beaver Area.

In 1985, Freeport lost an odd-sounding 5-3 decision to Jeannette for the conference title before what some believe was the largest crowd ever at Freeport Borough Field, since renamed James Swartz Memorial Stadium after the community's long-time public works director.

Freeport opened the 1985 playoffs at Washington and fell behind, 17-0. But a magnificent comeback, led by all-stater Jeff Christy, resulted in a 21-17 Freeport victory. It would be the 200th and final win in Earley's career because the following week, the Yellowjackets lost an overtime battle to Riverside, 6-0, in a quagmire at Butler High School.

Christy led the WPIAL with 203 points in 1985.

One More Run

Former Freeport player and assistant coach to Earley, Gary Kepple, took over the reins in 1986. The Yellowjackets would make one more run at a title, defeating long-time nemesis Jeannette, 28-21, at Valley Memorial Stadium. Freeport was 33 seconds away from its elusive WPIAL title at Three Rivers Stadium, but a touchdown by Steel Valley quarterback Marcel Weems led to a 20-14 victory by the Ironmen.

On October 23, 2009, Freeport recorded the 500th victory in school history with a 37-7 win against Deer Lakes.

Credit: Valley News Dispatch

Don Earley addresses his Washington Township team before taking the field against Avella in the 1961 WPIAL Class B title game.

Don Earley coached Freeport from 1967-85.

Credit: Bob Fair, Freeport, PA

Gene Sobolewski played for Freeport before moving on to Pitt. He coached at Clarion (PA) University for 23 seasons, including 11 as a head coach (1983-93). The Golden Eagles compiled a 144-86-3 record during his tenure.

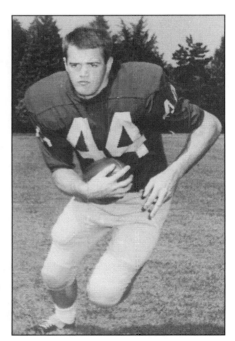

Credit: Bob Fair, Freeport, PA

Chip Young, shown here during his college days at William & Mary, was the first Freeport player named to the all-state team in 1963. He helped lead the Yellow-jackets to the WPIAL title game.

Credit: Valley News Dispatch

Fans line up outside Leechburg High School on Oct. 26, 1978 to get tickets for the 'Game of the Decade' the following night in Leechburg between the Blue Devils and Freeport.

Credit: Valley News Dispatch

Jeff Christy (40) makes some headway on Nov. 1, 1985 against Jeannette. Christy, later an NFL Pro Bowl center, scored 203 points that season.

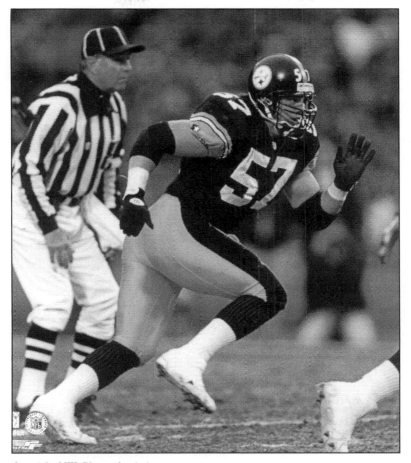

Eric Ravotti was an AP first team all-stater at linebacker for Freeport in 1988 before moving on to Penn State and the Steelers.

chapter 14

THE FACE OF FREEPORT FOOTBALL

When Bud Carson was head coach at Georgia Tech in 1970, the school band played an interesting variation of a popular commercial jingle.

At the end of the third quarter, the Tech band played the Budweiser theme song, ending the selection by yelling – "When you say Bu-u-u-u-d Carson, you've said it all."

In reality, when you say Bud Carson, you've said Freeport football.

From his start as a quarterback in the old single-wing formation, to his days as a North Carolina Tar Heel to being the architect of the Steel Curtain defense, Bud Carson never forgot his Freeport roots.

When he died on Dec. 8, 2005, it was discovered that he wanted to make a contribution to Freeport football two years after his death. His widow, Linda, notified the Freeport Area School District of Bud's wishes and made a $20,000 contribution from his estate to the school district.

Early in 2009, the district purchased a combo football/track scoreboard on the high school campus with the bottom part of the scoreboard carrying the inscription: Home of Coach Bud Carson.

Before making his mark in coaching, Carson was a stellar athlete for the Freeport Yellowjackets. Not only was he an all-Section basketball player and baseball player, he was part of the football program from 1945-47 and enjoyed the small-town atmosphere. "It was a great time to be in Freeport," Carson said in a 1995 interview. "All the vets were back from World War II, and everybody went to the football games – it was an all-encompassing activity."

After graduating from Freeport in 1948, it was on to Chapel Hill to play for North Carolina, a team just coming off a Sugar Bowl victory the previous season. Carson started at cornerback for three seasons and was an All-American honorable mention in his senior year.

After a stint in the U.S. Marines, Carson returned to Freeport in 1954, taking a temporary teaching assignment when the regular teacher was drafted. Bud told then-Freeport head coach Johnny Karrs that he would like to get into coaching.

Karrs had Carson apply for the job at Scottdale High School in Westmoreland County, where he led the Scotties to a 16-2-1 mark in two seasons before getting the call to become an assistant at North Carolina, South Carolina and Georgia Tech.

In 1967, he took over as head coach at Georgia Tech, replacing the legendary Bobby Dodd. He led the Yellowjackets to two bowl appearances in five seasons, but that wasn't enough to satisfy some demanding alumni, and he was dismissed.

But that turned out to be a break. Chuck Noll hired Carson as an assistant in 1972, naming him defensive coordinator midway through the season. The Steelers won their first division title that season and two years later, saw his defense compile two of the best playoff performances in NFL history. In the 1974 AFC title game, the Steelers defense held Oakland to a measly 34 yards rushing en route to a 24-13 victory and a berth in Super Bowl IX.

Carson lists as one of his biggest thrills as part of the Steelers staff, the arrival back at the Greater Pittsburgh Airport after the Oakland game. As estimated 50,000 jammed the airport and the parkway back to the City.

Two weeks later, however, Carson's rush defense was even better, limiting the Vikings to 27 rushing yards as the Steelers brought home a 16-6 victory.

Carson left the Steelers in 1978 and was an assistant coach with the Rams, the Colts, the Chiefs and the Jets before finally getting his first NFL head coaching job with the Browns in 1989. In what Carson regards as the biggest day of his football life, the Browns routed the Steelers, 51-0, at Three Rivers Stadium. After leaving Cleveland in 1991, he finished his career as an assistant with the Eagles from 1992-94.

He always kept in contact with brother Gib Carson and longtime friend Harry Crytzer to see what was happening around Freeport. When contacted by local reporters, he often asked first how everything was going in Freeport.

Credit: A–K Valley Sports Hall of Fame

Bud Carson lettered in three sports at Freeport before making his mark in the coaching ranks.

chapter 15

NEVER ON SUNDAY

Bob Malcolm had one of the A-K Valley's most successful coaching careers, guiding the West Deer American Legion to four state championships and 15 Allegheny County titles, leading the team from 1932-56.

But he is best known for a man of his convictions. Although he sent about 20 of his players to the pros and got many more into colleges for academic purposes, the convictions he brought with him are what he should best be known for.

One of those convictions was never playing any games on a Sunday. Period.

For example, in 1952, West Deer already had won the division, Allegheny County and regional titles and were in Reading for the state championship tournament. On Saturday, August 24, 1952, West Deer lost the first game of the tournament to Beaver Falls, 3-1. Later that day, West Deer rebounded and beat Barnesboro, 4-3. West Deer then had to play through the loser's bracket of the double-elimination tournament the following day. But Malcolm said he wouldn't play on a Sunday, and when the tournament officials wouldn't change the schedule, West Deer forfeited and headed home, since it was, technically, its second loss.

The story made nationwide headlines, but it wasn't the first time it happened. Former player Vince Taliani recalled a similar situation in the 1940s where West Deer refused to play a state playoff game on a Sunday. The team carpool was heading home from Reading when a Pennsylvania State Police team stopped the convoy near the Midway rest stop, hoping to persuade the team to turn back. Malcolm agreed to poll the players and found out they agreed with their coach and continued home.

The Inauspicious Start

The team was born during the Great Depression. American Legion officials urged Malcolm, a World War I veteran and a successful athlete at Freeport High School, to start a team based in the Curtisville section of West Deer Township.

While attending a Legion district meeting in Leechburg, Malcolm was told by Pittsburgh attorney Ben Giffen to start a team for the boys around the coal mining communities of West Deer. Joblessness and accompanying idleness of that era resulted in some to pursue avenues of destructive behavior. Activities like baseball could easily give teenagers a positive direction.

Early on, Malcolm shouldered the expenses of the baseballs, bats and other expenses out of his own pocket. Traveling to away games wasn't easy, either. The team members rode on the back of a coal truck.

Opposing teams razzed West Deer for their travel accommodations, but when the game started, it was all business – and the kids who rode in the coal truck would have the last laugh. It didn't take long for the program to get established. West Deer won the Allegheny County title in 1933, the second year of its existence.

Later, the players benefited from the donation of an old bus from Staley's Culmerville Auto Transit. The bus was dilapidated, but the players didn't seem to care. One night while returning home from a game at Mars, the bus broke down and the 25-player team hitch-hiked home, all with Malcolm's approval.

By 1939, the team brought home its first state championship. Another followed in 1943. By 1944, West Deer High School inaugurated baseball. The team went to the WPIAL finals in its first season.

In 1947, Malcolm left his job as paymaster Ford Collieries Co. and took a position with the Allegheny County Board of Viewers, the forerunner of the county assessment department.

Another state title came in 1949, just months after the high school team lost in the WPIAL finals to Vandergrift. The big thrill surrounding the '49 title run was the fact that the game was played at Forbes Field.

But before that, West Deer had to beat Beechview in a best-of-three series for Allegheny County honors. Malcolm's team came through in the clincher with a five-run outburst in the fifth inning. Stan Watychowicz relieved Phil Moretti and recorded the victory. In the state tournament, West Deer pulverized the Northwest Champions from the Erie area, 22-9. Victories over Wilson and Pottstown secured the state title under the lights before a huge crowd at Forbes Field.

After the forfeiture in 1952, West Deer returned in 1953 and won it all for a fourth time.

By the time the 1954 state tournament rolled around, Legion officials had gotten the message – a game involving West Deer for a Sunday was rescheduled for Monday. Malcolm's team eventually lost the state title game, but the point had been made.

Making the Big Time

Among the 20 players Malcolm sent to the pros was Al Federoff, born on July 11, 1924 in the Bairdford section of West Deer Township.

He signed with the Tigers in 1946 and immediately was sent to Jamestown in the old PONY (Pennsylvania, Ohio, New York) League. Federoff made it to Detroit in 1951 and played in 76 major league games.

He finished his playing career in the minors, spending four seasons with San Diego of the Pacific Coast League. Federoff played in 1,784 minor league games.

Watychowicz, who grew up in Indianola, signed with the Philadelphia A's after his stellar '49 season. He was assigned to pitch at St. Hyacinthe, Quebec, in the old Canadian Provincial League where he won 19 games and pitched a no-hitter against Granby.

In 1952, he was a September call-up for the A's. During the winter, however, he got another call, this time for Uncle Sam. After nearly two years in the military, Watychowicz was ready to be discharged when he got a bad break. Watychowicz fell off a tractor, hurting his shoulder,

Watychowicz tried to pitch, but rehabilitation in the mid-1950s was nothing near what it is today, and he never recovered from the injury.

The Stunning Ending

Though he suffered from diabetes, Malcolm's death on Feb. 12, 1957 was shocking to everyone who knew him.

He died of a heart attack in his Curtisville home shortly after returning home from Toledo, visiting with his daughter.

The Tarentum Valley Daily News ran a rare, front-page obituary that day. Tributes from across the state poured into West Deer. Even his opponents, particularly Tarentum manager Wes Cooper, forced to play second fiddle to Malcolm's teams, also offered a glowing tribute.

Malcolm had been the honoree at a dinner several months before, citing his 25 seasons as West Deer manager.

In 1958, the West Deer Legion team named the field adjacent to the West Deer Legion in his honor. On June 28, 2003, the field was rededicated the Bob Malcolm Field in the Superior section of the township.

Credit: A-K Valley Sports Hall of Fame

Bob Malcolm led West Deer American Legion to four state titles.

BACK ROW: Jim Hice, Tony Pleva, Rich Bowser, Stan Watychowicz, Al Rommes, Andy Massimino, Sonny Soloman, John Micklow, Donnie Allen, Dutchie Stepp.
FRONT ROW: Tom Tomayko, Larry Murray, Bill Hamilton, Phil Moretti, Jim Higgins, Ted Tabacchi, Bill Dlubak, Bill Suvoy. Bat boy is Ronnie Rommes.

Credit: Stan Watychowicz

The sign at the Bob Malcolm Memorial Field was re-dedicated June 28, 2003.

Credit: Stan Watychowicz

chapter 16

SMALL SCHOOL, BIG-TIME POWERHOUSE

One night in 1982, Jim Oberdorf was resting in his West Leechburg home when he heard a knock at the door. It was a couple of neighborhood girls who played softball for Leechburg High School. The girls were concerned that the school might abolish the softball program if no coach was found. Oberdorf agreed to run the team until somebody else could be found.

Well, 27 years and 23 straight WPIAL playoffs appearances, 17 section titles, three WPIAL titles and two PIAA titles later, Leechburg still hasn't had a coach emerge to replace Oberdorf. With 482 career victories after the 2009 season, Oberdorf is the second-winningest coach in WPIAL softball history.

It's been an amazing run for Oberdorf, who was a Pennsylvania State trooper when he took the job on what he thought would be on an interim basis.

The secret to Leechburg's astounding success has been deep, talented pitching.

From Janel Daugherty to Jennifer Wolfe to Jackie Mozga to Jenny Kulick to Stacey Pastva to Emily Sprankle to Emily Batiz, pitching always has been the key.

After being ousted from the WPIAL playoffs in the first round in 1987 and '88, Leechburg looked like it was on the verge of a major breakthrough in 1989. Entering the playoffs with a 19-0 regular season record, the Blue Devils played host to Fort Cherry. In pre-game practice, Jennifer DeCapite was hit in the face with a fly ball, and Jennifer Daugherty crashed into the left field fence chasing a fly ball and sprained her ankle. It just wasn't Leechburg's day as the Blue Devils dropped a 7-4 decision.

In 1990, Leechburg posted a 16-2 regular season mark, scoring 198 runs – an average of 12.5 runs per game. But Riverside silenced the Leechburg bats with a 5-1 victory.

Finally, Some Gold

Following four straight one-and-dones in the WPIAL play-offs, Leechburg finally brought home the WPIAL gold. After a 16-2 regular season behind freshman pitching sensation Jennifer Wolfe, the Blue Devils won their first playoff game with a 3-1 win over Burrell. Wolfe follwed that one with a 3-0 shutout over Mars. But perennial contender Sto-Rox loomed in a semifinal matchup at Oakmont's Riverside Park.

In the pre-game huddle, Oberdorf told the girls one run might win it.

It was a good call because in what was billed as a battle of the Jennifers – Wolfe against Savant, the only run of the game came when Duang Fouse singled and took second on a wild pitch. Fouse moved to third on Wolfe's groundout and came home on Jennifer Daugherty's single.

That put the Blue Devils in the WPIAL title game against New Brighton.

Wolfe, who had yet to yield an earned run in the playoffs going into the finals, was in the circle again for the championship game. The teams battled to a 2-2 stalemate in regulation, with Leechburg finally pushing across two runs in the top of the ninth to secure a 4-2 decision to win the WPIAL title.

It was the first of three titles in five years for the Blue Devils. Leechburg returned in 1992, prospecting for more WPIAL gold. Wolfe started the postseason with a 6-0 victory over Burrell, and followed that effort with a three-hitter in a 1-0 victory over Mars.

The day after Jay Leno took over for Johnny Carson on NBC-TV's The Tonight Show, Leechburg knocked off Carmichaels in a relative slugfest, 7-6, putting the Blue Devils into another championship game.

J.R. Stull, who had suffered through an 11-game hitless streak, donned a pair of eyeglasses and proceeded to drive in four runs with a single and a triple as Leechburg defeated Riverside, 4-3.

The Blue Devils weren't through yet, however, as they won their PIAA opener over Conneaut Valley, 2-0. A 6-0 victory over Brockway followed in the quarterfinals.

In the semifinals, Glendale committed six errors and Leechburg took advantage with Wolfe firing a two-hitter to win, 6-0.

It was on to Shippensburg University for the state title game. Wolfe, who threw 200-250 pitches daily in her cellar during her formative years, had a 4-1 lead over Springfield Montco going into the seventh inning at Seth Grove Stadium. Wolfe yielded just her third walk of the season in the seventh. A single, a fielder's choice and a bunt single later, Montco had the tying run on second base. But a groundout to third ended the game and Leechburg headed home to a huge parade down Market Street to recognize the school's first state title.

Wolfe and Jackie Mozga shared pitching duties over the next two successful seasons, but after Wolfe graduated in 1994, it was up to Mozga for another championship run.

Leechburg started the 1995 WPIAL playoffs with a 10-0 whitewash over neighboring Shannock Valley and a 5-0 blanking of Northgate. That put Leechburg in the WPIAL semifinals for the fifth consecutive season. Mozga held Sto-Rox in check and, despite stranding 10 baserunners, eked out a 1-0 victory.

Mozga was masterful in the WPIAL finals, striking out 19 Riverside batters in a 2-1 victory. Jamie Berger's single drove home Michelle Fouse with the winning run.

Leechburg entered the PIAA playoffs with a 3-0 win over Westmont Hilltop. In the quarterfinals, Leechburg led Sto-Rox, 4-1, with the bases loaded and one out in the seventh. The next batter popped up. When second baseman Jennifer Bowser heard the umpire shout an infield fly rule decision, she was startled and dropped the ball. Bowser alertly threw to third base to pick off a runner and end the game.

Leechburg defeated Riverside one more time, 3-2, and had its ticket punched for another PIAA title game berth at Shippensburg on June 15, 1995. Mozga was at her best again, as the Blue Devils brought home another state title, this time a 3-0 shutout over Annville-Cleona. Back-to-back triples by Beth Defilippi and Fouse were the key hits.

The victory gave Leechburg a 151-10 record since the start of the 1989 season. Mozga graduated with an all-time mark of 43 wins and one loss. Her father, Carl, coached many of the 1995 seniors in back-to-back Senior Division Little League titles in 1991 and '92.

Leechburg continues to churn out quality teams, while contending schools come and go. On May 17, 1997, Leechburg opened the WPIAL playoffs with a 4-3 win in 12 innings at Ford City's Pattonville VFW Field. Danielle Reinke was on second and got the steal sign from Oberdorf. The Ford City catcher threw the ball into leftfield, sending Reinke home to win the game. Leechburg was so happy to get out of there with a win that the team seemed to head to the bus the same time Reinke was crossing the plate with the game-winner.

Reinke summed up the program's legacy in a game two years later.

On May 27, 1999, Reinke's thumb hurt so badly, she could hardly catch some of Stacy Pastva's deliveries. She wouldn't go to the doctor's, feeling that he wouldn't let her play anymore. The team trainer treated Reinke several times during the game against Burgettstown at Penn Township Park. Needless to say, the game went into extra innings. With Melissa Klingensmith on second, Reinke had barely enough strength to grip the bat and slap a single to drive home the winning run in a 7-6 victory. In a post-game interview, Reinke said it best when she remarked about her hometown school:"This is where I want to be. People ask why I would want to go Leechburg, but this is the best place in the world to be."

Leechburg has continued to bedevil opponents in the 21st Century. But what must be pointed out is that prior to 1999, there were only two classifications in WPIAL softball – Class AAA and AA. Leechburg played in Class AA and often defeated schools two or three times its size such as Center and Riverside.

The PIAA religned to three classes in 1999 and to four classes in 2005.

Leechburg made three consecutive WPIAL title game appearances in 2003-05 – losing the '05 game in the final inning. Oberdorf has been around long enough to see some strange plays. In the 2005 PIAA second round at California (Pa) University, the Blue Devils were awarded a run on an illegal pitch to take a 1-0 lead. In the bottom of the fifth inning, a Beth-Center batter was initially ruled out because her uniform number was different than what was on a lineup distributed by the school to game officials and the media. However, the state rules interpreter who happened to be at the game ruled that it was a correctible error and Megan Appel was allowed to bat. She drew a walk that started a four-run rally and led to a 4-1 Beth-Center victory.

The Blue Devils continue to win and now Oberdorf is not only the coach, but he's the team bus driver.

So it can easily be said the team isn't going anywhere without him.

Credit: Valley News Dispatch

It is June 13, 1992 and the Leechburg softball team is honored with a parade down Market Street.

Through 2009, coach Jim Oberdorf has been credited with 482 softball victories with Leechburg.

chapter 17

UNIVERSAL ACCLAIM

When Chuck Wagner got his first head coaching job in 1961, John F. Kennedy was in The White House.

He is now coaching under his 10th U.S. presidency. Wagner has coached while JFK, LBJ, Nixon, Ford, Carter, Reagan, Bush I, Clinton, Bush II and Obama have served as the nation's Chief Executive.

But throughout all those presidencies, Wagner has been a winner in more ways than one. He has two WPIAL titles, 12 playoff teams and, with 240 career victories, ranked seventh on the all-time WPIAL coaching list. But beyond the W's, Wagner has done all this with a goodwill toward all he has come in contact with.

Late in his career, Wagner has become somewhat of a combination of mentor/consultant/philosopher.

A player from his first season, John Miceli, put it best. When Miceli was being inducted into the A-K Valley Sports Hall of Fame in May, 2009, he said during his acceptance speech: "If there's a better man out there than Chuck Wagner, I haven't met him." Wagner goes to great lengths to get his players into college and even greater lengths to keep in contact with them once their playing days are over.

Wagner made his coaching debut on Sept. 9, 1961, when his Oakmont Oaks won at Verona, 32-6. He followed the legendary Elmer Gross at Oakmont, and filled those big shoes well, finishing 6-3.

Verona was Oakmont's biggest rival, and the two teams played to open the season instead of closing the season as is the custom. That allowed the buildup to the rivalry games to take place in the waning weeks of summer. Fans of both teams would watch the opponent, then tell the respective coach what the other was doing. "Verona coach Joe Zelek and I were friends, and we knew what each other would like to run," Wagner said with a laugh. "Every once in a while, we'd run something we knew we'd never use in a game, just so the fans would go back and tell the coaches."

The First Championship

By 1964, Wagner had won his first conference title, copping the AIC Class B crown with a 20-7 victory over Washington Township in the conference playoff game against another coaching legend, Don Earley.

While that title game served as a springboard to Oakmont's 1965 championship season, the Oaks realized there was plenty of work to be done. After all, six of Oakmont's nine regular season games were on the road.

But the Oaks started out the season in a big way. On the first play from scrimmage, Oakmont scored on a 70-yard pass from Stan Flowers to Rich Springer at West Mifflin South en route to a 30-0 victory. Victories followed at Mars (39-6), Coraopolis (20-13) and Blairsville (12-0).

The Oakmont machine was nearly throttled in the rain and mud at Coraopolis. The Oaks fell behind, 13-0, in the first half, but gained momentum with two third quarter touchdowns to tie the game at 13-all.

But in those days, a loss or tie would disqualify a team from WPIAL title consideration. With 40 seconds left in the game, Springer threw an option pass to Sherron Montague at the 20-yard line. Montague would race 80 yards for the touchdown to hand Oakmont a 20-13 victory.

In Week Five, the Oaks finally got to play a home game in the friendly confines of Riverside Park, defeating Arnold, 13-6. Arnold was coming off a WPIAL title game appearance the previous season. Victories followed against Verona (26-6) and East Deer (13-0). Next loomed a test from Washington Township, where Ed Fitzgerald had taken over for Earley in the school's final season before being absorbed by Kiski Area.

The Oaks beat Washington, 34-0, and Avella, 25-7, to finish the regular season undefeated and earn a berth in the Class B title game at Ken High Memorial Stadium against local rival Apollo, a conference team that Oakmont didn't play in '65.

Starting tackle Rich Cecil, who would go on to play at West Virginia University, was doubtful for the game with an elbow chip fracture.

After getting treatment at Harmarville Rehabilitation Center, which was actually located in Harmarville at the time, Cecil managed to play against Apollo.

A strong fourth quarter enabled the Oaks to come away with a 26-13 victory and the WPIAL crown at Ken High Memorial Stadium. Springer scored three touchdowns and Montague added the other.

In 1966, Oakmont again made postseason play under Wagner, going 6-2-1 with the tie coming in the AIC Bowl against Arnold, a school that was playing the last game in its history before being consolidated with New Kensington.

In 1967, Oakmont lost just one game, a Week Three encounter at Coraopolis, 19-7. The Oaks would win their remaining games, including a 27-6 decision over East Deer-Frazer in the AIC Bowl.

The 1968 season got Oakmont another trip back to the WPIAL Class B championship game. The Oaks got revenge against Coraopolis with a thrilling, Week Three victory, 21-20, before what is generally considered one of the five largest crowds ever at Riverside Park. The only regular season loss came to West Deer, a school coached by Wagner's buddy, Don 'Pappy' Boulton, whom he would later combine forces with to field some outstanding teams at Springdale. West Deer was a Class A school, so the loss didn't eliminate the Oaks from WPIAL title consideration.

Oakmont beat Apollo, 34-0, on the road to conclude the regular season and earn a berth in the WPIAL title game. That one didn't have a happy ending as Chartiers-Houston, led by Jerry Patterson, the first 4,000-yard career rusher in WPIAL history, chopped down the Oaks, 31-0.

But something even more ominous than the loss to Char-Houston loomed over Oakmont – a chill stronger than any November breeze coming off the Allegheny River. Of Oakmont's nine regular season opponents, seven would be swallowed up soon after by a school consolidation. Penn Claridge, Coraopolis, Homestead, Verona, East Deer-Frazer, West Deer and Apollo were in their final days. Only Mars and Blairsville, a school no longer a WPIAL member, exist today.

With Pennsylvania moving from about 2,000 community-based school districts to the current 502, consolidations and mergers were constantly taking place. With the size of Oakmont and nearby Verona, it was only a matter of time until those two schools were swallowed up in some manner.

The first plan would be to have the Plum Borough School District take over Oakmont and for Penn Hills to pull in Verona. But Wagner and other civic and educational leaders had a better idea – combine Oakmont and Verona.

The wheels started turning, and eventually the state Department of Education approved the idea and the two schools were on their way to consolidating. The announcement became official in the fall of 1969.

Oakmont and Verona, oddly enough, played their last game against each other. On Nov. 14, 1970, the Oaks and the Panthers met in the AIC Bowl at Highlands High School field. Four weeks earlier, Oakmont, hoping for a WPIAL title berth in the school's final season, instead tumbled from the undefeated ranks with a 20-14 loss against Verona. In the final week of the regular season, Oakmont lost to Peters Township, 35-22, while Verona defeated Saltsburg, 20-14, to set up the grand finale. Rich Cecil ran in the first two Oakmont TD's, the second culminating a 15-play drive. Cecil scored a third TD after the Oaks took the second half kickoff. Quarterback Bill Braham scored the final TD in Oakmont history with 4:27 left in the game. Verona's lone score was on a 47-yard run by Bill 'Skip' Bonner with 1:18 to go as Oakmont prevailed, 28-6.

The Riverview Years

Wagner led Riverview to a 6-3 record in the first year of the school's existence. Riverview was placed in Class A, as the AIC B Conference was disbanded after 1970, what with all the school mergers dissolving the member schools and others like Shannock Valley, Saltsburg and Blairsville leaving the WPIAL.

The WPIAL changed the Class A designation to AA in 1973, though as the 1970s progressed, Riverview chose to play in the higher classification to keep their long-time rivalries intact.

Riverview, despite being one of the smallest schools in the AIC, still could compete to an extent. Things came to a head on

Oct. 11, 1974, when the Raiders lost a heartbreaker to Deer Lakes, 13-8. Wagner said he was retiring as the head coach, the athletic director, and manager of Riverside Park. Fortunately for high school football, Wagner decided to stay on, and Riverview would win the conference title three years later. Once again, Wagner used the AIC Bowl, winning 28-7 over Freeport in 1976, as a springboard to a conference title. The Raiders tied Freeport, 0-0, to end the 1977 regular season. But the first game of the Class AA playoffs proved to be a pivotal moment in school history.

South Allegheny, a school that recently dropped from Class AAA to AA, overwhelmed Riverview, 24-0, in a game that was not as close as the score indicated. Wagner met with his coaching staff soon after the game and decided it would benefit the school to eventually drop to Class A football. The reasoning was that instead of being a conference title contender once every 10 years, the Raiders could be a contender every year.

The plan worked, as Riverview tied Serra Catholic and Clairton for the first Eastern A Conference title in 1980. Though the school was the only A-K Valley team in the conference, Riverview quickly showed it could contend every year.

After the 1985 season, Wagner announced his retirement after 25 seasons and Jake Cappa was selected to replace him. Wagner would resurface for at Fox Chapel in 1988 before leaving there after three seasons, due to the illness of his wife, who eventually passed away.

The Dynamos Beckoning

By 1992, Springdale had hit the skids in high school football. The team had suffered 18 consecutive losing seasons and there was talk the Dynamos might form a combination team with Riverview. All parties denied the move was imminent, but the Allegheny Valley School District board knew it had to do something. The program won just 8 games from 1981-90 and was in the throes of a 26-game losing streak.

Directors visited Wagner and urged him to come out of retirement to try and resurrect what was once one of the A-K Valley's proudest football schools. Wagner agreed and went to work.

The first major accomplishment was getting the losing streak out of the way, which happened in Week Eight. Springdale beat Leechburg, 12-6, ending the losing streak at 35 games, third longest in WPIAL history.

In 1994, Springdale won its first four games for the first time since 1964, setting up a rarity in Dynamoland for Week Five – a good, old-fashioned showdown. In one of the largest crowds ever at Veterans Memorial Field, Riverview shut out the Dynamos, 22-0. But no matter – Springdale football was back.

After 19 straight losing seasons, the Dynamos posted a 6-4 record, missing the WPIAL playoffs after coming up short, 22-20, against Clairton in Week Nine. Springdale would have sporadic success, missing the playoffs in 1999 because of a 6-3 upset by Duquesne over Clairton on the final day of the regular season, but they were no longer being defeated by 30- and 40-point margins constantly.

One off-field action contributed to eventual success. Paul Jack, a former Dynamos quarterback and assistant coach, told the school board in the late 1980s, that the school system was allowing students to start first grade as early as age 5. When the children got to high school, Springdale basically had 15- and 16-year olds playing often times against 17- and 18-year olds. It would take a while, but eventually Allegheny Valley School District children entered first grade later than in the past.

Forgetting the Past

On Oct. 31, 2001, the orange & black Dynamos celebrated Halloween with a 28-8 victory over West Shamokin. Just as Wagner often used the old AIC Bowl as a springboard to great seasons, Springdale's Week Ten nonconference game proved to be the same tonic. The Dynamos finally broke through, making the 2002 playoffs and ending a 29-year postseason drought. Springdale lost an opening round playoff game to Sto-Rox, 35-10. But no matter, the Dynamos had finally broken down the playoff door.

The 2003 season ended with a second-place finish in the conference and a home game to open the playoffs. A WPIAL representative checked out Veterans Field late in the season and declared the stadium playoff-acceptable, meaning the Dynamos could open the postseason at home. Several times in the past, the WPIAL did not approve facilities that weren't up to standards.

In the first playoff game ever at 'The Vets,' the Dynamos blanked South Side Beaver, 21-0. The following week, Springdale shut down long-time powerhouse Monessen, 22-7. That set up one of the greatest football games in A-K Valley history.

Rochester came into the Class A semifinal at Highlands Golden Rams Stadium as a favorite. After all, the Rams had won three WPIAL titles in a row and were trying to become only the second school to ever win at least four in a row.

Rochester led, 7-0, at the half. But Springdale had two lengthy possessions to start the second half. The Dynamos took the second half kickoff a kept the ball for 15 plays before losing possession on downs at the Rams 19. After forcing a Rochester punt, Springdale was on offense for 16 more plays, again coming up short. But the time the Rochester defense spent on the field took its toll.

Dan Arnone recovered a fumble at the Rams 21. Quarterback Jon Molnar took it from there with runs of 13 and 8 yards to tie the game with 7:34 left in the fourth period. Both teams exchanged touchdowns and extra points in the first overtime. In the second overtime, Andrew Bosman and Sam DiGiovine exchanged 25-yard field goals.

But in the third overtime, Brent Whiteleather scored a touchdown. DiGiovine's extra point attempt, however, went wide right and Springdale took over. On third-and-one, Molnar followed guard Colin Dugan into the end zone to tie the game. Rochester called a time out to try and ice Bosman, but the Dynamos sophomore booted the extra point to send Springdale into the title game. In summer 2009, Bosman was a U.S. Marine Corporal, serving in Iraq.

The Dynamos again were underdogs in the finals against Sto-Rox, a team led by Adam DiMichele, then the WPIAL's all-time leading passer. The Vikings had scored 125 points in the three playoffs games to get to Heinz Field. In fact, Sto-Rox had scored 40 more or more in its last 10 games.

But Springdale figured the best way to handle DeMichele was to keep him off the field. And the Dynamos did exactly that keeping the ball on the ground to the tune of 321 yards team rushing, building a 21-7 halftime lead and rolling to a 30-13 victory.

The Springdale defense also was up to the task, forcing four Vikings turnovers and holding Sto-Rox to just 53 yards rushing. Wayne Mundekis had 106 yards rushing and 2 TD, Jon Molnar had 2 TD runs and one TD pass, while Mike Landers picked off two DiMichele passes.

The Dynamos won the line of scrimmage and Wagner had his second WPIAL title, 38 years after the first one in 1965 at Oakmont.

Wagner, because of both his longevity and demeanor, has respect wherever he goes. When the WPIAL had a meeting for coaches and athletic directors in February, 2004 after the PIAA changed the football format that would have reduced the playoffs to two teams from each conference instead of four, Wagner passionately spoke of how much it meant to Springdale to enter the playoffs after suffering 26 losing seasons in 27 years. The auditorium was silent. When Chuck Wagner spoke everyone listened. Springdale went on to make the playoffs the following five seasons, including 2007 when the Dynamos again visited Heinz Field, this time losing to Serra Catholic, 10-6.

Wagner has become a WPIAL icon. When someone needs advice, they seek out Wagner. When Ron Gevaudan took over the struggling Carlynton program, he had dinner with Wagner to pick his brain about turning around a football program.

Wagner shows no signs of slowing down, outlasting most of the 10 presidents.

Credit: A-K Valley Sports Hall of Fame

Chuck Wagner is one of the WPIAL's most respected coaches. He has 252 coaching victories, seventh on the all-time WPIAL list.

chapter 18

A GOLD MEDAL CAREER

Usually, the Olympics bring out the casual sports fan who likes to see quirky, but endearing events seen once every four years or a chance to flash some patriotic pride for American athletes who come from all corners of the country.

But in 1988, local fans got a chance to root for someone with Alle-Kiski Valley roots as Leechburg native Mickey Morandini took the field for Team USA, and ended up winning the gold medal in Seoul, South Korea.

When Morandini returned to Leechburg after the Seoul Games, he proudly showed off his medal and fans were treated to seeing a symbol of athletic prowess.

Morandini made the Olympic team after a grueling and demanding tryout process that followed a stellar career at Indiana University. The 1984 Leechburg graduate had to switch positions, making the team as a leftfielder after playing shortstop during his high school and collegiate careers.

But Morandini defied the odds and became one of 20 players on the U.S. team. After a barnstorming tour of the country that included four losses in seven games against powerhouse Cuba, the team headed for South Korea with a veritable galaxy of future major league baseball stars.

Much of the attention focused on pitcher Jim Abbott, a University of Michigan grad known for his success despite being born without a right wrist and hand. Abbott was the No. 1 pick of the California Angels and fellow hurler Andy Benes was the No. 1 of the entire draft, selected by San Diego. Other future major leaguers included Robin Ventura and Tino Martinez. Ventura once hit in 58 straight collegiate games for Oklahoma State.

The USA team survived pool play and defeated Puerto Rico, 7-2, in the semifinals and Japan, 5-3, to win the Gold Medal.

It was the culmination to a great calendar year in 1988 for Morandini. He was the Phillies fifth round pick that year after making his second consecutive All-American team and his third straight All-Big 10 team.

The Start

When selected by Philadelphia, it marked the second time he was chosen for a team called the Philles. As a nine-year old in Leechburg Little League, Morandini was selected in 1976 by Andy Lucchino, manager for the Phillies, who saw extraordinary talent, even in a player so young.

Morandini continued his climb through the Little League ranks, becoming the first 13-year-old in Leechburg Little League history to make the Senior Division all-star team. At the time, the age group was 13-15, making it remarkable for anyone 13 to be picked.

As a 14-year-old in 1981, he played on a Pennsylvania District 26 all-star runner-up, and a championship team in 1982. He also excelled in basketball.

Blue Devils coach Larry Ondako made him a starter as a ninth grader in the 1980-81 campaign. He was a basketball product developed in the Catholic Youth Organization (CYO) basketball program at the Leechburg Catholic Center.

Morandini changed his shooting technique and became a prolific scorer, setting the Leechburg career record of 1,675 points, also one of the top totals in local history. But Ondako was most pleased with the fact that Morandini led not only in scoring, but in assists the final three seasons. As a senior, Morandini led the Blue Devils to an undefeated regular season, losing in the second round of the WPIAL playoffs.

In baseball, he led the Blue Devils to the 1983 finals before losing to California Area. In the opening round of that tournament, Morandini pitched all 12 innings in a 4-3 win over Ford City. After a win in the opening round of the PIAA playoffs, Leechburg lost to eventual state champion Riverview.

In 1984, Morandini again led Leechburg to the WPIAL playoffs. Perhaps his greatest performance was against Carlynton in a playoffs game at Pullman Park, Butler. Morandini drove in five runs with a two-run triple, a solo homer and a bases-loaded double in his final scholastic appearance. He finished with a .490 career batting average with the Blue Devils.

Though he had a chance to play Division II or III college basketball, there was no doubt Morandini would cast his lot with baseball. He accepted a baseball scholarship to the University of Indiana in Bloomington.

He was named to three different All-American teams in his junior season. Morandini was selected by the Pirates after his junior season, but decided to return to the Hoosiers for his senior season.

In his first season with the Phillies' farm team in Spartansburg, S.C., he played 63 games and hit .338 (78-for-231), clubbed 16 doubles, scored 43 runs and stole 15 bases. Morandini received the Paul Owens Award as Philadelphia's minor league Player of the Year.

At the end of 1989, he was sent to the Philles' Clearwater, Fla., team in the Instructional League where he learned to play second base from former Pirates and Phillies star Dave Cash. Morandini was soon on the fast track to the big leagues. He made his major league debut on Sept. 1, 1990.

The Triple Play

Nothing in baseball is rarer than an unassisted triple play. But Morandini turned the ninth unassisted triple play in baseball history on Sept. 20, 1992. It came in a game against the Pirates at Three Rivers Stadium

At the time, the Pirates were roaring towards their third straight National League title while the Phillies were headed for another last-place finish.

On a sunny Sunday afternoon with the score tied at 1-1 in the sixth inning, Andy Van Slyke was on at second and Barry Bonds at first. With both runners breaking, Jeff King hit a liner near second that Morandini caught on the fly moving to his right. Morandini stepped on second base for the second out and tagged Bonds for the third out.

Though rare, Morandini was prepared for the triple play. He used visualization – planning on how situations would play out if he got the ball. King would be more successful later in the game, singling home Cecil Espy in the bottom of the 13th inning to give the Pirates a 3-2 victory.

The Phillies would finish in last place that year, but 1993 was altogether different. Philadelphia climbed out of the cellar and soared all the way to first place, winning the National League East and defeating Atlanta in the National League Championship Series with a 6-3 victory to secure a berth in the World Series.

The Biggest Stage

Morandini was set to play on baseball's biggest stage. By then Morandini was sharing time at second base with Mariano Duncan. He got his first World Series hit in Game 6, but that one was decided by a walk-off home run by Toronto's Joe Carter to hand the Blue Jays their second straight world championship. In 1995 coming out of the baseball strike, Morandini was named to the National League all-star team. After being traded to the Cubs, he played in the National Divisional Series in 1998 as Chicago lost to the Braves.

Morandini spent the final portion of the 2000 season with Toronto. His last big league game was on Oct. 1, 2000 when Toronto lost to the Indians at Jacobs Field. That same day, Three Rivers Stadium, the site of Morandini's triple play, hosted baseball for the final time.

Morandini's final career numbers were: 1,298 games played, 5,135 at bats, 1,222 hits for a .268 average.

Currently, he is the varsity coach at Valparaiso High School in western Indiana.

During spring training, 2009, Morandini was invited to the World Champion Philles training came for a two-week instructional stint. Morandini liked it so much that he is seriously considering a major league coaching job once his three young sons are grown.

Credit: Valley News Dispatch

It is Oct. 1, 1988 and Mickey Morandidni poses with his Olympic gold medal on his return to Leechburg from the Seoul Games.

Leechburg's Mickey Morandini pitched all 12 innings in a WPIAL win over Ford City at Butler's Pullman Park on May 31, 1983.

chapter 19

REACHING THE WINNER'S CIRCLE

Coach Ray Bartha has over 500 victories in over 30 years as Apollo-Ridge High School's girls basketball coach.

But there's one victory that will always be treasured.

The Lady Vikings, after eight previous WPIAL playoff appearances, some of which ended in early-round disappointments, finally got to enter the winner's circle on March 9, 1991. In a Saturday afternoon encounter at Pitt's Fitzgerald Field House, the Vikings defeated Brentwood, 54-51, in a thriller that will be remembered for many years.

Apollo-Ridge entered the Class AA playoffs as the No. 1-seeded team with a 24-0 record. The Vikings had made the semifinals just once in the past, losing to North Catholic in 1982. Four times Apollo-Ridge was sent packing with an opening round loss. The 1990 playoffs saw an overwhelming victory in the first round against Wilmington, 70-28, on the Kiski Area High School floor. But things were much different in the second round as the Vikings dropped a 51-46 decision to Brentwood at Fox Chapel.

It was the second playoff loss to Brentwood, with the first coming in 1979.

With only starter Heidi Guido graduating, Apollo-Ridge was poised for a deep title run.

What made the season particularly satisfying for Bartha was the fact that he had two daughters – Shane and Jennifer – in the starting lineup. Other starters included Daina Cleveland, Jill Rollinson and Brande Schade.

In what was supposed to be a key test for the Vikings on a frigid January night, Apollo-Ridge traveled to Armstrong East, a recent merger Shannock Valley and Dayton, two solid girls basketball programs.

Instead, the Vikings barely broke a sweat, winning by a 70-44 bulge. It advanced Apollo-Ridge to 16-0 overall, and it was the 15th consecutive time the Vikings held the opposition to less than 50 points. East Allegheny tallied 56 against Apollo-Ridge on opening night.

With the top seed in tow, Apollo-Ridge opened the playoffs with a resounding 51-31 win over Springdale at Armstrong Central High School, home of the temporary merger of Kittanning and Ford City high schools.

The quarterfinals were another story. The Vikings barely survived Wilmington, the team it pounded by 26 points the previous season. Many skeptics insisted Apollo-Ridge played too soft of a schedule.

Rollinson injured her ankle in the first half and the Greyhounds were hitting their three-point shots. Wilmington led, 46-42, with four minutes left in the game when Apollo-Ridge's defense went to work, outscoring the Greyhounds, 11-5, over the final minutes of play to emerge with a 53-51 victory at the New Castle Fieldhouse.

"We had 'em all the way," coach Bartha would say. "We needed to have a close game."

Shane Bartha led the way with 21 points, including the late basket that gave the Vikings the lead for good. Cleveland added 20 points, 12 rebounds and six blocked shots.

Apollo-Ridge squared off against another local team, Deer Lakes, in the semifinals at Butler High School. The Vikings, a three-point victor over the Lancers during the regular season, beat Deer Lakes by a 49-39 margin to earn its first WPIAL title game berth.

Defense carried the Vikings game after game, and the Class AA championship game would be no different. Apollo-Ridge kept Brentwood off the scoreboard from the 6:37 mark of the second quarter until the 2:18 mark of third quarter. Brentwood had led, 21-13, before their long dry spell.

Apollo-Ridge had a 42-32 lead after three periods, but trouble loomed. Daina Cleveland and Shane Bartha both fouled out during the fourth quarter, Jill Senapole and Erin Buchner had to come off the bench to hold off the Spartans. A key steal by Rollinson with 1:43 left gave the Vikings possession. Rollinson was fouled with a minute left and made a free throw to put the Vikings up, 54-49. With nine seconds left, Schade missed a foul shot and Brentwood rebounded. A three-point attempt by Pam Artman hit the rim at the buzzer, setting off a wild Apollo-Ridge celebration. Only three Vikings scored in the title game as Shane Bartha collected 24 points, Rollinson added 19 and Cleveland scored 11. Apollo-Ridge didn't have much time to celebrate. The Vikings were back an action two nights later. With Easter falling in late March, the PIAA decided to condense the basketball playoffs into three nights the first week. Apollo-Ridge had to play powerhouse Girard, and team that was upset early in the District 10 playoffs by Kennedy Christian. Girard handed Apollo-Ridge a stunning, first-round loss, 55-49, at Armstrong Central, only 53 hours after the Vikings earned WPIAL honors.

Though Apollo-Ridge hasn't been able to return to the WPIAL finals, the program is one of the most consistently successful operations in WPIAL girls basketball. Bartha's teams have made the WPIAL playoffs 21 times in his 33 years at the helm.

Bartha has 518 career victories and his teams have won 10 section titles and made four PIAA tournament appearances. His junior high teams posted seven undefeated seasons.

Bartha has coached 45 postseason games, similar to two extra seasons when placed together.

A secret to Bartha's success is the Top Gun instructional program which has taught basketball skills to hundreds of youngsters over the years.

On June 22, 2009, the Apollo-Ridge School Board appointed Bartha as coach for a 34th consecutive season.

Ray Bartha has led Apollo-Ridge to 21 playoff berths in 33 seasons.

Credit: Valley News Dispatch

Apollo-Ridge guard Shane Bartha (52) fires up a shot against Brentwood in the WPIAL Class AA title game at the Pitt Field House on March 9, 1991.

Credit: Dan Angeloni, West Deer Alumni Association

The East Deer-West Deer football rivalry featured The Antlers, a trophy which went to the game's winner for at least one year, until the subsequent game. If the winner repeated, it got to keep the trophy for at least another year. But in 1951, East Deer defeated West Deer, 14-6, in a driving snowstorm. That meant West Deer's Donnie Allen had to hand over the trophy to East Deer's Leroy McCaskey. Looking on is East Deer coach Warren Heller, West Deer coach Vince Antonelli, Allen, McCaskey, Ed Frena of East Deer, East Deer principal Andrew Petor and West Deer captain Larry Rommes. As an added benefit, the winning team's school often got a day off.

Credit: A-K Valley Hall of Fame

Washington Township graduate Bob Long was the first from the A-K Valley to play in a Super Bowl game. Here, Long hauls in a touchdown pass for the Green Bay Packers during a game against the Vikings at Metropolitan Stadium in Bloomington, Minn. The stadium is now site of the Mall of America.

chapter 20

RACING TO THE TOP

Lernerville Speedway in the Sarver section of Buffalo Township is regarded as one of the top dirt tracks in the country, a remarkably successful facility for racing fans who come from far and wide for events.

But it wasn't always that way for the track and owner/promoter Don Martin.

Long before Lernerville had its inauspicious beginning in 1967, Martin was a big race fan. Upon his discharge from military service in the 1950s, he became a car owner with Dick Swartzlander. Later, Martin owned a number of cars himself, ranging from a coupe-bodied Modified to an ex-Indy roadster that ran against Sprints at tracks around Western Pennsylvania.

Martin won his share of races, but the effort certainly wasn't lucrative. His main job was operating a trucking company and he never planned on owning a track. But things rarely turn out the way they're planned.

In1967, Earl Bauman, Dale Hafer and Bucky Fleming started work on a quarter-mile track at the location of Lernerville Park, a former amusement park dating back to the 1940s. The track was located practically across from Martin's trucking firm. Bauman, Hafer and Fleming needed help getting things going, and Martin was there to help.

The group had planned to begin racing in the spring of 1968, but Buffalo Township passed an ordinance that would have kept the track from opening. To beat the effective date of the ordinance, the group hurriedly opened the speedway for two races in October, 1967.

The owners had to skimp on a lot of things to get the track grandfathered before the ordinance kicked in. Martin was one of the first promoters, however, to guarantee purses, and that attracted racers to Lernerville.

The first race was a 100-lap event for Modifieds that brought cars from the old Penn-Western Racing Association and the

Sportsman cars that raced at Butler, Mercer, Blanket Hill and Tri-City. Johnny Axe of New Castle won the first race with a number 34 Chevy coupe. Butler's Harry Hein finished second and Ed Lynch Sr. took third, representing the pre-race favorite, Penn-Western.

Other winners in the inaugural year included Jim Minton and Russ Woolsey.

But despite the contribution from top racers, the early years were unsuccessful at the gate, and Martin had to buy out two of his partners a year later.

Part of Martin's vision was a racetrack with a family atmosphere. One way to attain that atmosphere was to not sell beer. Though that surely would have made the track's bottom line healthier, but Martin stuck with his philosophy in the hope that people could bring children to the races and develop another generation of racing enthusiasts.

In 1981, Martin bought out Bauman's interest and became sole owner. Bauman, however, helped out at the track as an assistant promoter until his death in 1985.

Martin died in 1993, just a year after the track defied all odds and celebrated its 25th anniversary. For his contributions to Sprint Car Racing, Martin was posthumously inducted into the National Sprint Car Hall of Fame.

Martin already had been inducted into the A-K Valley Sports Hall of Fame in 1984.

Helen Martin, Don's widow, and daughter Patty Roenigk designated Dave Bauman, Jim Roenigk and Albert 'Ouch' Roenigk as track co-promoters. Bauman was killed in a terrible skiing accident in 1998 and Jim Roenigk left to pursue other avenues a year later.

Garry 'Arch' Hunter and Albert 'Ouch' Roenigk were named co-promoters by the owners in the 1999 and 2000 racing seasons. By 2001, Ouch Roenigk was the sole promoter.

In 2004, Barb Bauman Bartley and Tom Roenigk, also known as Lernerville Motorsports, took over as co-directors and leased the track from the Martin family. Then, the duo leased the track from DIRT Motorsports in 2005.

Later in 2005, Lernerville speedway was sold to DIRT Motorsports, which continues to operate the track.

From those halcyon days of 1967, Lernerville has grown to become one of the country's best dirt tracks. The whir of engines on a Friday night has become part of Alle-Kiski Valley culture. Yes, they now sell beer at Lernerville. But one bit of logic was that selling beer would lessen the incentive for someone to get drunk in the parking lot before entering the grandstand and being disruptive during the evening. The track can control beer sales and consumption, and it works to everyone's advantage.

Features such as the World of Outlaws and school bus races also have become Lernerville staples.

The track has been three times from a small quarter mile to a large quarter, then to a 3/8 –mile track, then to its current size as a small half mile.

Seating also has increased several times to the current capacity of about 12,000.

Credit: *Valley News Dispatch*

Don Martin stands near the sign welcoming race fans to his Lernerville Speedway on June 28, 1991 along State Route 356.

Credit: Valley News Dispatch

Lernerville's racing nights often are plagued by bad weather. But at least for one night, fans could see a rainbow during the evening.

This is an overview of what the track looks like today.

chapter 21
FINDING THE RIGHT SIZE

The creation of Quad-A football changed the landscape of WPIAL like nothing in the past. Up until 1980, the WPIAL had a tidy arrangement of Class AA, A and B.

Some schools winced at the though of playing the largest schools around. So much to the point that Franklin Regional, Churchill and Moon high schools bolted the WPIAL rather than play the likes of Penn Hills, Butler and Mt. Lebanon.

The large schools were so dominant that a 5-A class was being talked about. The WPIAL had to do something, or more schools were threatening to jettison the organization.

For the 1982 and '83 seasons, the WPIAL came up with two tiers of Quad-A – the 14 largest schools would play in Quad-A, Division I, while the next 14 schools in size would play in Quad-A, Division II.

The Plum Mustangs were one of the first schools to take advantage of that arrangement, winning the Class AAAA, Section 3 title in 1982, then coming away with the Quad-A, Division II title in 1983.

Plum won the conference in '82 with a perfect 6-0 slate. The Mustangs finished the regular season at 9-1, the only loss a 24-21 setback against Central Catholic. In the WPIAL playoffs for the smaller tier of Quad-A schools, the Mustangs knocked off Chartiers Valley, 28-7, for only the second playoff victory in school history. Plum was eliminated in the semifinals by Ringgold, 18-13.

Plum's ascent, however, to the top of the WPIAL mountain in 1983 wasn't easy. Expectations were high since a number of the players from the previous season were returning. Plum started out 2-0, but lost three of the next four games.

After six weeks, Plum looked ordinary with a 3-3 mark after a loss to Hempfield in a non-conference game. But the final seven weeks were anything but ordinary. Mustangs coach Al 'Abby' Mauro switched halfback Paul Palamara from halfback to fullback and he responded with a record-setting performance on Oct. 28,

1983. He set a school record 306 yards rushing against Greensburg Salem as the Mustangs routed the Golden Lions, 42-0. In fact, Plum's stellar 4-4 Defense didn't yield a point the final four games of the regular season. The Mustangs blanked Latrobe (18-0), Laurel Highlands (22-0), Greensburg Salem and Kiski Area (39-0). That allowed Plum to finish 5-1 in conference play – the only loss was to Fox Chapel. What's more impressive was a dismantling of Ringgold, 38-0, in the opening round of the play-offs. Palamara continued his torrid pace with 204 rushing yards and three touchdowns.

In the semifinals, Plum faced heavily-favored Upper St. Clair. With 4:12 left in the game, quarterback Jimmy Miller's 5-yard pass to Jeff Hahn lifted the Mustangs to a 12-7 victory.

The WPIAL decided that three of the five title games would be played at Three Rivers Stadium. Plum would be facing powerful New Castle in a game that would be televised by KDKA Channel 2. But the Mustangs and their growing legion of fans were undaunted. The fans, in fact, started a huge car caravan from the school's campus to the stadium that stretched for miles.

And all those fans liked what they saw. With the scored tied 6-6 late in the fourth quarter, Plum tallied two safeties in the final 3:44 of the game to record a 10-6 victory.

Mauro, who won a WPIAL title at Burrell three years later, was inducted into the A-K Valley Sports Hall of Fame in 1998. Palamara, who later starred at Indiana (Pa.) University, was inducted into the Plum Sports Hall of Fame on Nov. 12, 2009.

Credit: Valley News Dispatch

The Plum Mustangs carry coach Al Mauro off the field following the team's WPIAL Quad-A championship at Three Rivers Stadium on Nov. 26, 1983.

chapter 22

THE SUDDEN DYNASTY

During the merger mania of the 1960s where so many schools were consolidating that it was sometimes tough to keep track of them all, most of the newly-merged schools needed an incubation period for everybody to adjust to the new surroundings. Not so with Valley High School basketball. The Vikings won a section title in their first season and didn't stop there.

In the first 12 seasons of Valley basketball, starting with the inaugural 1967-68 campaign and going through to the 1978-79 state championship team, the school compiled a 232-62 record for a .789 winning percentage.

The superb record makes the consolidation of New Kensington and Arnold high schools look smoother than it really was. For the first three school years, Valley High School operated from two different buildings – the New Kensington campus and the Arnold campus.

Mike Rice, who had coached Ken High over its last four seasons, was selected to run the new, joint program. Players from the Arnold building had to get to the New Kensington building after dismissal. There were no activity buses.

"We'd get out of class at Arnold and had to catch a ride to Ken High or walk over the hill," said center Craig Confer.

It all came together for opening night as Valley won its first game, a 76-64 decision over Duquesne. The Vikings lost their second game to Penn Hills, then embarked on a 12-game winning streak.

Triumph & Tragedy

It was obvious that the new team had talent, but despite all of the success that first season, there was a lingering thought as to how much better the team would have been if tragedy and economic reality hadn't stepped in.

On Jan. 10, 1968, tragedy befell the new program when senior forward Ron Waugh suffered a coronary while sitting on the bench during Valley's 86-59 win over Burrell, the first meeting between the two schools.

"We were close, just like brothers," said fellow senior Al Jackson. "It happened right beside me on the bench."

Two years earlier, budding star Perry Ludy left New Kensington when he was recruited by a California high school. At the time, California was considered the Land of Milk & Honey, where seemingly everybody could go and get a fresh start.

In Ludy's case, it was a single mother with six children to raise receiving government assistance being promised a job in the Golden State, with the Ludy children having a shot at college educations. So Ludy was off to Oxnard High School, located about 60 miles north of Los Angeles. He was named the nation's Optimist Club Boy of the Year in 1969, where he went to Washington, D.C., shaking hands with President Nixon at the White House and later addressing the U.S. Senate.

Ludy appeared on the Tonight Show, where he matched wits with Johnny Carson and Ed McMahon. Ludy was recruited by some 20 to 30 colleges, finally settling on Northwestern University. He played in the Big 10 Conference two years before heading back to California when he feared his younger brother, Brad, might go astray.

After a redshirt year, Ludy finished his collegiate career at UC–Santa Barbara. Ludy has been a rousing success in the business world, having held executive positions with Proctor & Gamble, San Diego's Imperial Corp., Pizza Hut and Sears Auto Glass. He then started his own company – USA–GLAS Network, where Sears Auto Glass eventually bought products from him.

Brad turned out OK, too, growing to 6-foot-7 and playing professional basketball in Norway.

The Shot that Shook WPIAL Basketball

Despite Waugh's tragic death and Ludy's absence, stars like Torrance Lyle, a junior guard, came to the forefront with 534 points. Valley knocked off Har-Brack on the final night of the regular season, forcing a one-game playoff with the Tigers for the Section 1 title and a berth in the WPIAL playoffs. The Vikings won the showdown, 81-68.

On March 4, 1968, Valley faced Farrell, the dominant WPIAL program of the era, before 11,000 fans at the Pittsburgh Civic Arena. The Vikings were heavy underdogs. The Steelers were without their legendary coach, Ed McCluskey, who was in New York City for an eye operation. Assistant Sam Jankovich handled the team.

Valley had the lead from the 6:51 mark of the second quarter to the 6:45 mark of the fourth quarter. The score was knotted at 54-all after regulation time.

Farrell took a lead with 45 seconds left in the overtime, but missed a foul shot with nine seconds remaining. Llewellyn Johnson got the rebound and found Jackson heading upcourt. Jackson got off a shot from 23-feet away. The high, arching shot fell through the hoop and set off a wild celebration, as the Vikings pulled out a 58-57 victory.

"When that shot was in the air, I thought I missed, then I felt the presence of my friend and I saw the ball going through," Jackson said.

The Vikings lost in the semifinals to Donora, 72-54, as future baseball star Ken Griffey Sr. scored 24 points as Valley finished its inaugural season 22-3.

Even with the Donora loss, a new WPIAL basketball powerhouse was born.

More Success

Valley went 16-6 overall in its second season, finishing second in the section. The following season, the Vikings finished in a first place tie with Highlands in Section 1-A.

Although the schools are just four miles apart, the tiebreaker game was scheduled for Geneva College in Beaver Falls, some 55 miles away. The Civic Arena was being used that night – likewise, Pitt's Fitzgerald Field House and Carnegie-Mellon's Skibo Gym. The WPIAL, insisting the game be held on a college floor, shipped the game to Geneva. The crowd followed, packing the Beaver Falls facility as Highlands secured a 57-50 victory.

Valley next won a section title in 1973, compiling a 12-0 section mark and won 20 games in a row at one point. The Vikings returned to the Civic Arena for the first times since 1968, winning a

61-59 thriller over previously undefeated Jeannette. But three nights later, Valley was hammered by eventual WPIAL champion Ringgold, 66-39. Ringgold was led by Joe Montana, who was more well-known for basketball in high school than in football, and Ulice Payne, who would go on to play for Marquette's 1977 National Championship team.

Valley finished at 21-2.

The B.B. Era

The following season, the Vikings finished 16-6 overall and runner-up in the section to Burrell.

But emerging that season for Valley was scintillating sopho-more guard Baron 'B.B.' Flenory. Mixing the ability to either shoot from the outside or slash to the hoop, Flenory presented a host of dilemmas for defenses.

Flenory gained national prominence as a ninth-grader, ap-pearing in *Sports Illustrated*'s Faces in the Crowd section for his 83-point performance against Deer Lakes Junior High.

What made the feat really remarkable is that Flenory sat out the first quarter because he didn't wear a necktie to school on game day.

In the 1974-75 season, things really came together for Flenory and a number of other teammates, including guard Roger Galo, sophomore Benjy Pryor and juniors Ed 'Jim-Jim' Hughley and Gerald Williams.

As the team kept winning, the Valley gym was the place to be. Despite a severe population drop in New Kensington and Arnold, the gym was packed on game nights. Interest was so intense that Westmoreland Cable Channel 3 televised three games live in 1974 and '75. If there were some tickets remaining, Channel 3 General Manager Nelson Goldberg would buy up the remaining tickets to assure the school district of a sellout.

Valley was cruising toward a section title, but on the final day of the regular season, the Vikings were upset by Highlands, 70-62, necessitating a section playoff at the Civic Arena.

Valley thrived on the big 'Arena floor, dispatching North Hills to win the Section 5-AAA title, 64-49. In an outstanding quarter-finals battle, the Vikings edged South Hills Catholic, 56-55, in overtime. In another hard-fought battle, Valley got by Hempfield, 70-65, before huge throng swelled by 26 buses from Hempfield. That set the Vikings up for the finals, where Uniontown prevailed, 68-61.

It was on to the PIAA playoffs, again on a college floor, where Flenory dazzled the crowd at Edinboro University by pouring in 49 points. Valley won the school's first state playoff game with ease, 84-54, over Meadville.

The Epitome of Ugliness

Of the more than 1,000 basketball games that Valley has played, none was uglier than the March 15, 1975 second round game against Fifth Avenue at Charleroi High School.

Archers coach Elmer Guckert brought his formidable lineup of senior Henry Montgomery, junior William Clarke and sophomores Sam Clancy, Warner Macklin and David Kennedy into the game. What followed was an afternoon of taunting, verbal threats, fans rushing the floor and officials more concerned with their personal safety than calling a basketball game.

Fifth Avenue grabbed an early lead that grew to 38-28 by halftime. A Valley mounted a comeback, however, the atmosphere grew ominous. During timeouts, Fifth Avenue fans came out of the stands to join the Valley huddle. Coach Rice's clipboard was shattered by a Fifth Avenue player and the officials tried to sell every call made against the Archers. Valley's 12-2 run to end the third quarter tied the game at 50-all. Things clearly were getting out of hand as Valley took a 57-54 lead on Galo's fast break with 4:27 left in the fourth quarter.

Fifth Avenue fans stormed the floor, causing a 7-minute delay. Only two policemen were on hand. State Police at a nearby barracks were summoned, but order was restored by the time the troopers arrived.

With one minute left in the fourth quarter, the alternate official seated at the scorer's table was sent to the locker room by Pittsburgh City League athletic director George Cupples because he could not guarantee the safety of three officials.

Flenory's foul shot with 2 seconds left in regulation tied the game at 60-60 and sent it into overtime. Reserve David Trent's third basket of the overtime gave Fifth Avenue a 69-68 lead with 10 seconds left. Pryor was gang-tackled attempting a lay-up that would have won the game for Valley. Referee Max Crease raised his hand as if to call a foul. But the buzzer sounded, and Crease headed for the locker room.

The New Kensington-Arnold School District filed a protest, but to no avail as the Vikings season ended at 23-5. The next Fifth Avenue game against Aliquippa was played behind closed doors. Fifth won, 53-49, but lost the PIAA semifinals to eventual state champion Schenley.

In the 1975-76 season, with only Galo graduated, Valley again made another run, winning the section convincingly and finishing the regular season 21-1. The only loss was to North Catholic in a non-section encounter.

Flenory set the school's single-game scoring record of 52 points in a game against Norwin in December, 1975.

The Vikings got a first round bye and defeated Sto-Rox, 83-73 on the Civic Arena floor. Valley was tested by a gritty Monessen team in the semifinals, winning 77-75. That put the Vikings in the Class AAA title game for the second straight year.

This time around, Valley fell victim to Farrell, the same school in the 1968 game that put Valley on the basketball map. The final score was 58-53.

It was on to the PIAA playoffs once again for the Vikings, who began the state tournament with a resounding 78-54 victory over Warren at Edinboro. But looming in the second round once again was Fifth Avenue. This time the game was played at California (Pa) University and went off without incident. Valley led by nine points and was holding for the final shot of the half. But the lightning-quick Macklin stole the ball and was fouled going for the hoop. So instead of a possible 11-point lead, the Valley advantage was cut to six, and the Archers never looked back, winning 76-67. Fifth Avenue eventually won the state title, defeating Norristown, 53-42. It turned out to be the last game in school history, as Fifth Avenue and Gladstone were merged with a portion of Pittsburgh's South Side to form Brashear High School. The Archers finished only 12-0, starting their season late because of a Pittsburgh Public Schools teachers strike.

Flenory later was named to the Parade All-American team, one of only 12 Pennsylvanians ever honored. He would go on to a stellar career at Duquesne University and was one of the final cuts of the Boston Celtics in 1980.

Flenory was named to the Pennsylvania Basketball Hall of fame in 2008.

Flenory, Williams and Hughley all graduated, and Mike Rice also left, accompanying Flenory at Duquesne as an assistant to head coach John Cinicola.

Valley finished 24-3.

Not Much of a Rebuild

With three starters and their coach departing, some thought it was rebuilding time at Valley.

If it was, they showed an odd way of rebuilding.

With new coach Jim Patterson, an assistant under Rice, starters Pryor and Cliff Guy returned. Lance Ballard, Ollie Jackson and Jerome McDew also saw their playing time increase, and they were joined by a solid sophomore class that included Billy Varner, Ron 'Mack" McNabb and Gosby 'Goose' Pryor.

Valley hardly missed a beat, going 19-3. The Vikings missed the playoffs however, because two of the three losses were section games against Fox Chapel, the eventual WPIAL and PIAA champion. It was the final season the WPIAL would take only section champions to the playoffs.

In 1978, Valley tied North Allegheny and North Hills for the section title. A 3-way playoff was needed to determine the top two teams who would go to the playoffs. The Vikings lost to North Hills, then beat North Allegheny for second place. Valley was ousted in its first playoff game by Penn Hills, 78-66. The Indians featured 7-foot-2 center Kevin Hall, who later became an actor. After receiving a scholarship to George Washington University, he went to Hollywood and eventually landed the lead role in the TV series Harry and the Hendersons, a sitcom about a family that runs over Bigfoot while vacationing in the Pacific Northwest, and takes him home, becoming part of the family. In 1990, Hall was involved in a serious auto accident of his own. During surgery, he allegedly received a blood transfusion tainted by the HIV virus. He later contracted AIDS, going public with the illness along with his wife, actress Alaina Reed. Hall died on April 10, 1991.

Valley finished the 1977-78 campaign 18-8, eagerly anticipating the following season. The Vikings escalated the quality of their non-section schedule, adding teams like defending state champion Schenley to the December card. An extra challenge materialized when Varner, one of the top players in the state, was injured. Patterson had to throw Mike Fuquay into the lineup instead of bringing the sophomore along slowly as planned.

When the Section 5-AAA season was completed, Valley and Fox Chapel were tied for the top, necessitating a one-game playoff. The crowd arrived early and packed the Penn State-New Kensington Fieldhouse. Fans who couldn't get in milled around outside to get scoring updates. Many probably thought the updates were bogus because Valley breezed to a 77-52 victory.

In the WPIAL Class AAA first round, the Vikings overwhelmed West Mifflin North, 86-65, setting up a quarterfinal showdown with neighboring Burrell. The two schools were no longer in the same section and split a pair of non-section games earlier.

Burrell staged a big second half surge before 7,040 fans and held on for a 50-48 victory, despite the Civic Arena clock skipping two minutes along the way.

Putting it All Together

Valley would be among the first schools to be placed in a mini-bracket of the four quarterfinal losers to determine the last two PIAA playoff spots from the WPIAL.

The Vikings made the most of their second chance, knocking off Chartiers Valley and, one more time for good measure, Fox Chapel. That allowed Valley to enter the PIAA tournament as the No. 5 seed from the WPIAL.

The Vikings PIAA tournament bracket, however, appeared formidable. The opening round game would send Valley headlong into a late-winter snowstorm to Windber High School to face an Altoona team that included 7-footer Ricky Tunstall and 6-8 Louie Schmitt.

Despite the disparity in height, Valley pulled out a 63-59 victory. It seemed like every team had at least one big star in that era. Three nights later, Valley won a PIAA second round game for the first time, defeating Pittsburgh's South Hills High School. But there was little time for celebration as a matchup with Schenley loomed.

Before a packed house at Indiana (Pa.) University's Memorial Fieldhouse, the Vikings dethroned Schenley in a big way, 75-45. The victory, shocking by its margin, would have ramifications for years to come. It effectively ended the dominant era by the Pittsburgh City League, and Schenley, winners of four state titles in 13 years, wasn't the same for a least the next decade. In the subsequent 30 years, the City League would win just two PIAA titles – Perry in 1991 and Schenley in 2007.

But there was more work for Valley to do in 1979. A narrow victory over reigning WPIAL champion Beaver Falls put the Vikings into the state title game against Allentown's William Allen High School. A crowd of 7,131 at the Civic Arena watched Valley bring home the state championship to New Kensington and Arnold. The last seconds of the game were poignant as Varner's dunk seemingly put the exclamation point on a remarkable era for Valley High School and Western Pennsylvania in general.

After 1979, the steel industry collapsed and people relocated to other parts of the country to find work. Plus, school populations also plummeted as members of the Baby Boom Era (born from 1946-64) finished their high school careers.

From 1964-82, teams from the West won 17 of a possible 18 state championships in Class AAA, the largest enrollment division.

Credit: Valley News Dispatch

Valley's Benjy Pryor makes a move on Hempfield's Doug Waszo on March 3, 1975 at the Civic Arena. Valley won the WPIAL semifinal contest 70-65.

Credit: Valley News Dispatch

Valley's B.B. Flenory goes to the hoop on March 3, 1975 at the Civic Arena. Flenory became a Parade All-American in 1976. Note the absense of balconies at the Arena.

Credit: Valley News Dispatch

Valley's Bill Varner is guarded by Burrell's Joey Myers on March 2, 1979 at the Civic Arena in a WPIAL quarterfinal game won by Burrell, 50-48.

Credit: Valley News Dispatch

The Valley Vikings pose on the floor of the Pittsburgh Civic Arena moments after winning the PIAA title on March 24, 1979.

The Top of the Mountain

PIAA Class AAA championship game March 24, 1979
Valley 72, William Allen 66

Score by quarters: Valley 18 18 22 14 - 72
                        Allen 18   9 18 21 - 66

Individual scoring: V: Goose Pryor 11 0-0 22, Dale Parson 2 0-0 4, Billy Varner 10 8-8 28, Ron McNabb 6 0-0 12, Chipper Harris 2 2-2 6, Mike Fuquay 0 0-0 0, Joe Marzullo 0 0-1 0. Totals: 31 10-11 72.

WA: Bill Driesbaugh 7 4-4 18, Mitch Schmidt 7 8-10 22, Sean Ward 3 5-6 11, John Carter 1 0-0 2, Keith Bruan 4 0-0 8, Terry Heffner 2 0-2 4, Tim Hess 0 1-2 1. Totals: 24 18-24 66.

Total fouls: Valley 19, William Allen 13. Attendance: 7,131

chapter 23

THE MIRACLE IN THE MUD

Of the thousands of football games played in the Alle-Kiski Valley since 1898, relatively few have had a lasting impact. One game that did, however, was the Nov. 17, 1995 WPIAL Class AA semifinal between Burrell and New Brighton at Baldwin High School's Rosemarie Cibik Stadium. WPIAL game site policy changed after that night.

Burrell upset New Brighton, 14-8, on a 69-yard return of a fumble recovery by defensive end Jason Gregg.

The stage for this memorable game actually was set about three days earlier, when an early snowstorm blanketed western Pennsylvania. The WPIAL had set semifinal games for the weekend, and concern was raised about field conditions, especially since few schools had artificial turf at the time.

Baldwin officials assured the WPIAL office that the field would be ready for the Bucs and the Lions. On the day of the game, Baldwin representatives got a truck with a snow plow attached to scrape the snow off the field, but the truck got stuck. Two-and-a-half hours before game time, a crane had to lift the sinking truck from the field.

Once the truck was removed, Baldwin staffers filled in the area with topsoil, making matters worse.

New Brighton came into the game as the favorite. The Lions were the defending WPIAL champions and had taken the measure of Apollo-Ridge, 39-12, the week before while Burrell had survived a titanic, triple-overtime struggle against East Allegheny, 27-21.

The Bucs wanted to strike quickly the first time they had the ball, because the field conditions would deteriorate quickly. Quarterback Kevin Horwatt hurriedly led Burrell on a 73-yard drive following Gene Nicastro's pass interception. Late in the third quarter, Ed Flowers of New Brighton scored on a two-yard run and tallied the two-point conversion.

The Lions were taking time off the fourth quarter clock when a botched handoff by New Brighton quarterback J. D. Basile was quickly recovered by Gregg. The play, however, was nullified by a motion penalty. On the following play, the handoff again was botched. This time Gregg picked up the football and took off for the end zone. He had to escape a sweeping attempt of a tackle at the 35 by Florence, kept his balance and continued his run into folklore.

"We talked about needing to come up with the big play, and they lined up to run the same play," Gregg said.

The problem was, no one seemed to know who scored. The mud was so bad that jersey numbers had been obscured. It was nearly 10 minutes before confirmation came to the press box that Gregg had made the play.

Burrell won, 14-8, and made more history the following week when the Bucs defeated Washington, 14-13, in the first overtime championship game in WPIAL history.

A victory over Tyrone in the PIAA semifinals preceded a loss to Harrisburg Bishop McDevitt in the state finals.

As to the impact of the game, the WPIAL has an unwritten policy of attempting to hold all neutral site games on artificial turf.

Credit: Valley News Dispatch

Burrell's Jason Gregg picks up a fumble and races 61 yards for a touchdown as Burrell upset New Brighton, 14-8, on Nov. 17, 1995.

places that have changed

1947

Here's how Memorial Stadium in New Kensington looked in 1947 and 2009

2009

Credit: Valley News Dispatch

Arnold played its home games at Valley Camp Field, behind the present location of National Materials Corp. In this April 30, 1962 photo, Arnold's Denny Fiorentino is hit by a pitch from Ken High's Bruce Carson. Vic Bush is the catcher.

Valley Camp field (today)

Credit: Fox Chapel Area School District

A capacity crowd watches Aspinwall in its final year of football in 1960 at its stadium at the foot of the Highland Park Bridge. Today, two youth baseball fields occupy the former gridiron.

Aspinwall Field (today)

Credit: Bell Township High School yearbook

In 1951, the Bell Township majorettes had plenty to cheer about because their team was ready for its third straight undefeated season. Today, the former stadium is a vacant meadow.

Bell Township (today)

Credit: Valley News Dispatch

East Deer-Frazer's Walt Shaw scores on a 2-yard run against Etna on Oct. 25, 1958 as the Bucks posted a 33-12 win. Note the former JFK Elementary School in background.

East Deer Community Park (today)

Credit: AK Valley Historical Society

The Creighton Tigers semi-pro football team played at Creighton Field. Note the PPG Creighton plant in the background.

The old Creighton Field is now the home of Weleski Transfer and Storage. The old East Deer High School now East Deer Personal Care Home is in the background.

Credit: Valley News Dispatch

The old East Deer High School gym had fans seated close to the action. In this Dec. 9, 1960 photo, tossing the pass is East Deer's Harold Coley. Wearing No. 25 in the dark jersey for Washington Township was Larry Cignetti, later head football coach at Leechburg and Apollo-Ridge.

Credit: Fox Chapel Area School District

Fans in the old-fashioned gyms were right on top of the action, as Aspinwall's Jim Grabowski demonstrates in a game at the old Aspinwall High School gym.

Credit: Courtesy Apollo–Ridge School District

Here is a look at Elders Ridge warming up before a game in its final season of 1968. The former school is now vacant.

Elders Ridge (today)

Credit: Courtesy John Heinz History Center

Here is a rarely-seen photo of Forbes Field in its football configuration, which went from home plate to right field. The Carnegie Tech band is entertaining (note the kilts).

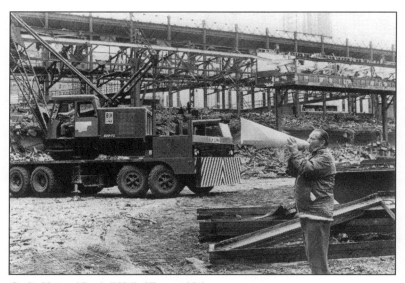

Credit: National Baseball Hall of Fame and Library.

Forbes Field undergoing demolition in 1971.

Credit: Valley News Dispatch

On May 2, 1960, Freeport's Guy Conti is out at the plate as Ken High's Dan McLaughlin makes the tag. Aldo Bracco is the umpire. The Northern Westmoreland Career and Technology Center sits where the baseball field was.

Baseball field (today)

Credit: Valley News Dispatch

Plum played host to West Deer on Oct. 20, 1958 at Pivik Field. In 1961, the Mustangs moved to the current field. Today, soccer is played at Pivik Field.

Pivik Field (today)

This is how New Kensington High School looked in 1950.

Today, the site is the Ridge Avenue Apartments.

Credit: Riverview School District

Verona played its home games at Cribbs Field, nestled between city blocks. The field is named after Hyatt M. Cribbs Jr., and was dedicated April 23, 1923 by his parents Hyatt M. and Ida M. Cribbs. Today, youth baseball, softball and varsity soccer call Cribbs Field home.

Cribbs Field (today)

Credit: Valley News Dispatch

West Deer's Larry Guerrieri (30) scores on a 97-yard punt return against East Deer at Braves Stadium on Oct. 25, 1963. Below: Braves Stadium hosts midget league football today.

Braves Stadium (today)

Credit: Ford City 1941 yearbook

PPG Field in Ford City was used for high school football, baseball and ethnic drum & bugle corps presentations until Eljer Plumingware expanded in 1956.

PPG Field in Ford City (today)

Credit: Fox Chapel Area School District

Oakmont defeated Aspinwall, 13-6, at Scaife Field in 1956. Located a few blocks from the current Riverside Park, Scaife Field was known for a soupy terrain where the baseball infield was.

Oakmont Scaife Field is the site of a trucking company today.

Courtesy: Valley News Dispatch

Aspinwall High School students occupy the outline of the new Fox Chapel Area High School on Groundbreaking Day, Jan. 26, 1960. The school opened its doors in Sept., 1961.

Courtesy: Veltri's Restaurant, Plum

Springdale once played football at Mellon Field until 1938 when Veterans Memorial Field was built as part of a Works Progress Administration project.

177

Courtesy: People's Library of New Kensington

Ken High played its home games into the 1940s at Herr Stadium in the Parnassus section of New Kensington. The stadium was named after long-time school director Benjamin Herr. Today, it's the site of the Fort Crawford Elementary School.

Herr Stadium (today)

Hall of fame quarterback Jim Kelly played on the old East Brady Field in the late 1970s before obtaining national stardom. East Brady High School closed in 1991 and was absorbed by the Karns City School District.

chapter 24

THE FAB FOXES

It took 58 years for an Alle-Kiski Valley basketball team to win a PIAA championship.

But the first to do it, the 1976-77 Fox Chapel Foxes, easily ranks among the best local teams of all-time.

Fox Chapel, under coach Rick Keebler, compiled a 29-1 record. A great starting five consisting of Stu Lyon, Gene Thorpe, Dan Brudnok, Dave Damico and Frank Rocco, along with sixth man Ron Urso brought a brand of quality ballhandling, crisp passing and solid defense to the table.

While the team was exciting to watch, an argument can be made that it also the greatest team the fewest people saw. That's because many regular season games were played in the afternoon, in what became known as the year of the energy crisis.

Severe cold hit the Pittsburgh region in January, with temperatures falling as low as -17 degrees. Many schools were closed, as temps stayed below freezing for the majority of month. Extra-curricular activities such as basketball were cancelled, with natural gas and oil in short supply, cars wouldn't start in the morning. School buses couldn't start, either. Same went for gasoline trucks that carried fuel to service stations.

When things got back to normal, basketball games were moved to daylight hours in the hope of using less energy. The thermostat at the Fox Chapel gym on practice days was set at 50-55 degrees.

Because the Foxes were winning, the games home games drew well simply because the students stayed after school. But overall, with the move to daylight hours, attendance plummeted.

A Valley home game against North Catholic drew 37 fans on a weekday afternoon. But the Vikings, winners of the section titles three of the previous four seasons, were looking forward to a showdown against undefeated Fox Chapel.

After a three-week delay, the undefeated Foxes finally got a shot at Valley for undisputed possession of first place in Section 5-AAA. Fox Chapel withstood a furious fourth-quarter comeback by Valley to hang on, 51-49. Valley had the ball with three seconds left, but an inbounds pass hit the rafters at the Valley gym, and the Foxes recorded their first-ever victory over Valley.

Fox Chapel also won the return match the following week, 76-61, to clinch its first section title in 10 seasons. It proved to be the final season where only section winners made the WPIAL playoffs.

The dream of an undefeated regular season campaign vanished in the penultimate game, a stunning, 66-54 loss at North Allegheny. The Foxes, however, capped the regular season with a 102-76 thrashing of Shaler.

The Postseason

Fox Chapel rolled to playoff victories over Uniontown, Beaver Area and Norwin, setting up a great finals matchup with favored Beaver Falls.

In a tightly-contested game at the Civic Arena, Fox Chapel prevailed, 50-46. Brudnok's basket off a pass from Lyon gave the Foxes the lead, 44-43, with 3:26 remaining.

As the PIAA tournament opened, Fox Chapel served notice that it would be too tough to beat, grabbing impressive victories over Erie Academy (79-54) and Erie Cathedral Prep, 68-52.

That set up a trip to Hershey, where both the semifinals and the finals would be played on consecutive nights.

In what amounted to an unforgettable classic on statewide television, Fox Chapel needed two overtimes to squeak by Norwin, 64-63.

Lyon's basket with 33 seconds left in regulation sent the game into overtime. A Lyon shot at the end of the first overtime was swatted away, necessitating another extra session.

This time, Lyon fed Urso for a key basket. It's would be Urso's only basket of the game. Urso then added two free throws with 34 seconds remaining to put the Foxes in command.

Lyon, despite playing with four fouls, led Fox Chapel with 22 points while Brudnok added 15.

Despite such an excruciating game, the Foxes still had enough left in the tank to finish off Steelton-Highspire the following night. The Steamrollers, who knocked off Reading in their semifinal, were led by Greg Manning, who scored 57 points in the quarterfinal game against Nanticoke at the Harrisburg Farm Show Arena. Manning, whose 57 points remains a PIAA tournament game record, scored 31 against Fox Chapel, but it wasn't enough. Instead, the Foxes controlled the boards and rolled to an 81-71 victory. Thorpe led the way with 26 points, while Lyon added 21.

Courtesy Fox Chapel Area School District

Fox Chapel became the first A-K Valley School to win a PIAA state title in 1977 at Hersheypark Arena.

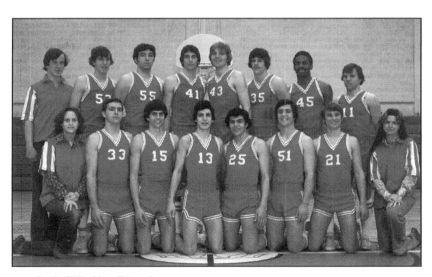

Credit: Valley News Dispatch

Here is the 1976-77 Fox Chapel basketball team: Front row, from left, student manager Liz Hutchings, George Brandner, Dave Damico, Art Morgan, Bob Napoli, Dave Dacus, J.R. Miller, student manager Dee Dee Haines. Back row: student manager Glenn Burdick, Ed Sauer, Joe Nypaver, Stu Lyon, Dan Brudnok, Frank Rocco, Gene Thorpe, Ron Urso.

chapter 25

THE JACK (HEIMBUECHER) OF ALL TRADES

Throughout the years, many local coaches have excelled in more than one sport.

Don Earley, for instance, won WPIAL championships in football and track, and won 100 basketball games. Burrell's Tom Henderson has coached WPIAL contenders in football and wrestling, likewise Knoch's Dale Mahan in track and basketball.

But for Springdale's Jack Heimbuecher, winning was a way of life for all seasons.

Heimbuecher coached Springdale High School to the 1973 WPIAL football championship. A year earlier, he guided Springdale American Legion Post 764 to the Pennsylvania state title. In 1976, he got the Dynamos to the finals of the WPIAL high school baseball playoffs and, in 1989, was Chuck DeVenzio's top assistant in Springdale's drive to the WPIAL basketball title year.

But Heimbuecher is best known for baseball. Besides the high school coaching and American Legion coaching, he ran the Little Pirates in the 1960s, the elite team of high school players of its day. After retiring from Springdale, he was an assistant coach at Indiana University in the Big 10 Conference. From 1994 until he died on April 19, 2000, he coached at Flagler College in St. Augustine, Fla. A Korean War veteran, Heimbuecher was Post 764 Commander in 1979-80.

Heimbuecher's calling card was discipline and fundamentals – and no compromises.

When a player arrived at the field, he was expected to be ready to play. His uniform was laundered and his shoes were shined. It didn't matter if Springdale had an afternoon game followed by a night game the same day, your uniform was expected to be cleaned and your shoes shined.

And don't even think about wearing your shirttail hanging out or putting your cap on backwards or sideways.

Players were expected to know how to bunt and move runners up. Even the Nos. 3 and 4 batters in Springdale's lineup were expected to bunt when the situation called for that strategy.

Anyone who won a starting job found out it wasn't permanent. In 1970, Rich DiSanti, Springdale's regular third baseman, was injured and missed playing time while he recovered. When DiSanti told Heimbuecher he was ready to go, there was one problem – DiSanti had to win his job back from the person who replaced him. Heimbuecher was running a baseball team, not a jobs service.

1972 American Legion

Heimbuecher managed the Post 764 Legion team from 1970-84. The first step towards the '72 state title was winning the Allegheny County championship at Lawrenceville Field, Pittsburgh. Like most inner-city fields built to accommodate city blocks, the right field in Lawrenceville was so short that a ball hit over the fence from rightcenter to the rightfield line counted as just a double.

But with superb pitching, Springdale Legion didn't have to worry about quirky ground rules. Terry Dreher, one of the state's youngest Legion players that year at age 15, fired a two-hitter and struck out 12 in the county semifinals as Springdale posted a 5-0 victory. In the county final, Tom Eaton pitched a three-hitter and struck out seven as Springdale beat Ninth Ward, 5-1.

In Western Regional play, John Duff's ERA of 0.67 actually rose, with Springdale winning over Washington, 5-1. Tom Eaton then went the distance in a 12-3 victory over South Whitehall, qualifying Springdale for the state tournament.

Springdale didn't have to travel far as Freeport played host to the double-elimination tournament to decide the state champ. Duff moved his record to 12-2 with a 5-0 victory over Coplay.

Next, Don Papich's home run was the key blow in a 5-1 win over South Scranton. With Dreher on the mound and shortstop Skip Yakopec driving in three runs, Springdale defeated Valley View of Archbald, PA in the state semifinals, setting up a clash with Chambersburg.

On August 19, 1972, Springdale became the first team from the West to win a state title since Lower Burrell seven years earlier with 3-1 victory. Springdale took advantage of four Chambersburg errors in the fifth inning and Eaton pitched no-hit ball into the sixth.

Springdale had won 25 of its last 26 games.

In the Mid-Atlantic Regionals in New Jersey, Springdale opened play with a 4-3 victory over the Maryland state champion from the Baltimore area.

But in Game Two, Springdale dropped a 9-2 decision against Ewing, the host team. Springdale recovered to defeat Wilmington Manor, Del., 7-4, before being eliminated by Ewing, 4-3. Springdale had the bases loaded and one out in the seventh, but could push across just one run, dashing hopes of playing for the national championship in Memphis, Tenn.

1973 Springdale Dynamos

After its archaic system of allowing only undefeated and untied to play for the championship, WPIAL football underwent a major change in 1973.

Conference champions, no matter what their record was, would be admitted into a playoff.

And Springdale was the first team to take advantage of that new policy.

Following a loss to Richland in the season's opener, 18-0, Springdale wouldn't lose the rest of the way and won the third WPIAL football title in school history with a 20-14 nailbiter over Union Area.

The Dynamos started their roll with a 22-14 victory over Hampton, followed by a convincing, 36-13 win over Mars. Next, Springdale took the measure of Riverview and coach Chuck Wagner, 22-6.

Heimbuecher felt the turning point came in Week Five with a narrow, 30-24, decision over Leechburg. The Dynamos defense had to make some critical stops to preserve the victory. After a close call in defeating Leechburg, Springdale's offense kicked into high gear with victories of 56-16 over Ford City and 47-0 over Kittanning. That set up a Week Eight showdown with Freeport at Tarentum's Dreshar Stadium.

Springdale moved its home games to Tarentum from 1973-76 while Veterans Memorial Field underwent a major renovation. Beating Freeport, though, was easier said than done. After all, the stellar, first-team defense of the Yellowjackets had given up just seven points over the previous seven weeks.

But Springdale was ready to play, overwhelming Freeport, 35-6, before one of the largest crowds ever at the historic Tarentum facility. Sam Sack rushed for 135 yards in 31 carries to pace the Dynamos.

The Dynamos then secured a WPIAL playoff berth by winning at Apollo-Ridge, 42-14. The first playoff game involving a team with a conference defeat in WPIAL history was set to take on Burgettstown to open the postseason.

In what had to be one of the coldest November nights on record in Armstrong County, Springdale took the field at Kittanning with swirling, snowy winds and a hardscrabble playing surface. The Dynamos adjusted to the Arctic-like conditions and prevailed, 22-12. The strange bracket had Springdale getting a bye in the semifinals and a championship game date against Union Area at Thomas Jefferson High School in Pleasant Hills the night after Thanksgiving.

It looked like it would be a rout early, as Springdale jumped out to a 20-0 lead. But the Scotties scored twice in the second half and were driving for a tying touchdown. Sack intercepted a pass with four minutes to go in the game. The Dynamos couldn't move the ball, however, and Union regained possession. Sack then broke up a Scotties pass at the Springdale 10 and registered another pick-off on the following play to preserve the victory.

The Runners-up

Springdale came within two outs of winning a WPIAL baseball crown in 1976.

What was remarkable about the team was the fact that the Dynamos rolled through the regular season often defeating much larger schools, such as Butler, which had an enrollment six times the size of Springdale. In section play, Springdale beat schools like Highlands and Kiski Area with much larger student bodies.

There were no enrollment classifications, everyone was lumped together. After a 21-4 regular season, Springdale opened the playoffs with a 5-0 victory against Mohawk High School at Mars behind the shutout pitching of Clint Courtney. Jeff Boyer followed that with a 2-0 whitewash of Kittanning at Highlands High School.

In the quarterfinals, a major challenge loomed as New Brighton, led by Terry Francona, had received national recognition. *Sports Illustrated*'s Faces in the Crowd section featured Francona, who brought a 6-0 record into the game, with 68 strikeouts and an .028 ERA to go with his .769 batting average.

What's worse, Courtney's glasses were broken and he had lost a contact lens. Pitching with one contact in, Courtney was helped by Randy Runyan's double and triple en route to an 8-3 victory.

Springdale dispatched Washington, 7-2, in the semifinals and faced Elizabeth-Forward, one of the WPIAL's bigger schools, for the title at Highlands.

Jeff Ewing's suicide squeeze brought home Joe Leskovic with the first run. Brian Holton, who would later pitch for the Dodgers, held the Springdale offense in check for much of the sweltering afternoon.

The Dynamos scored twice in the top of the seventh to go back in front, 3-2. But in the bottom of the seventh, an overthrow at third base brought home the winning run.

Heimbuecher was hoping to add a companion WPIAL baseball title to compliment the one his friend, DeVenzio, won in 1954. In 1978, Springdale appeared poised to win another state Legion title.

Again, travel was not an issue as Springdale hosted the event at the high school and at Veterans Memorial Field. Springdale started out strong in the winner's bracket, defeating Bessemer, 4-1, and Northeastern, 5-2, in the same day.

But Boyertown proved to be Springdale's undoing, winning 6-4 at the Vets' Field. Following a victory over Rhawnhurst , Springdale had another shot at Boyertown, but came up short, 8-0.

It was an unprecedented third straight state title for the Boyertown program.

Heimbuecher was inducted into the A-K Valley Sports Hall of fame in 1985. A year after his death, Heimbuecher was the recipient of the prestigious Red Cox Award at Flagler College.

Cox was the recreation superintendent of St. Augustine for 37 years.

Courtesy Springdale American Legion Post 764

Here is the 1972 Springdale state championship American Legion team. Front row from left: Coach Frank Basilone, Bill Walsh, Bob Korpany, John Duff, Tom Eaton, Don Papich, Mike Simcic, Skip Yakopec, Terry Dreher. Rear: coach John Fugal, Dan DeStout, Jim Basilone, Eddie Stack, Jeff Marino, Dennis Runyan, Frank Burger, Craig Turley, Don Kovich, statistician Dave Berth, manager Jack Heimbuecher.

Credit: Valley News Dispatch

The Springdale Dynamos, with coach Jack Heimbuecher kneeling in front, celebrate the WPIAL Class AA football title on Nov. 23, 1973 at Thomas Jefferson High School stadium.

chapter 26

MAKING THE RIGHT CHOICE

Sometimes, it seems like doing the right thing goes unrewarded. But for Riverview High School baseball coach Bill Beebe, he did the right thing and the Raiders became the first A-K Valley school to win a PIAA baseball championship.

On June 17, 1983, the Raiders were set to play Schuylkill-Haven in the Class AA title game. At the time, there were no pitching limitations in Pennsylvania high school baseball. A pitcher could pitch every inning for his team, which is exactly what a California Area High School player did in 1982.

One day earlier, Riverview defeated Mount Union in the PIAA semifinals, 2-1, in nine innings behind the stellar pitching of Ed Rayburg. Beebe could have elected to throw Rayburg in the finals, but the veteran coach would have nothing of it.

"It's not worth ruining a kid's arm over one game," Beebe said. Instead, Beebe gave the starting nod to Bobby Shoop, though Rayburg was having a great season with a 12-1 mark. Schuylkill-Haven meanwhile, went with Bobby Farr, who had pitched the preceding day.

As the temperature hovered near 90 degrees, Beebe thought Farr would tire. In the fourth inning, Farr gave up four walks and his defense committed a critical error and Riverview scored four runs and eventually won a 4-3 decision.

The Raiders had some talented teams the previous two seasons, but everything seemed to come together in 1983 as they posted a 22-2 mark.

Beebe credited two games against Carlynton as the turning point of the season. In the first game against the Cougars, Riverview pulled out a 1-0 decision in nine innings. Carlynton pitcher Greg Gazella struck out 23 Raiders in one of the best individual efforts in WPIAL history. In the second Section 14-AA game against the Cougars, Gazella struck out 13, but Riverview still won, 3-2.

"Mr. Beebe always had a saying, 'whatever it takes,'" Rayburg said in a 1993 interview commemorating the 10th anniversary of the title drive. "Well, that guy struck out 36 batters and still didn't win."

The Raiders went undefeated in section play and lost in the WPIAL semifinals to California. The PIAA admitted the top four teams from the WPIAL tournament, so the Raiders' season was still alive.

Riverview opened the PIAA tournament with an 8-1 decision over Curwensville. Rayburg struck out 12 and Shoop went 4-for-4. In the quarterfinals, a local team, Leechburg, provided the opposition. Future Olympic gold medalist and National League all-star Mickey Morandini pitched for the Blue Devils, but Riverview prevailed to move into the state's final four.

At the time, both the semifinals and the finals were held at Shippensburg University. Players from the four Class AAA teams and the four Class AA teams were housed in the school's dormitories as players got to experience a college-type atmosphere .In fact, the Raiders got to room with Allderdice of the Pittsburgh City League and some players formed friendships.

When it came time to play the state semifinals, Riverview had to face not only a talented, 18-0 Mount Union team, but 90-degree heat greeted the Raiders at Seth Grove Stadium. Sophomore catcher Mike Juliano doubled in the second inning to score Craig Komratz and give the Raiders a 1-0 lead. Mount Union tied the score by getting a run off Rayburg in the fifth.

Riverview looked ready to win the game in the seventh, but Mount Union's Steve Brookheimer pitched out of a jam to send the game into extra innings.

In the ninth, Rayburg hit an one-out double down the right-field line and went to third on Komratz's single. Jeff Peters followed with a grounder that Mount Union tried to turn into a double play, but the throw to first was a bad one and Rayburg scooted home with the winning run to send the Raiders into the title game.

Beebe understood the nuances of baseball, as he was talented himself in his playing days. In 1961, Beebe made the American Legion all-star game and played the outfield with Joe Namath of the Beaver Falls Legion team.

Beebe told his players to be patient, with Farr pitching his second game in as many days. Schuylkill-Haven took a quick, 3-0 lead.

Riverview didn't panic, and the Raiders were able to break through in the fourth inning to take the lead. That was enough for Shoop, who yielded just one hit over the final three innings. The big win was improbable, but perhaps even more improbable was the reaction back home. The Raiders' drive to the state championship pushed the U.S. Open, being held at rain-drenched Oakmont Country Club, off the front page.

Ford City would win a state title four years later, but that has been it for A-K Valley schools.

Credit: A-K Valley Sports Hall of Fame

Bill Beebe's 1983 Riverview High School baseball team was the first from the AK-Valley to win a PIAA state championship.

chapter 27

THE LADY IS A COACH

Credit: Bell Township yearbook

Pauline Rugh Smith in 1949

It was 1943, the middle of World War II, and the men were away fighting in Europe and the Pacific.

It's been well-documented how women took over traditional male roles during the time, such as working in industry. But the traditionally-male jobs the women took over didn't stop with Rosie the Riveter — at tiny Bell Township High School, it included football coaching. Indeed, with all the male faculty members away at war, Pauline Rugh Smith was asked by Bell principal Quentin Kintigh to take over the football coaching job.

"And for no explainable reason, I said 'yes,'" recalled Rugh Smith in a 1999 interview.

There were 35 boys out for the Lions football team. If Rugh Smith hadn't stepped in, the team would have disbanded. The boys didn't care that Rugh Smith was the only female high school head coach in the country – they wanted to play.

It didn't take long for people everywhere to take notice. Rugh Smith came home after practice one night and saw photographers from all 3 Pittsburgh newspapers in her driveway. It wasn't long before it made national news. The situation caught the ear of famous national radio news commentator Lowell Thomas, the Tom Brokaw of his day.

Penn State football coach Bob Higgins invited Rugh Smith to sit in on a few practices and sent her away with some plays for the Lions to use during their season.

During the season, a crew from Look Magazine, one of the key ways Americans received their national news each week, also showed up at the Rugh farm.

But despite the uniqueness and all the publicity, Bell Township failed to win a game that season. The closest the Lions would come was a 13-7 setback.

"My husband and I rationalized the coach would have been ostracized for losing to a woman," she said when being inducted into the A-K Valley Sports Hall of Fame in 1999.

Even though the Lions were winless, the school attained its goal of keeping the football program alive. A number of schools who shut down their football programs during World War II found it difficult to re-start them.

By 1944, male teachers started to return home from war duty. Rugh Smith remained on the staff as a health and phys-ed teacher and girls basketball coach.

Rugh Smith later became a guidance counselor when Bell was consolidated to form Kiski Area in 1962.

She died on July 3, 2009 at age 88.

chapter 28

THAT MAGICAL YEAR

Most any high school student wants a memorable senior year. It's your final shot in the school system and the memories that take place have to last the rest of your lives.

Arnold High School's 1964-65 year contained a treasure trove of sports memories.

First of all, Arnold saw a temporary swelling of its senior ranks. Burrell High School opened about four miles away with solely juniors and sophomores. Ken High said it could no longer take students from Burrell as it had its own overcrowding problems with more than 1,500 students.

So nearly all the Burrell seniors, many of whom already had been part of the Arnold student body, were finishing up their high school years on Alcoa Drive.

Expectations were high as the 1964 football season approached. After all, the Lions had compiled a 35-5-1 record over the past four seasons under one of the top coaches around, Frank Martin.

Arnold started quickly out of the gate, shutting out three of its first four opponents, including Plum (6-0), Freeport, the WPIAL runner-up from the previous season (21-0) and cross-river rival Tarentum, 20-0. Only West Deer was able to cross the goal line in a 34-7 setback to the Lions in Week Two.

Despite some great teams over the years, Arnold had never finished a season undefeated. As the Lions rolled past Penn Claridge (28-6), Ford City (28-7) and Oakmont (21-6), fans began to dream of a WPIAL championship.

Things were falling into place for Arnold as other schools exited the unbeaten ranks. Plus, the Lions got an extra home game with Hampton's Fridley Field under construction forcing the Talbots to play all away games in 1964.

Fans flocked to George Leslie Memorial Stadium, a quaint facility tucked into a hillside adjacent to the high school building. The stadium was named after the first Pennsylvania serviceman killed at Pearl Harbor on Dec. 7, 1941.

In Week Eight, once-beaten Leechburg rolled into town and Leslie Memorial Stadium was bursting at the seams. Though the actual seating capacity was less than 2,000, as many as 5,000 fans crammed their way in to watch Arnold win a critical game. Touchdowns by quarterback Tony Silvestrin and fullback John Henry Favors powered Arnold to a 13-7 victory. Leechburg rallied late, driving to the Arnold 29, but a pass from Paul Noonan to Jerry Booker was broken up at the goal line by Carl Brooks. Leechburg would go on to win its next 23 football games, including two WPIAL titles.

The following week, Arnold blanked Hampton, 14-0, setting up a showdown in Springdale to see if the Lions would qualify for the WPIAL title game.

Montour, the defending champion, already had qualified for the title game, amassing the most Gardner Points among Class A schools. If Arnold would lose to Springdale, Southmoreland, a first-year merger between Scottdale and East Huntingdon high schools, would oppose Montour.

Just 16 Tickets

The buildup to the Springdale game was huge. Springdale's Veterans Memorial Field held about 3,000, but there were under 800 reserved seats available.

Part of the buildup was fueled by Arnold's anger in only getting 16 reserved tickets for their fans. The Allegheny Valley School District provided Arnold with 140 reserved seats – 40 comps, 84 for parents of the 42 players, leaving just 16 tickets for Lions fans. Ken High offered its field and Arnold offered up Leslie Memorial Stadium, but that would have given the Lions seven home games. Springdale was adamant that the game would stay put.

Lines to get into the field started early. Westinghouse Electric's Cheswick plant let its workers out early at 4:00 so they could get to the big game.

Those who got in late missed what's arguably the biggest touchdown in Arnold history. On the third play from scrimmage, Dynamos fullback Bob Hepler was stood up by Chuck Johnson, enabling lineman Bill Baker to grab the ball and race 36 yards for a touchdown. Silvestrin's extra point was good.

Springdale scored in the third period, but the extra point was missed and Arnold held on for a 7-6 victory and a shot a WPIAL honors.

The Lions, however, were beat up physically by then and Montour posted a 19-7 victory in Arnold's only WPIAL football title game appearance.

Diamond Dandies

Several months later, Arnold would ride its wave of success to the WPIAL baseball title game.

The Lions were magnificent in 1964, outscoring the opposition 54-4 in section games. But Arnold was eliminated in the WPIAL playoffs with a loss to Penn Hills at Sokol Camp Field, Lower Burrell.

Although Lions coach Jim Marino had some holes to fill, the 1965 team featured depth and versatility. Only section winners were admitted to the WPIAL playoff field, but Arnold qualified in a big way as Joe Unites pitched a no-hitter against Har-Brack, winning 2-0 to sew up the section title. The game was played at the Valley Camp Field, located behind the American St. Gobain plant, affectionately known to generations of Arnold residents as "the Glass House."

The Lions dressed at the high school and ran the six blocks to the field. Some would be buttoning their shirts and putting on their belts while running downhill. It wasn't wise to be late on Marino's watch.

Arnold played much larger schools en route to the WPIAL crown. There were no enrollment classifications at the time. The Lions beat Greensburg, 5-2, in the playoff opener on a one-hitter by Jim Fantuzzo. In the quarterfinals, Unites was one strike away from a no-hitter, but settled for a one-hitter in an 8-0 victory over North Hills.

In the semifinals at Kiski Area High School, Fantuzzo relived Unites as Arnold held on for a 3-1 victory over Gateway, as the Lions got their tickets punched for the WPIAL title game at Forbes Field on June 15.

Arnold was a huge underdog against Beaver Falls and it was no wonder why. Tigers pitcher Jim (Jumbo) Suskiewicz, in his six appearances leading up to the title game, tossed a no-hitter, two one-hitters and two two-hitters and struck out 92 batters in 48 innings.

With Beaver Falls ahead,1-0, Lions centerfielder Alan Baroni nailed a runner trying to score to end the second inning. That seemed to turn the tide as Arnold exploded for five runs in the third inning. In the fourth, the Lions chased Suskiewicz, marking the first time since Little League play that the big righthander was knocked out of the box.

Arnold won the game, 11-1, behind Fantuzzo's pitching. Johnson, who died on April 17, 2009, had two RBI each in the quarterfinal, semifinals and championship game.

The Lions were feted after the game with a motorcade through town and dinner at the IAES Club. Two months later, many Arnold players performed on the Lower Burrell American Legion state championship team.

Two years later, Arnold played its final athletic event, a 4-1 baseball loss to Ken High on May 20, 1967.

George Leslie Memorial Stadium, where the Arnold Lions once roared, is now the home for Ar-Ken Rens youth football. The stadium was named after Leslie, the first Pennsylvania serviceman to die in the Japanese attack at Pearl Harbor Dec. 7, 1941.

Credit: *Valley High School football program*

Here is the 1964 WPIAL runner-up: Front row, from left: Bob Colella, Alan Baroni, George Joseph, Bob Palochik, Bill Richards, Joe Unites, Roger Stiveson, Ron Andring, Frank Lombardo. Second row: Joe Morabito, Pat Meredith, Ed Pelchar, Mike Farinelli, John Ciciarelli, John Mazur, Eugene Aftanas, Jimmy Fantuzzo, student manager Danny Marra. Third row: Student manager Bill Acre, Les Kearley, Tony Silvestrin, Pete Gavasto, Bill Baker, Chester Napierkowski, Dennis Bejester, Dennis Olszewski, Tony Bagetta, Jerry Peconi, head coach Frank Martin. Last row: Assistant Ollie Phillips, Steve Vasilopus, George Hustak, Rich Sampson, James Bellavia, Frank Pharturos, Chuck Johnson, John Henry Favors, assistant Dick Romito.

Credit: *Valley News Dispatch*

Arnold coach Jim Marino accepts the WPIAL baseball championship trophy on June 15, 1965 at Forbes Field. The catcher is John Mazur.

Credit: Riverview School District

Riverview's Lucas Heakins, the A-K Valley's all-time leading rusher, talks with WTAE Channel 4's Andrew Stockey after the Raiders won the 1997 WPIAL Class A title at Three Rivers Stadium.

Credit: Comcast Communications

Broadcasting legends Bob Tatrn and Joe Falsetti covered events for more than 40 years. Their first assignment was the Arnold-Beaver Falls WPIAL baseball title game at Forbes Field on June 15, 1965.

a day at the races...

VALLEY HEIGHTS RACE TRACK

Valley Heights race track in New Kensington, built in the early 1920's, was originally built for horse racing but used mostly for auto and dog races. It was destroyed by fire in 1952. In late 1950's Ryan Homes developed the Rivercrest housing developement on the site.

Pit crews and drivers watch the flag man prior to start of a race at the Valley Heights Race Track in New Kensington. Notice the American flag in the rear has 48 stars. Note the absence of development in the Mount Parnassus section of Lower Burrell in background.

Pace car from Jerome Motors New Kensington, PA., set to lead the racers around the Valley Heights Race Track.

The track was located about 200 feet behind Denny's Restaurant. This view is from Campbell Avenue.

chapter 29

WORTH MORE THAN THE PRICE OF ADMISSION

For those in the media who cover high school sports, many often hear of the latest or newest 8th-grade hotshot or junior-high stud that's on his way to varsity stardom.

Anyone covering Valley High School basketball during the 1988-89 season certainly heard about this kid at Valley Middle School that can leave his feet at the foul line and dunk.

Hearing is one thing – but seeing is believing.

The momentous career of Valley's Tom Pipkins will be remembered as long as basketball is played in the A-K Valley. Pipkins had the unbelievable ability to take control of a game through a combination of shooting, stealing and rejecting. Opponents often watched him in awe instead of guarding him.

The opposing players, monetarily, got to watch Pipkins whoosh by them for free. As for the paying customers, The Pipkins Show was worth more than the price of a ticket.

After playing on a Pittsburgh Area Youth All-Star team in Las Vegas before entering the ninth grade, Pipkins made quite a splash in his varsity debut on Dec. 8, 1989. With 5:43 left in the first quarter at Highlands High School in the A-K Tip-off Tournament, he scored the first two of 2,838 points on a dunk. He would go on to score 10 points on that opening night as the Vikings dropped a 53-51 decision to Kiski Area.

The second night didn't disappoint, either. Valley played Highlands in what remains tied for the third-longest game in WPIAL history, a four-overtime Vikings victory, 61-54. Pipkins and sophomore teammate Jay White had 16 points each.

It didn't take long for Pipkins to garner WPIAL-wide attention. He scored 25 and 28 points, respectively, in the Indiana Christmas Tournament. In his section debut in early January, Pipkins poured in 28 against Freeport – with all the points coming in the first three quarters of an eventual 60-50 victory over the Yellowjackets.

Valley would fall short of the 1990 playoffs, but everyone knew

Pipkins and the Vikings were going to be a force to be reckoned with over the three subsequent seasons.

In the 1990-91 season, Valley won Section 6-AAA and made the WPIAL playoffs for the first time in six years. That must have seemed to be an eternity for the Vikings' discernable fans.

The school started a rivalry with North Catholic that would last for much of the decade. In the first meeting between the two schools, it was old-fashioned basketball at its best — all 10 players went the entire way. Neither team made any substitutions as the Vikings pulled out a 70-67 victory, giving Valley a 12-1 start, the school's best since the 1975-76 season.

Valley opened the postseason as the No. 2-seeded team in Class AAA and defeated Jeannette, 84-67, at Norwin High School. Cable TV viewers of that game saw something that would be a constant at the time — Pipkins signing autographs for youngsters after the game.

Valley lost a quarterfinal game to Aliquippa, 78-65. The team would prove to be a nemesis of the Vikings. But it was enough to get into the PIAA tournament as the No. 8 team from the WPIAL.

In the school's first PIAA game since winning the 1979 state championship, Valley defeated Brookville, 65-46, at Clarion University. In the second round, Valley was eliminated by Blackhawk, 51-42.

In the 1991-92 campaign, the Vikings repeated as section champs and opened the playoffs by hammering Greensburg Salem, 86-59, at Kiski Area High School. But Pipkins was hobbled in a quarterfinal round game that was dropped to Steel Valley, 64-59, at Penn-Trafford High School.

The Vikings, however, made the PIAA tournament as the No. 7 seed and won big in the opener, 97-66, over Penn Cambria at St. Francis College of Loretto. But in the second round, the Vikings squandered a late, nine-point lead and fell to Aliquippa, 58-55.

As Pipkins' senior year approached, expectations were high at Valley. Pipkins needed just 41 points to reach the 2,000-point career scoring mark and 417 to break Don Hennon's all-time WPIAL record of 2,376.

203

That Championship Season

The season was supposed to have started with the annual A-K Tip-off Tournament on Dec. 10, 1992. But a massive snowstorm that day delayed the tournament until Saturday where an afternoon session was followed by an evening session.

It didn't take long for Pipkins to reach the 2,000 milestone. He did it in the championship game of the tournament with 5:37 left in the fourth quarter against Wilkinsburg, becoming the seventh WPIAL player to reach the magical mark. Pipkins took a pass from Billy Coury and slammed the ball through the hoop.

After a third-place finish in the prestigious Blackhawk Christmas Tournament, Pipkins began to close in on Hennon's record toward the end of January. In a Jan. 26, 1993, game at Penn Hills, Pipkins came within three points of the WPIAL mark before sitting out the final 4:21 of the game.

The Valley gym was packed long before the tip-off on Jan. 29, 1993 as the Vikings had a non-section encounter against South Park. Out-of-state license plates adorned some cars in the parking lot, while other vehicles had license plate liners from dealerships far from New Kensington. It seemed as if everybody wanted to be in on history.

As usual, Pipkins didn't disappoint. Coach Tom Myers called a time out with 4:18 remaining in the first quarter. Myers designed an alley-oop play that worked to perfection as Coury lobbed a pass to Pipkins, who, in what became his signature for big shots, slammed the ball through to break the record. The game was stopped for about five minutes as the media, particularly the Pittsburgh TV stations, all wanted to talk with the new scoring leader. Pipkins brought the game ball over to his father, Tom Sr., in the stands and action resumed. Pipkins would go on to score 29 points as Valley routed the Eagles, 97-63.

As Valley finished the section season undefeated at 12-0, there was work yet to be done. There was a nagging feeling that the Vikings hadn't gone as far in the playoffs as their previous seedings indicated.

Valley was the No. 1-ranked Class AAA team and the Vikings took no mercy on Derry Area in the opening round. Valley led 45-

10 at halftime and rolled to a 90-35 victory. The quarterfinal round game was won over Jeannette, 71-48. Up next was Beaver Falls in the semifinals, and Valley was slightly disappointed that Seton-La Salle would knock off Blackhawk 72-62, in a game that preceded Valley's 75-64 victory over Beaver Falls. The Vikings were hoping to play Blackhawk, the team they lost to in the PIAA playoffs two seasons ago and the team that beat them in the Cougars' Christmas tournament game.

As Valley was set to make its first championship game appearance in 17 years, weather forecasts called for a major storm as fronts from the west and the southeast were set to collide. Still, a huge crowd gathered at the Pitt Field House to watch the Class AAA finals.

After coming up short in 1975 and '76, Valley finally won its first WPIAL title with a 52-46 win over Seton-La Salle. Pipkins scored 30 of his team's 52 points, including 14-of-18 from the foul line. But Pipkins will be most remembered for one of the greatest defensive plays in WPIAL title game history. In the third quarter, Rebels guard Eric Binkowski looked like he was charging downcourt for an easy lay-up. But Pipkins came out of nowhere, leaping over Binkowski and swatting the ball away from the hoop. After the game, Pipkins' handprint was on the banking board.

As the crowd left the Pitt Field House, they were greeted by what became known as the "Storm of the Century." The WPIAL, regretfully, tried to play the first of five title games the following morning. But conditions had become so dangerous that the league postponed the remainder of the championship games four days in a row while the region dug out of a 24-inch snowfall.

The Vikings opened the PIAA playoffs, blowing out Penn Cambria, 82-50, and St. Marys, 77-43. In the quarterfinals, Valley won a hard-fought game against Perry, 61-51, putting the Vikings a game away from the state title game.

On the Butler High floor, Pipkins showed the scoring didn't have to be all about him. With the score tied, 4-4, Pipkins spotted Nate Cope open, heading downcourt. He threw a perfect pass to Cope, whose layup gave Valley the lead for good with 4:08 left in the first quarter. Less than two minutes later, the pair combined on a similar play.

In a pattern that was part of the Pipkins years, fans watching the first game of a playoff doubleheader would stay for the second game. The baseline bleachers at the Pitt Field House weren't pulled out, causing a seating shortage. It also caused the Valley and Hickory students sections to be seated on the same side of the arena. Not a good mix.

After tension continued brewing, a fight erupted, stopping the game with 2:06 left in the first half. Valley students eventually were moved to the upper deck on the opposite side to watch their Vikings roll to a convincing, 70-51 victory. Pipkins had a dramatic, alley-oop dunk with 1:15 to go, putting the finishing touch on a prospective trip to Hershey.

The Vikings shot just 32.9 % from the field as Pottstown won the state title with an 85-66 victory before 7,121 fans at Hersheypark Arena.

Pipkins scored 28 in his final Valley appearance before heading to Duquesne University, where he remains among that storied program's all-time scoring leaders.

No one has really come close to Pipkins' career total of 2,838 points. With the PIAA recently trimming the basketball season by two games, a future challenger to Pipkins would have eight less games to try and reach the mark.

One final footnote about Pipkins' Valley career: He never fouled out of a game.

Here is a list of the Top 10 scorers in WPIAL history as of March 10, 2009:

Name	School	Senior Year	Points
1. Tom Pipkins	Valley	1993	2,838
2. Kevin Price	Duquesne	1994	2,635
3. Kevin Covert	Neshannock	1995	2,612
4. Vince Graham	Belle Vernon	1995	2,429
5. Don Hennon	Wampum	1955	2,376
6. Dan Fortson	Altoona/Shaler	1994	2,331
7. Drew Schifino	Penn Hills	2000	2,318
8. Terrell Pryor	Jeannette	2008	2,285
9. Ben McCauley	Yough	2005	2,284
10. Brandon F-Cheatham	Blackhawk	2001	2,278

Credit: Valley News Dispatch

Tom Pipkins became the WPIAL's all-time leading scorer with this dunk on Jan. 29, 1993.

chapter 30

THE COACH'S COACH

For more than 25 years, coach Tom Myers dominated A-K Valley basketball.

He resurrected programs at Highlands and Valley, winning a WPIAL title with Valley.

And, for good measure, led Burrell to a 2006 WPIAL playoff berth to put the finishing touches on an outstanding career. Not only did he win 330 varsity basketball games over his career, but his tenure also served as an incubator as a number of his assistants have gone on to experience success with their own teams.

Besides leading his teams to 14 WPIAL playoff appearances, assistants such as Rich Falter (Highlands), Dave Fuhrman (Bradford), Mark Ziemianski (Burrell), Brian Sharick (Burrell) and Mark Jula (Butler, North Allegheny and Center) are among those who have learned the game from Myers and have led their own teams to playoff berths.

A 1964 Ken High graduate, Myers learned his basketball from one of the best – former Valley and Ken High coach Mike Rice.

Myers began his coaching climb by leading St. Margaret Mary grade school in Lower Burrell to a 1975 state championship. As the 1978-79 season got underway, he moved up the hill to Burrell High School where he assisted Tony Sellari in the Bucs' run to the WPIAL title game that season and a section title the following season.

Starting in 1980, he took the struggling program at Highlands and guided the Golden Rams to five consecutive WPIAL playoff berths. By the time 1989 rolled around, Valley was coming off a 4-17 season, and it was time to head across the Allegheny River. Myers had the Vikings in the playoffs during his second season in New Kensington.

His arrival coincided with Tom Pipkins starting his renowned career as a ninth grader. Myers led the Vikings to the WPIAL Class AAA championship in 1993. Even after Pipkins graduated, there were five more playoff trips for Valley.

Myers had the uncanny ability to adapt a coaching style to the type of talent he had on his teams. At Highlands, he played a slowdown game, often scoring in the 20s or 30s, defeating Quad-A schools like Penn Hills and Central Catholic that Highlands had no business beating.

Credit: Valley News Dispatch

At Valley, his teams were built around the gifted Pipkins, and often played an up-tempo game. "Basketball is a game of strengths and weaknesses," Myers always said. His game-planning

Valley coach Tom Myers discusses strategy during a time out on March 31, 1993, at the Pitt Field House as Valley faced Hickory in the PIAA Class AAA semifinals.

was like that of a football coach, spending hours watching film of opposing teams and devising a plan to utilize his team's strengths and exploit the opponents' weaknesses.

Three-hour practices were the norm for Myers. He would run one play over and over again until the players got it right. Often that one play, when executed successfully, would make the difference in a close game.

Not only was game preparation vital, but he was at his best during games. Myers often called time outs at a strange time, but it was the right time to get a point across.

After leaving Valley in 2002, Myers had a brief stint at Penn State's New Kensington campus, leading the Little Lions to the playoffs. But recruiting players to a non-scholarship setting wasn't quite what Myers was looking for.

After a break of a couple of years, Myers closed out his career at Burrell, leading the Bucs to a 15-10 record. That included a playoff victory over Northgate, 58-53, on Feb. 17, 2006, the final victory of his career.

chapter 31

THE LITTLE SCHOOL MAKES IT TO
THE BIGGEST STAGE

On March 17, 1963, St. Joseph High School of Natrona played for the Pennsylvania Catholic Interscholastic Athletic Association (PCIAA) Class B basketball title.

But the route St. Joseph took to the championship game was long and arduous in a number of ways.

High school basketball teams today basically have the benefit of spacious, well-lit facilities, chartered buses to away games and camcorders taping upcoming opponents.

But the Spartans had nothing in the way of amenities. In fact, the school never had a home gym until December, 2008.

The Spartans used the old Har-Brack gym, now the Highlands Middle School. They played home games on Wednesdays and Saturdays, scheduling around Har-Brack and its opponents. Practice? Good luck with that. Coach Joe Nee's team practiced in the upstairs at the old Polish Falcons Club in Natrona. There was no heat or no showers. A section of the one wall was burned out and only a tarpaulin protected the area from the outside elements. Lighting? Don't squint. There were two light bulbs hanging from the ceiling.

"When it got cold, I had the players practicing in their street clothes," Nee recalled. "We didn't have the best equipment, but sometimes, I think that brought us all closer together" Away games? No buses, the Spartans just car-pooled it.

Often, St. Joseph took the floor without knowing much about their opponents. Being the only school in the Catholic League Section 2 that wasn't located in, or adjacent to, Pittsburgh, Nee didn't have a scouting budget that modern teams have.

"I never believed in scouting too much," Nee said. "I figured they just had to beat us."

Instead, teams were forced to adjust to St. Joseph's fast-break offense and full-court defensive pressure. Not many teams were successful.

One team that did solve the St. Joseph scheme was St. Casimir of Pittsburgh, which was led by future Duquesne University stand-out Ron Guziak.

After the loss to St. Cas, the Spartans shifted into high gear and crushed section-leading St. Anselm of Swissvale, 83-49. That one was followed by victories over Braddock St. Thomas, Sheraden Holy Innocents, and two McKees Rocks schools – St. Mary's and St. Francis de Sales.

The biggest victory of the 1962-63 regular season was a 43-39 victory in the return match against St. Casimir. With starting guard Joe Zalenski injured, reserve Ron Bowman came off the bench to score eight points.

After defeating St. Casimir again in the section tie-breaker, St. Joseph qualified to play St. George of Pittsburgh's Allentown section in a best-of-three series to decide the Pittsburgh Diocean crown.

The Spartans blasted heavily-favored St. George, 76-54 and 62-43 to win the series in two games.

A playoff victory over Latrobe's St. Vincent Prep put St. Joseph into the western Pennsylvania final against Elk County Christian. A sellout crowd of 1,400 at the Arnold High gym watched the Spartans knock off ECC, 75-59. Dave Krumenacker led the way with 30 points. Lou Demharter chipped in with 13 as the little school from Garfield Street in Natrona that didn't have a place to call its basketball home suddenly had earned a berth in the PCIAA title game in Scranton.

The opponent would be St. Rose of Carbondale.

The team finally got a chance to ride a bus and stay in a hotel. But the Spartans failed to get much sleep the night before the big game. It was St. Patrick's Day Eve and an Irish bagpipe band marched through the hallways while Nee's squad tried to get some shut-eye.

Around the same time, several busloads of St. Joseph fans left Natrona at midnight and arrived in Scranton at about 10 a.m. The trip took 10 hours, Remember, there were no highways like the Route 28 Expressway or Interstate 80.

Back home, there were unseasonable temperatures of 70 degrees that day, creating a serious 15-mile ice jam along the Allegheny River that had local residents quite worried. The Kinzua

Dam in the upper Allegheny River region was still a few months from completion, so residents in riverfront towns were still at the mercy of high waters when snow and ice would melt too quickly. But the fans arrived in Scranton in time to join 3,500 others who jammed the Scranton CYC for the championship game. St. Joseph led, 11-9, at the end of the first quarter and 26-23 midway through the second period, but the Spartans frontcourt was in foul trouble.

The Roses took a 31-30 lead at halftime and were in front, 49-45 at the end of three quarters.
St. Joseph narrowed the gap, trailing 55-54 with 1:18 left in the game. The Spartans stole the ball, but lost it back quickly with 1:05 left as the Roses started to freeze the ball. St. Rose was forced into a jump ball with 46 seconds left. Three other jump balls would take place in the next 10 seconds.

Under today's rules, St. Joseph would have gotten at least two possessions out of bounds, but jump balls took place after every stalemate then. A foul shot by St. Rose with 12 seconds left would be the final point of the game. A desperation shot by Ed Thimons with three seconds left went off the boards.

The Spartans, with only 18 boys in their overall senior class, fell just short of a state championship.

Tom Antkowiak led St. Joseph in scoring with 20 points before fouling out with 1:47 left in the fourth quarter. Demharter had 10 points and Zalenski 6. Krumenacker had 4 before fouling out midway through the third period.

The Spartans ended a memorable season at 21-4.

Mr. Joseph Nee
Coach

Mr. Ronald Slater
Assistant Coach

Members of the 1963 St. Joseph High School basketball PCIAA runner-up were, front row, from left: Rich Demharter, Joe Zalenski, Tom Conroy, Ed Thimons, Tom Severn, Ron Bowman. Back row: Head coach Joe Nee, assistant Ron Slater, Lou Demharter, Dave Krumenacker, Tom Antkowiak, Ron Krasewski and Bob Chistri.

chapter 32

HIS TEAM, HIS TOWN

Many successful high school football coaches are the ones that blend in with their communities.

One of the best examples of that is long-time Kittanning coach Harry Beckwith. He seemed to personify Kittanning through and through. Beckwith was the right coach for the right community. He was old school before old school became a popular catch phrase, fitting in so well at an old, riverfront, industrial community. Of course, Beckwith had a built-in advantage since he grew up in Kittanning, playing for Dave 'Red' Ullom, the man for whom the school's stadium has been named.

Beckwith took over for Ullom in 1974 and, just a year later, led Kittanning to the Allegheny Interscholastic Conference title. The 1975 team made the WPIAL playoffs for the first time, defeating Union Area in the Class AA first round at Leechburg's Veterans Stadium, 32-8. In that era, only the conference winners entered the WPIAL postseason. The Wildcats clinched the title on the final night of the regular season at Freeport. With Freeport in punt formation in a scoreless game, the Wildcats broke through and blocked the punt out of bounds for a safety and gained the momentum that led an 8-0 victory.

The Union win put Kittanning in the WPIAL finals at Mt. Lebanon Stadium against Beth-Center. With no score, a Kittanning punt went straight up into the air, giving Beth-Center generous field position. That was the turning point in a 13-0 Beth-Center victory.

Beckwith thought his team was even better in 1976, going 10-0 and defeating a solid Freeport team – again in the regular season finale – 29-22 - before one of the largest crowds ever at Kittanning.

But the dreams of a return trip to the Class AA finals were shattered by a 22-16 setback against Brentwood in the playoff opener.

Beckwith had a unique pre-game drill where his running backs would run through a gauntlet made up of tackles and linebackers. During the season when Beckwith would be asked to be a guest on various radio and cable television shows, he'd always ask to bring his players along. Since some teenagers are inherently shy, this helped the players to mature and speak in public situations, helping them as they progressed through college and working lives. Even in the years Kittanning fell short of a playoff berth, Beckwith continued to develop some outstanding individuals and teams. One example was Mitch Frerotte, linebacker and tight end who went on to Penn State and later, played in three Super Bowls with the Buffalo Bills, a team he made as an undrafted walk-on. As 1986 approached, it was time for a change in scenery, but Beckwith didn't stray too far from home, taking over at Ford City, a school that had never experienced a trip to the playoffs. In just his second season there, the Sabers made the postseason behind Gus Frerotte, Mitch's cousin and Beckwith's future son-in-law. In 1990, Beckwith faced, perhaps, his biggest coaching challenge when Kittanning and Ford City merged to form Armstrong Central High School. The move put former rivals now wearing the same jerseys. Early on, Beckwith said any player who didn't think they could be part of the new environment could leave. One Kittanning player took Beckwith up on his offer. After he left, Beckwith told the remaining players it "was now my way, or the highway."

The Cougars quickly jelled and exceeded all expectations, qualifying for the playoffs. Armstrong Central lost in the playoff opener to Kiski Area, but Beckwith received plaudits for the way he handled a thankless situation.

In 2001, Beckwith was named to the Pennsylvania Coaches Association Hall of Fame as he prepared for his final season. He finished his 37-year coaching career -28 as a head coach - with his eighth WPIAL playoff team. The Wildcats dropped a double-overtime thriller to Blackhawk, 27-21.

His final record was 150-99-9, including a 127-77-5 mark at Kittanning.

But the record Beckwith is most proud of is another one that is 150. That's at least the number of players Beckwith helped get into college and have found success in the legal, medical and educational professions.

Credit: 1999 Kittanning High School boosters

Harry Beckwith.

chapter 33

A RECORD-SETTING ROLE

When Gus Frerotte stepped on the field for the Minnesota Vikings on Sept. 17, 2008, he set a record.

Not an NFL record, but an Alle-Kiski Valley record. Frerotte became the first local player to play 15 seasons in the NFL, breaking the mark of 14 seasons set by Har-Brack High School graduate Dick Modzelewski.

The 2008 season also saw Frerotte tie an NFL record. On Nov. 30, he tied the mark for the longest pass from scrimmage, a 99-yard TD pass to Bernard Berrian. But the 2008 season was bittersweet for Frerotte, after leading the Vikings to an 8-3 record, he suffered a back injury. Tavarius Jackson, whom he had replaced

Credit: Valley News Dispatch

Ford City's Gus Frerotte (12) looks for a receiver against Kittanning on Sept. 16, 1988.

when named the starter by Vikings coach Brad Childress, returned to the lineup.

Frerotte was released by the Vikings on Feb. 27, 2009, after the team signed backup QB Sage Rosenfels.

The Start

Gustave Joseph Frerotte was born on July 31, 1971, in Kittanning.

He emerged as the starting quarterback for Ford City High School in 1987, as a junior. Frerotte led the Sabers to their first WPIAL playoff berth that season as the runner-up team in the Allegheny Football Conference. It was the first time Ford City had made the playoffs after inaugurating football in 1908.

Frerotte played for coach Harry Beckwith, who would eventually become his father-in-law. In 1986, Frerotte's sophomore season, a teachers strike in the Armstrong School District prevented Beckwith from coaching in four of Ford City's nine games. In the spring of 1987, Frerotte played centerfield for the Ford City state championship baseball team.

But in '87, the football program turnaround began. Mid-season victories against long-time powers Jeannette and Freeport propelled the Sabers to claim a playoff berth.

It would be only the fifth winning season in a 29-year span for Ford City. The Sabers lost a first-round playoff game at Sto-Rox. In 1988, Frerotte made the most of a Ford City team plagued by injuries and inexperience. The 1988 team returned only eight starters, but Frerotte finished eighth in WPIAL passing with 1,443 yards. His 101 completions included 12 TD passes, enough to get noticed by the University of Tulsa.

College Days

At Tulsa, he finished second all-time in career passing with 5,480 yards, behind former teammate T. J. Rubley. During that time, Frerotte completed 423-of-860 passing attempts with 32 touchdowns.

As a senior, his 2,871 passing yards were the most by a Golden Hurricane quarterback in 28 years. As a sophomore, he handled Tulsa's punting duties, averaging 35.5 yards per punt. As a redshirt freshman, he started eight games in 1990 when Rubley was injured, a role that would be recurring throughout his NFL career. In an even bigger event during his collegiate days, he started dating his future wife, Annie. Beckwith made it abundantly clear during high school that his attractive daughter was off limits to team members. But while studying nursing at the University of Pittsburgh, Annie experienced a bad break-up, and Beckwith advised Gus to help her through the difficulty. The two have been together ever since and are the parents of Gunnar and Gabriel.

The Pros

Frerotte was selected in the seventh round of the 1994 NFL draft by the Washington Redskins. Earlier in the draft, the 'Skins picked University of Tennessee quarterback Heath Shuler in the first round, the third overall pick.

During the 1995 season, however, Frerotte was starting in place of Shuler because of injuries and Shuler's difficulty adjusting to the rigors of the NFL. By 1997, Frerotte had been named to the Pro Bowl.

Many, though, remember that season as the one where Frerotte rammed his helmet into a padded wall at Giants Stadium while celebrating a Redskins touchdown and a 7-7 tie. He injured his neck during the TV Sunday Night Football encounter. Here's a brief rundown of Frerotte's pro career:

- In 1999, he was the backup in Detroit to Charlie Batch and started a rare Lions playoff game when Batch was injured.
- In 2000, he started for Denver after Brian Griese was injured, leading the Broncos to the playoffs and stayed in the Mile High City the following season.
- In 2002, he joined the Bengals and won the starting job, but three games into the season gave way to Jon Kitna under the head coach Dick LeBeau, who was fired shortly afterwards.
- In 2003-04, his first stint with the Vikings, he backed up Daunte Culpepper, but started twice and went 2-0.
- In 2005, he earned the starting job in Miami, leading the Dolphins to an upset victory over Denver in the opener. He started 15 games and Miami finished 9-7.

- In 2006, he began a two-year stint with the Rams as a backup to Central Catholic High School graduate Marc Bulger. He started several games in 2007 when Bulger was simply beat up from St. Louis losing so many linemen to injuries. After coach Scott Linehart, who was Frerotte's offensive coordinator in Miami was let go, Frerotte was released on Feb. 28, 2008.

- In 2008, he inked a two-year, $3.75 million deal with Minnesota for his second go-around in the Twin Cities. In his 15 pro seasons, Frerotte has passed for 21,191 yards and 114 touchdowns.

chapter 34

THE MAGNIFICENT COMEBACK

Memorable comebacks are part of sporting folklore. But the comeback staged by the Deer Lakes High School girls basketball team on March 29, 1985 was truly memorable. The Lady Lancers, down by 17 points at halftime, pulled together and tripped Palmyra, 45-43, in the PIAA state girls Class AAA finals at Hersheypark Arena. Through 2009, it is the only time an A-K Valley girls team has won a state title.

But the road to Hershey was filled with impediments, not the least of which is a powerhouse that still reigns today.

In the 1983-84 season, Deer Lakes laid the framework for its state title run. The Lady Lancers drew a first-round bye in the Class AAA playoffs in the first season of four classifications. Deer Lakes defeated Swissvale in the second round before losing to Canevin. It was enough to qualify for the PIAA playoffs, where the Lancers knocked off Cambria Heights, 57-47, at St. Francis College, Loretto. But Deer Lakes lost a 33-32 heartbreaker to Hickory in a second round PIAA game on the small floor at Clarion Area High School.

Coach Don Favero wanted the taste of success to linger doing the off-season. To that point, Favero mailed a post card of Pitt's Fitzgerald Field House, site of the WPIAL finals, to each of his players during the summer.

The Lancers began their drive to the state title with a resounding, 57-6 win over Riverview to start the season. Deer Lakes completed the pre-section part of the season by winning all six games. The closest encounter was a 15-point victory over Turtle Creek.

The Lancers won their first two Section 8-AAA games before colliding with North Catholic. Then as now, the Trojanettes were the program teams must go through to win a WPIAL title. It was a one-sided collision as North Catholic humbled Deer Lakes, 79-56. Undaunted, the Lancers kept winning, defeating their next six opponents before another confrontation with North Catholic. This time Deer Lakes decided to hold the ball and keep the score down. That made for little action, and Comcast TV-3 announcer Bob Tatrn recited the Gettysburg Address to fill some air time as the Lancers spent considerable time passing while the clock ran. The strategy didn't work as North Catholic managed a 14-6 victory to take a two-game lead in Section 8-AAA.

Deer Lakes won the final two games of the regular season by generous margins over Hampton and Kittanning. That impressed the WPIAL Basketball Steering Committee enough to slot the Lancers as a No. 2 seed and the team received a first round bye.

In the WPIAL quarterfinals, Deer Lakes eased by Swissvale, 66-43, and Carlynton, 63-48, in the semifinals to set up a date for the WPIAL title against none other than North Catholic. Getting to the finals was nothing new for the Trojanettes. They were the two-time defending PIAA champion and were in their eighth consecutive WPIAL title game. With top-notch forward Monique Wade out of the lineup, Deer Lakes aggressively attacked the hoop, taking a 10-9 lead after one quarter. North Catholic answered with a strong second quarter to take a 23-21 halftime advantage.

But few could have imagined what would happen in the third quarter. Deer Lakes held North Catholic scoreless, and the Lancers' defense frustrated attempts to get the ball into Amy Santa, the tallest girl on the floor at 5-feet-11. A 23-21 deficit had turned into a 33-23 lead at the end of three periods. North Catholic came within six points of the Lancers, but that's as close as it would get, as Deer Lakes posted an impressive 42-32 victory.

Shawn Rearick had 11 points and Erica Goodrich 10 to lead the Lancers.

Getting the top seed from the WPIAL in the PIAA tournament, Deer Lakes took the measure of Franklin Area, 55-41, in opening round play at Westminster College. The Lancers defeated Turtle Creek for the second time that season, 50-37, at Chartiers Valley High School. Deer Lakes had never been as far as the PIAA quarterfinals, but the trip to New Castle High School was a success as the Lancers beat back an upset attempt by Sharon, 42-35. But at the same time Deer Lakes was eliminating Sharon, Altoona's Bishop Guilfoyle surprised North Catholic, 45-43, at Indiana (Pa.) University. That meant Deer Lakes wouldn't have to face the Trojanettes for the fourth time that season.

But Guilfoyle was no pushover for Deer Lakes. In a testament to how far girls basketball had come, the PIAA semifinal was the sole game scheduled at Indiana (Pa.) University's Memorial Field-house. A huge crowd watched the Lady Marauders take a 39-33 lead after three quarters. But Deer Lakes rallied and took the game into overtime and outscored Guilfoyle, 8-3, in the extra session to prevail, 55-50, setting the stage for the big trip to Hershey to face Palmyra. The Cougars defeated Harrisburg Bishop McDevitt, 46-40, in a game at Steelton-Highspire High School. The Deer Lakes-Palmyra matchup was what would become a rarity in PIAA basketball – two public schools vying for the state title.

In the first 12 years of Class AAA girls basketball, this and the 1990 matchup between John S. Fine High School of Nanticoke and Beaver Falls were the only times two public schools met for the Class AAA title.

It was evident early on that Deer Lakes would have its hands full as Palmyra jumped out to a 10-5 at the end of one period. The Lancers shot poorly (6-for-19) in the first half as Palmyra kept feeding the ball inside to take a 30-13 halftime lead. At the intermission, Favero told his players to press for the first 10 minutes of the second half. The Cougars did manage to take a 34-15 lead on a basket by guard Tammy Powell.

But Deer Lakes proceeded to rattle off 13 unanswered points to get back into the game.

Palmyra was racked by seven turnovers in the quarter as the Lancers cut the lead to five by the start of the fourth period.

Deer Lakes continue to narrow the gap before finally tying the game at 43-all. Terri Gizenski picked up Palmyra's 23rd turnover of the game and fed Rearick, open on the left wing, for the decisive shot with 9 seconds left.

Gizienski and Rearick led Deer Lakes with 11 points each. Amy Alger, who would later attend Duquesne University, led the Cougars with 12 points.

Goodrich and Suvoy each had 7 rebounds to pace the Lancers. Fans met the team the following afternoon at Allegheny Valley Exit 5 of the Pennsylvania Turnpike and paraded the newly crowned state champs through West Deer.

Deer Lakes 45, Palmyra 43, PIAA Class AAA girls title game March 29, 1985.

Score by quarters:

Deer Lakes 5 8 19 13 - 45
Palmyra   10 20   7   6 - 43

Individual scoring: DL: Terri Gizienski 5 1-3 11, Erica Goodrich 4 2-2 10, Kathy Suvoy 2 1-3 5, Missy Overly 3 0-0 6, Shawn Rearick 5 1-2 11, Valarie Chauvin 1 0-1 2. Totals: 20 5-11 45. P: Amy Alger 4 4-5 12, Missy Brubaker 4 0-0 8, Vinetta Daiga 2 0-0 4, Tammy Powell 3 0-1 6, Jenny Spahr 2 0-0 4, Chris Bucher 1 0-0 2, Lisa Brannon 1 0-0 2, Sue Shay 1 3-4 5. Totals: 18 7-10 43.

Credit: Valley News Dispatch

Coach Don Favero (holding game ball) and the Deer Lakes Lady Lancers celebrate winning the PIAA Class AAA championship on March 28, 1985.

chapter 35

THE PRIDE OF DUCKTOWN

Don't look for Ducktown on a map.

It might be too small for a map, but the denizens of Ducktown have more collective pride than a major city.

Ducktown is a little neighborhood on the western side of the railroad tracks between Natrona and Natrona Heights. Its population is comprised of families who earlier emigrated from Poland and other Eastern European areas – people with immense pride. Nobody is rich in Ducktown and nobody cares that they're not rich. The area gets its name from the fact that many people raised ducks and, when the time came, made duck soup and pillows with duck feathers.

The area really swelled with pride during the eras of the football Modzelewski brothers.

Ed (Big Mo) Modzelewski and Dick (Little Mo) Modzelewski both started their careers at Har-Brack High School, both went on to the University of Maryland and both went on to notable NFL careers.

The Modzelewskis were two of six children. Another brother, Gene, played one season with the Browns before fulfilling a military commitment while another brother, Joe, was successful in boxing.

Ed

Edward Modzelewski was born on Jan. 13, 1929.

His route to football stardom was truly unconventional. He quit school at age 15 and joined the Merchant Marines. When his family discovered that a number of ships were being sunk in the North Atlantic, a local priest intervened to get Ed his release. He later worked in a slag dump, but he missed football and decided he better go back to school, re-joining the Har-Brack program in time for his junior season. His bruising, bowl-you-over style and his blocking ability soon won him a starting job in 1946.

In '47, Har-Brack was undefeated and a WPIAL title contender. A late-season game against Munhall matched two 8-0 teams. On the first play of the game, quarterback Ralph Atkinson lateraled to Ed, who threw the ball 60 yards downfield. The receiver was so surprised that he stepped out of bounds at the 2. With the Tigers ahead late in the game, 13-12, Har-Brack was trying to run out the clock when Ed broke up the middle for an 80-yard touchdown run.

The following week, Ed scored both Tigers touchdowns (his 13th and 14th of the season) in a 13-0 victory over Vandergrift and his popularity soared. He actually got his nickname from a confused young schoolgirl on an academic quiz. She was asked what was 'Big Mo?' The answer that the judges were looking for was the battleship U.S.S. Missouri from World War II. Instead, she answered: "That's Ed Modzelewski, he plays football for Har-Brack."

The answers were published in a newspaper and a nickname was born.

The 1947 season didn't have a happy ending for Har-Brack as the Tigers were blown out by Ken High, 28-0, in the WPIAL title game at Forbes Field. Ed, however, was named second team AP all-state running back.

The Tigers were 15-4-1 during Ed's career.

It was on to the University of Maryland for Ed, where he led the Terapins in rushing as a sophomore in 1949 with 589 yards in 120 carries. He was an AP All-american honorable mention in 1950 and a second-teamer on the AP's 1951 team.

The 10-0 Maryland team, ranked third in the country, was invited to play No. 1 Tennessee in the Sugar Bowl. The Terps knocked off the Volunteers and Modzelewski was voted game MVP with his 153 yards rushing.

On Jan. 2, 2009, Ed was at the 75th Sugar Bowl where the 74 previous MVPs were honored at halftime.

In 1952, Ed was the first round draft pick of the Steelers and the sixth selection overall in the NFL Draft. It remains the highest draft position ever for an A-K Valley football player.

In 1953 and '54, Ed joined the Air Force. He was stationed in Washington, D.C., at Defense Command Headquarters.

After his military service, Ed was traded to the Cleveland Browns in time to be part of the team's 1955 NFL championship as a fullback with NFL legends Otto Graham at quarterback and

Paul Brown as the head coach. He gained 619 yards in '55 during the 12-game regular season.

In 1957, Jim Brown arrived from Syracuse University and Ed was moved into a reserve and special teams role. He was selected in the 1960 NFL expansion draft by the Cowboys, but never suited up, retiring at 31.

One of his biggest football thrills came at age 79 on Oct. 17, 2008. Ed flew some 2,500 miles from his home in suburban Cleveland to watch his grandson, Anthony Giacobbe, play football for the first time at Analy High school in Sebastopol, Calif., located in Sonoma County, north of the San Francisco Bay Area.

Giacobbe, a running back who also wears the No. 36 his grandfather wore for the Browns, scored a touchdown in the first quarter of a game against Case Grande.

"I looked up into the stands, and he was going crazy; it was a great feeling I will never forget," Giacobbe told the *Sonoma West Times & News*.

Dick

Richard Blair Modzelewski was born on Feb. 16, 1931. Dick was a lineman for Har-Brack who had a reputation for always being prepared to play. He often blocked for brother Ed in the Tigers backfield.

Dick missed part of his sophomore year with a broken fibula, suffered in a game against Ford City in 1946. He recovered enough to be an integral part of the 1947 Har-Brack WPIAL runner-up. In 1948, Dick was named an all-state lineman in 1948 and his stock among college coaches rose. He was being recruited by South Carolina, Notre Dame and Georgia, but decided to follow his brother to the University of Maryland.

During his Har-Brack years, the Tigers compiled a 23-6-1 record.

Maryland was one of the country's top programs under Jim Tatum, pulling off a 22-game unbeaten streak at one point. In 1950, Dick started in his sophomore season, taking over when Ray Krouse was injured.

Maryland attained a No. 3 national ranking in 1951. In one game that season against North Carolina, Dick made 12 solo tackles and was part of a defense that held the Tar Heels to 40 yards net rushing.

He again cleared the way for brother, Ed, in the 1952 Sugar Bowl, where Ed was game MVP as the Terps' went 11-0.

Dick was a second team All-American selection by the AP in 1951. But in 1952, he won the Outland Trophy, symbol of being the country's top lineman. It was the first major award bestowed upon a Terrapins player.

He found out about winning the Outland Trophy while playing in an all-star collegiate game in Arizona.

"I always credited Joe Blair, the Maryland publicity director who's from Freeport, for promoting me," Dick said in a 2006 interview with the Pittsburgh Tribune-Review.

Dick was a second-round draft pick by the Redskins in 1953 and played in the Nation's Capital through 1954. He clashed with 'Skins' coach Joe Kuharich in 1954, ultimately signing with the Calgary Stampeders of the Canadian Football League. The Redskins filed a successful court injunction to void the contract.

The Redskins swapped him to the Steelers on March 1, 1955, where he would rejoin Ed. But Ed was traded to the Browns when Cleveland needed a replacement for retiring fullback Marion Motley.

Dick then was traded twice in a four-day period in 1956. On April 24, 1956, the Steelers sent Dick to the Detroit Lions who, three days later, shipped him to the New York Giants for, of all people, Ray Krouse, whose 1950 injury paved the way to Dick's prominence.

That proved to be a huge break for Dick's career as the Giants won the 1956 NFL title and would play in five more NFL title games while with New York.

By then, Dick was on his way to established an NFL record for durability, playing in a then-record 180 consecutive games.

The Greatest Game

While with the Giants, Dick was part of the original "Fearsome Foursome" defensive line that included Roosevelt Grier, Andy Robustelli and Jim Katcavage.

To end the 1958 season, Dick was part of what has been called the NFL's Greatest Game, the title game against the Baltimore

Colts on Dec. 28, 1958 at Yankee Stadium.

The Colts won, 23-17, in overtime. It is, to date, the first and only NFL title game to go into overtime. It can be argued that few sporting events in American history had the impact of that game, one of the first to be nationally-televised. An estimated 45 million people watched the game. The audience would have been somewhat higher, but the game was blacked out in the New York City area, due to the NFL's blackout rule, which was rescinded by the U.S. Congress in 1973.

The game is considered by many as the contest that catapulted pro football to the No. 1 spot in favorite sports among the American populace.

And Dick Modzelewski was at his best on the national stage, sacking Colts quarterback Johnny Unitas three times that day. Dick had a shot at a fourth sack, but Unitas surprised everybody by calling a draw play on 3rd-and-17.

Dick asked Johnny how he could call a draw play on third and 17 and Unitas replied: "We got a first down, didn't we?" With a 17-14 lead late in the game, it looked as if Dick and the Giants would be celebrating a second NFL title in three seasons. But Unitas directed the Colts into field goal position – a strategy that would later be dubbed "The Two-Minute Drill." Steve Myhra's field goal sent the game into overtime, a concept everybody was unfamiliar with. In fact, the Baltimore bench was puzzled when the officials told the Colts to send out the captains for a coin toss. The Giants won the flip, but had to punt. Baltimore drove 80 yards for a touchdown, but it wasn't easy. With the ball at the New York 8, TV screens across the country suddenly went blank.

A fan came onto the field, and play had to be stopped. It turned out the person was an NBC employee who was ordered to go on the field and create a distraction while the network frantically tried to fix the problem.

It turned out a simple plug was pulled out, so play resumed and Alan Ameche's 1-yard run gave the Colts the historic victory. Dick often said that no one playing in that game realized the historic impact it would have.

Dick played five more seasons with the Giants, never missing a game. New York lost its third straight NFL title game to the Bears in 1963.

On March 4, 1964, Dick was traded to the Browns for wide receiver Bobby Crespino. The Browns hoped Dick would supplement defensive tackles Jim Kanicki and Frank Parker, but he was rushed into the starting lineup following Parker's injury in the season's opener.

The Browns would go on to win the NFL title that season, 27-0, over Unitas and the Colts. No Cleveland team has won a pro sports title since. Oddly enough, Ed Modzeleweski won a title with Cleveland in his first year in 1955 and Dick did the same in '64. The Browns reached the title game again in 1965, but lost to the Packers. In his final season of 1966, Dick was joined by brother Gene.

The Coaching Years

After a stint as a Browns scout in 1967, Dick joined the team's coaching staff and nine years later, was named defensive coordinator by coach Forrest Gregg. When Gregg was fired with one game left in the '77 season, Modzelewski was named interim head coach for one game, a 20-19 loss to Seattle.

In 1978, new Browns head coach Sam Rutigliano abolished the position of defensive coordinator and offered Dick the defensive line coach's job. Sensing a demotion, Dick went to the Giants for one season.

In 1979, he resurfaced as defensive line coach with the Cincinnati Bengals. After being seemingly dismissed after another wholesale coaching change, Gregg was named to head the Bengals and he brought Dick on as defensive coordinator.

In 1981, Cincy put together a memorable season and finally, Dick Modzelewski got to be part of a Super Bowl team. Despite a 26-21 loss in Super Bowl XVI to the 49ers, Dick stayed on with Gregg two more seasons, then followed Gregg to the Packers for four seasons.

After Gregg resigned as Packers head coach, he joined the Lions for two seasons as defensive line coach before calling it quits in 1989.

Both Ed and Dick Modzelewski are members of the University of Maryland Hall of Fame and the A-K Valley Hall of Fame.

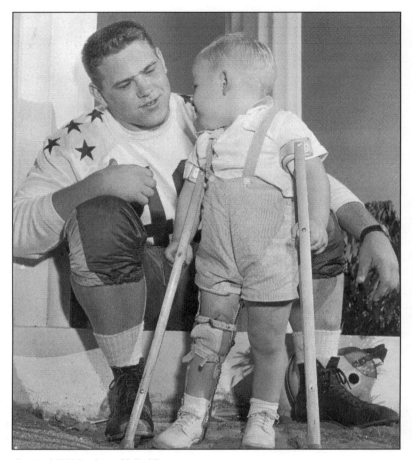

Credit: A-K Valley Sports Hall of Fame

Dick Modzelewski meets Tommy Hellmuller in Miami prior to North-South Shrine all-star game on Christmas night, 1952. Little Mo played for the South team in a 21-21 tie.

Credit: Dom Corso, Brackenridge, Pa

Ed Modzelewski, left, is greeted by Browns head coach and owner Paul Brown and quarterback Otto Graham after he was traded to Cleveland in 1955.

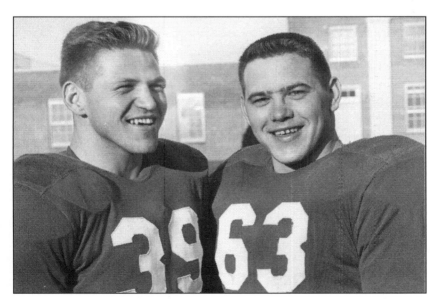

Credit: Dom Corso, Brackenridge, Pa

Ed (left) and Dick Modzelewski pose on the University of Maryland campus in the early 1950s

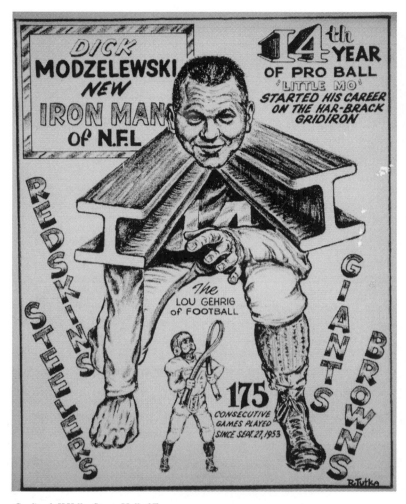

Credit: A-K Valley Sports Hall of Fame

Dick Modzelewski became the NFL's Iron Man for his consecutive games played streak.

chapter 36

GETTING TO THE FINISH LINE

Clang!

That was sound for much of the evening when Leechburg played California Area in the WPIAL Class A basketball championship game on March 2, 2007 at Duquesne University's Palumbo Center.

The Blue Devils were seemingly letting a shot at WPIAL gold slip away by missing an extraordinary amount of free throws. But when the chips were down, Nick Matviko calmly canned a pair of foul shots with 4.7 seconds to go in the game to lift Leechburg to a 60-59 victory, and the school's lone WPIAL basketball title. Matviko led Leechburg with 23 points, while Steve Predebon added 22 as the Blue Devils returned home to a raucous late-night parade down Market Street upon their arrival from the game. It was a wild ride to the championship. A year earlier, Leechburg appeared on its way to its first WPIAL semifinal appearance since 1966 when the Blue Devils led Clairton by 20 late in third period, only to lose by 11 in overtime, a 31-point shift in 14 minutes of basketball.

But with the fact that only leading scorer Andy Tressler was graduating, expectations were high going into the 2006-07 campaign. Head coach Damian Davies beefed up the non-section schedule, playing Class AAA schools like Knoch (twice) and Valley, and a Quad-A school, Brashear, from the Pittsburgh City League. Another Class AAA school, New Castle, was scheduled for the final week of the regular season at Penn State's New Kensington Campus, the that game was cancelled because of wintry conditions.

Leechburg did well against schools three or four times its size, losing by just three to Knoch, for example. That would bode well for the Blue Devils in the postseason.

A key section victory against Duquesne was, perhaps, the highlight of the Section 4-A campaign because the Dukes were ranked among the top 10 teams in the state at the time. A running lay-up with 0:07 left in the game by Matviko gave Leechburg its first lead of the night. The Blue Devils trailed by eight with 3:45 left in the game. But two 3-pointers by Jon Takosky kept Leechburg's hopes alive, setting the stage for the big basket by Matviko to lift Leechburg to a 60-58 win.

Predebon tallied 20 against the Dukes, Matviko followed with 17 and the largely unheralded Takosky wound up with 14 in one of the best performances of his career.

A final playoff tune-up against Riverview, however, did nothing but make the check-engine light come on. The Blue Devils fell victim to Riverview's slowdown game, and never got out of the blocks. Leechburg trailed by 12 at the half and lost by nine, 46-37, to finish the regular season with a 12-10 mark.

But the Blue Devils recovered nicely in the playoff opener, outgunning Our Lady of the Sacred Heart (OLSH), 84-68, at North Allegheny High School. Predebon's 32 points led the way for Leechburg. Todd Rupert was 9-of-10 from the foul line. A quarterfinal victory over Western Beaver followed, setting up a showdown against No. 1-seeded Serra Catholic at Keystone Oaks High School.

Predebon and Matviko caught fire early, as the Blue Devils rolled out to a 24-14 halftime advantage. In fact, Predebon had 16 points in the first half, more than the entire Serra team.

Leechburg led the No. 1-ranked team in the state, 55-46, with 49 seconds to go. Only a trio of 3-point baskets by Serra made the final score look close.

Predebon finished with 29 points and Matviko added 18. Marc Rozanski led Serra with 15 points while Pat Grubbs, the 6-foot-8, 260-point center came up with 14, but he was frustrated much of the night by double-and triple-teams.

But after 88 years of basketball, Leechburg was finally going to the WPIAL championship game.

All Roads Lead to Palumbo Center

The Blue Devils headed to Pittsburgh brimming with confidence. But the California Area Trojans were riding a 20-game winning streak coming into the championship encounter. California came out ready to play, leading from the 6:53 mark of the first quarter until the 1:41 mark of the fourth period. It looked like Leechburg would have to settle for silver medals when the Trojans moved in front, 47-36, with 2:18 left in the third quarter. A traditional, three-point play with 5:29 to go by Matviko brought Leechburg's huge following to its feet as the deficit was cut to 51-48. Moments later, Matviko came up with the first of two steals in consecutive Cal possessions, making it 51-50.

"That changed the complexion of the game," Trojans coach Phil Pergola said of Matviko's thefts. The comeback was completed when Matviko's pinpoint pass to Predebon near the hoop put the Blue Devils ahead, 56-55.

A baseline jumper by Stephen Meidus with 8 seconds remaining brought Leechburg to with 59-58. Pergola called a time out to set up a play to break Leechurg's press. But a long pass downcourt by Chris McVicker forced Donte Valentino to step out of bounds, handing the ball back over to Leechburg.

Matviko was fouled going for a final-second shot. He sank free throws to make it 60-59. California had one more chance, but another long pass resulted in Matviko tipping the pass to Takosky as time expired.

It marked the first time a school from Armstrong County won a WPIAL basketball title since Shannock Valley did it in 1957. The fact that Leechburg was only 14-of-31 from the foul line was quickly forgotten.

Reaching the top of the Mountain March 2, 2007
WPIAL Class A title game
Palumbo Center, Duquesne University

Score by quarters: California Area   16   14   17   12 - 59
                   Leechburg   14   13   13   20 - 60

Individual Scoring: (CA) Donte Valentino 6 1 5-11 20, Travis Van Olst 2 0-2 4, Mike Hrivnak 1 1 0-0 5, John McVicker 2 0-0 4, Chris McVicker 4 1 4-4 15, Ben Carson 1 1 1-2 6, Waugh Carter 1 0-0 2, Michael Galis 1 0-0 2. Totals: 17 5 10-18 59. (L) Steve Predebon 7 1 5-11 22, Todd Rupert 1 1 2-3 7, Stephen Meidus 2 2-3 6, Nick Matviko 6 2 5-14 23, Sheldon Loughner 1 0-0 2. Totals: 17 4 14-31 60.

Credit: Valley News Dispatch

Nick Matviko (21) celebrates the WPIAL Class A championship with teammates at the Palumbo Center.

chapter 37

THE POWERHOUSE FROM SCRATCH

When Burrell High School emerged from nowhere to field back-to-back WPIAL football championships in 1967 and '68, the route to glory was quite unconventional.

Burrell defeated Freeport, 6-0, in consecutive WPIAL championship games in New Kensington, becoming the youngest school to win two straight titles. Not only was the score the same, the touchdowns were scored in the same end zone of the field – the one closest to Little Pucketa Creek.

The only difference was that Burrell had two different head coaches, and the stadium name was changed. Frank Martin piloted the first championship for the Bucs and Frank Solomond the second.

The 1967 game was played in what was called Ken High Memorial Stadium. By the time the 1968 game rolled around, the facility was changed to Valley High Memorial Stadium, reflecting the new name of the high school following the New Kensington-Arnold merger.

In the Beginning

Unlike most of the high schools in the 1960s that were created via consolidations of existing high schools, Burrell was carved out of fresh territory. Lower Burrell was one of the post-World War II suburban boomtowns. It was, basically, a rural community until the farmers began selling their land to developers when GIs returning from the war wanted to settle in, build homes and start families.

As a result, Lower Burrell's population of 4,214 in 1940 nearly tripled to 12,543 in 1960. In response to the major influx of families, Glade View Elementary School was built in 1949 and Bon Air in 1953. Already-existing Stewart Elementary, opened in 1932, was expanded in 1952. Glade View and Bon Air both added classrooms in 1958. The school district could barely keep up with the expanding enrollment, quickly running out of classroom space.

Stewart also served as the junior high for many years, but the need for a sole junior high building manifested itself. The independent school districts of Lower and Upper Burrell came together to form the Burrell Joint School District. The junior high school, housing students in grades 7-9, opened in 1960.

At the end of ninth grade, Burrell students had to choose a high school to attend. Most all went to New Kensington and Arnold high schools. But those two schools, particularly New Kensington – popularly known as Ken High – was bulging at the seams and said it could no longer take Burrell students. The need for a high school soon became evident. The school district purchased a flat tract of land on Puckety Church Road that was part of the original Wharton Family farmstead, first deeded in 1787.

The high school opened to strictly juniors and sophomores in 1964. Seniors from that academic year mostly attended Arnold, while some in the eastern part of town went to Kiski Area, a high school in its third year.

When the 1965-66 school year began, it marked the first time a Burrell student would spend all 12 years in the community.

The Rugged Start

Bob Haser was appointed not only school district athletic director, but interim head coach of all sports teams until a permanent coach could be found. He inaugurated junior varsity football in 1964, scheduling a game against any school he could find with an open date. One game was against The Kiski School varsity, which Burrell won, 7-0. Under PIAA guidelines, since the win came against a varsity team, in went into the books as a Burrell victory. Haser, who died on Feb. 8, 2009, always joked that he was the only Burrell coach to retire undefeated – at 1-0.

Gene Urbanski was selected as the first official head coach, but he lasted only one year as the Bucs struggled, going 0-8-1 and scoring just 40 points the entire season. Onto the scene came Frank Martin, who, two years earlier, led Arnold to the WPIAL title game.

With the impending merger with Ken High, Martin could see the handwriting on the wall – it was time to leave his beloved

Arnold to stake out new territory. Martin was Arnold through and through. He played there as a student and has lived across the street from George Leslie Memorial Stadium for more than a half-century. But with a number of Lower Burrell-bred players on the 1964 team, Martin knew there was talent in the fledgling school district. Burrell won just two games in 1966, both in shutouts over Knoch and Plum.

Few observers dared to predict what would come next. The Bucs opened the 1967 season with a 19-6 victory over Fox Chapel, a positive start, to be sure. But the following week, Burrell pounded Kittanning, 40-7, behind two touchdowns each from Lanny Murdock and John Suvoy. The Bucs defense set up five of the six touchdowns, and suddenly it seemed the young program was maturing.

For the first road game of the season, the Bucs played at Sewickley Area, traveling to a tiny stadium in the town of Hermanie. Martin rated Sewickley as a championship contender. The school won the WPIAL Class A title in 1960, so the program had lofty aspirations.

Instead, Burrell held the Bison to 64 yards rushing en route to a 24-0 victory. Though Burrell had outscored the opposition, 59-13 in its first two games, Martin still wasn't happy with the offense and inserted fleet halfback Tommy Greco, who responded with two touchdowns.

Martin had shown many times during his career that he would make a change if he thought it would benefit a given team in a given season. For instance, in 1961 while at Arnold, Martin employed messenger quarterbacks, alternating two players and giving the play calls to each as they re-entered the lineup every other play.

In Week Four, Burrell traveled to Swissvale for a key test. It would be the first foray into the talent-rich Mon Valley, where the Bucs would prevail in a Saturday afternoon encounter at Dickson Field. Following a street fight after a game with rival Braddock, officials compelled the Gold Flashes to offer daylight football. Burrell passed its test with ease, 46-14.

The Bucs returned home to play the injury-riddled Tarentum Redcats, a school in their final football season before being consolidated with Har-Brack to form Highlands. Tarentum was down to its third-string quarterback, Tony Prazenica. Original starter Joe 'Skip' Guyaux suffered a fractured wrist; second-stringer Gary Weleski suffered a broken ankle. Things didn't get any better after Prazenica left with a wrist injury in the second quarter. He was replaced by fourth-string quarterback Gary Cravener. It all added up to a 45-0 rout as the undermanned Redcats committed five turnovers. Suvoy scored three touchdowns in a 3-minute span. Big victories followed against Knoch and Ford City and, suddenly, talk of Burrell making it to the WPIAL championship game was realistic. A big game at Springdale loomed, and a Burrell victory there would give the Bucs Gardner Points from Springdale's five victories. Freeport, also undefeated, needed a victory over Richland to get credit for the six Rams victories.

Burrell and Freeport both held up their end of the bargain with victories. But the Bucs and the Yellowjackets got some unexpected help from 50 miles away. New Brighton tumbled Braddock from the undefeated ranks, 32-7, behind three long touchdown runs by Ron 'Po' James, who scored 200 points that season, a WPIAL record that stood for 18 years.

Earlier in the season, Donora, thought to be the top WPIAL team with all-state quarterback Bernie Galiffa and speedy running backs Malcolm Lomax and Ken Griffey Sr., sustained an upset. Since New Brighton had two ties blemishing its record, Burrell and Freeport stood one victory away from a clash for WPIAL honors.

Burrell defeated Plum and Freeport knocked off Leechburg to set up an all-A-K Valley treat for fans.

The Road to......Jeannette?

While local fans savored a local matchup, the game site was anything but local. The WPIAL Football Steering Committee announced the two schools, located just a few miles apart, would play at Jeannette's McKee Stadium on Friday, Nov. 17. Burrell and Freeport school officials were flabbergasted, feeling the game should be played at Valley High School. Steering Committee Chairman Michale J. Herk, Donora High School principal, said Valley's first senior class play was that night. Valley offered its stadium for Saturday, but the WPIAL said it already had set Friday as the date. Burrell's school board and Lower Burrell City Council fired off letters of protest, but the steering committee was unrelenting. Four days before the game, the WPIAL Board of Control switched gears and announced the game would be in New Kensington Saturday afternoon at 1:30 despite an already-scheduled children's play at the school auditorium.

The buildup to the game was massive. It was the perfect matchup of Burrell's power game vs. Freeport's speed. Fans were being asked to car-pool it to the game, since parking was limited by the play and by wet grounds. By game time, 10,000 fans jammed into the 8,000-seat stadium, the biggest crowd since the 1947 Ken High drive to the WPIAL title.

Late in the first quarter, Burrell quarterback Scott Swank burst into the end zone on a 5-yard run for the game's only score. Swank would later become chairman of the Chicago Mercantile Exchange.

Burrell's stellar defense made the early touchdown stand up, limiting Freeport's offense to just 95 total yards. The Bucs yielded just 39 points the entire season, including five shutouts.

The Bucs enjoyed their championship, but more success would lay ahead.

The Hunted Ones

Burrell, which surprised almost everybody with its 1967 title drive, quickly discovered it's easier to be the hunter rather than the hunted.

First, coach Frank Martin left to inaugurate the new football program at Highlands High School. The school system then elevated assistant Frank Solomond who, at 28, was one of the youngest head coaches in the state.

Solomon's debut was a success as Burrell blanked Fox Chapel, 26-0. That was followed by a 37-12 victory at Kittanning. Getting out of town was the toughest part of the night as the Burrell team bus was stoned while passing through the usually scenic riverfront area.

After an easy, 41-19 victory over Sewickley Area, the Bucs would host Swissvale, which featured running back Gus Dagnus, the subject of that week's Sport's Illustrated's Faces in the Crowd segment. But Dagnus quickly became a victim of the SI jinx, and the Burrell defense as the Bucs rolled to a convincing 45-0 victory.

Seneca Valley replaced Tarentum on the Burrell schedule, but it didn't matter as the Bucs rolled on, 38-0.

Another trip to Butler County loomed the following Saturday as Burrell visited Knoch.

The Great Escape

The morning of Oct. 12, 1968 was as typical as any fall morning with gray skies and intermittent sunshine.

But by the end of the day, Burrell's close call at Knoch was anything but typical.

Burrell needed to keep moving, as a loss or tie would eliminate the Bucs from contending for another title. Burrell had beaten Knoch by a combined score of 66-0 the past two seasons, so the Bucs wouldn't heed their coach's warning that Knoch was much better than its 1-4 record would indicate.

The Knights dominated the first half, leading 14-7 and driving on the Bucs just before the half. But time expired with Knoch on the Burrell 9. Solomond was livid in the locker room at halftime, as the Bucs were forced to switch to an unfamiliar passing game. Nothing seemed to be going right for Burrell as a 60-yard punt return for a touchdown by Suvoy was nullified because of a penalty. Burrell did score on a 42-yard pass from Jack Beattie to Walt Spak, but the extra point was missed and Burrell trailed, 14-13. With 2:42 left and possession on its 12, Burrell had one last gasp. After a loss to the 8, Beattie connected with Suvoy on fourth-and-14 for a 55-yard pass play.

Burrell moved to the Knoch 16, but a 15-yard penalty moved the ball back to the 31, giving Burrell an uncharacteristic 69 penalty yards.

On third-and-17, Beattie found Spak at the 10. Spak fought off two Knoch defenders and broke free for a touchdown with 0:04 left in the game.

After much-closer victories than the previous year over Ford City and Springdale, it was apparent that Burrell and Freeport were on a collision course for a title rematch. Donora, with Griffey and Lomax, couldn't accumulate enough Gardner Points.

Burrell needed a victory at Plum to seal up a title berth. But the Mustangs had other plans. With Burrell leading, 24-13, Plum scored with six minutes left in the game. The Mustangs tried an onsides kick and were successful when a Bucs player touched the ball at midfield. Plum drove to the Burrell 12, but two straight losses for eight yards set up a Spak fumble recovery, and the Bucs ran out the clock and right into another WPIAL title game. This time, the WPIAL didn't fool around with naming a mind-boggling site. It would be Valley – and that was that. This time around, it was Suvoy who scored the game's only touch-down as the Bucs survived a muddy field and a fast Freeport team for another 6-0 victory.

That put Burrell at the .500 mark – four years of football and two titles.

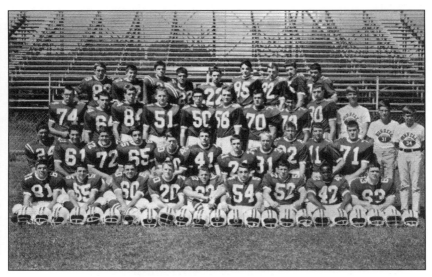

Credit: Burrell High School yearbook

Here is the 1967 WPIAL Class A champion Burrell Bucs. Front row, from left, John Husar, Steve Rowe, Max Krugle, John Suvoy, Tom Harris, Allen Conti, Ron Pelegrinelli, Tim Miles, Brad Post. Second row: Jeff Koziura, John Vasilopus, Tom Whitney, Jan Mohammed, Lanny Murdock, Tom Greco, Bill Ference, Sam Males, Howard Davis, Jack Beattie, Jeff Bartosiewicz. Third row: Steve Yacko, Rich Ogurchock, Jim Fox, Chuck Davis, Jack Villella, Ron Pazul, Mike Spires, Mike Solomon, Gene Regoli, student managers Bret Nelson, Jimmy Smith, Steve Booher. Back row: Walt Spak, Bill Wardle, Sonny Johnson, Dan DeCola, Joe Kurtik, Pete Szakacs. Dave Tobin, Mike Obertance, Howard Baer.

Credit: Burrell High School yearbook

The Burrell Bucs celebrate their second straight WPIAL title after a grueling 6-0 victory over Freeport on Nov. 16, 1968.

chapter 38

THE BEST TEAM THAT DIDN'T WIN ANYTHING

There is little doubt that the 1985-86 Kiski Area basketball team was one of the best in A-K Valley history.

The 27-5 team coached by Sam Intrieri won the hearts of many in Cavaliers Country, but, otherwise lost the Section 1-AAAA title to Norwin, lost the WPIAL finals to Norwin, and lost a heartbreaker in the PIAA finals to Carlisle.

But those second-place finishes don't detract from the stature of that team, as it was part of a great era in local basketball.

Although the school fielded great teams in football and baseball, Kiski Area had problems competing in basketball. Some years saw talented teams, but they just couldn't seem to take that step to the next level.

All that changed in the mid-1980s. Superb guards like Tony Petrarca and Adam Petrosky complimented big men like Phil Nevin and Dave Nabors. And workmenlike players such as Denny Wuyscik and Joel Hansen were complimentary.

The Cavaliers made the WPIAL playoffs for the first time in 1984. It was the year of the open WPIAL tournament where everybody who wanted in got in. But Kiski Area didn't need the open tournament format. The Cavaliers won a section title for the first time in school history.

It didn't take the fans long to realize what was happening. Kiski Area experienced its first basketball home sellouts as the school district has a chance to show some pent-up emotion towards the basketball program.

The Cavaliers made the most of their first playoff appearance, defeating Plum at home, 70-57, in the only year that the WPIAL has let teams play at home in the playoffs. A double-overtime victory over Gateway, 71-68, at the Valley High School gym was followed by a quarterfinal loss to Central Catholic. But it was enough to get the Cavaliers into the PIAA playoffs as the No. 8 team from the WPIAL.

Kiski Area played its first-ever PIAA playoff game at Altoona, as the Mountain Lions got to play on their home court. In some of the most disgraceful officiating ever seen, Altoona savored the home-cooking to the tune of a 55-53 victory. Altoona mugged 6-foot-11 center Nevin, and got away with it. After the game, Nevin had scratches over his upper chest signifying where fouls weren't called.

The PIAA didn't have any schools open the playoffs on their home court until 2009.

In the 1984-85 season, Kiski Area defeated Penn Hills in the first round, 59-52, at Valley High School. In the quarterfinals against Blackhawk at Butler, current Arizona coach Sean Miller's 35-foot shot as time ran out knocked off the Cavaliers, 56-55. Kiski Area took the measure of Erie Tech in the opening round of the PIAA playoffs before losing to Baldwin.

The Trek to Hershey

But with players like Nevin and the 6-5 Nabors gone, everyone knew Kiski Area in 1985-86 would be a guard-oriented team. The Cavaliers opened the season with a 78-73 victory over Central Catholic. On Dec. 7, 1985, Kiski Area edged Farrell, 60-58, with Petrarca pouring in 31 points and proving that the Cavaliers could win in what remains one of the toughest places to play in Western Pennsylvania.

Norwin, however, won both Section 1-AAAA games against Kiski Area, starting with a 73-65 win on Dec. 20. The rematch was Jan. 29, a game delayed one day because of snow. This time, Norwin got two free throws after time ran out in overtime, winning 64-62.

Late in the regular season, Kiski Area had a Saturday night game at highly-touted Meadville. Kiski fans chartered buses and watched the Cavaliers defeat the Bulldogs, 68-62. Victories like that impressed the WPIAL Basketball Steering Committee enough to seed the Cavaliers second in the playoffs behind Norwin, even though Kiski Area finished second in the section race. In the playoff opener, Kiski Area was victorious in a rematch with Central Catholic, 69-59, at Valley. The quarterfinals, held at Greensburg Salem, resulted in a 78-65 win over Laurel Highlands. It was time to head to Pitt's Fitzgerald Field House for the semifinals. Connellsville, a team the Cavaliers scored 99 points against in December, gave Kiski Area all it could handle before losing, 61-57, in Kiski Area's first-ever semifinal appearance.

In the finals, it was more of the same as Norwin stopped the Cavaliers, 62-50, to win WPIAL gold. Kiski Area got the No. 2 seed from the WPIAL in the PIAA bracket. The Cavaliers breezed to an 80-44 victory over District 9's Clearfield in the PIAA opener at Pitt. But it was what happened in the second game that really had an impact of Kiski Area's fortunes.

Meadville, the District 10 runner-up, shocked Norwin, 46-45, to abruptly end Norwin's season at 26-1.

"Coming home that night on the bus I told (assistant coach) Bill Ceraso I never saw this team more fired up," Intrieri said. "We beat Meadville during the regular season, and our players didn't think we could get past Norwin."

In the second round of the state tournament, the Cavaliers dispatched Erie McDowell, the District 10 champ, 65-50, at the New Castle High Fieldhouse. That set up a Tuesday-Thursday-Saturday format for the final three rounds. The PIAA condensed the tournament in order to get it finished before Easter Weekend.

It was back to New Castle for the quarterfinals against Farrell, another team the Cavaliers had defeated earlier in the season by two points. This time, Kiski Area emerged with a 49-46 victory as the Steelers employed a triangle-and-two defense in an attempt to stop Petrarca and Petrosky. Instead, another guard, Ken Tardivo, made a key shot to earn the victory.

Two nights later, the Cavaliers battled Meadville at the Pitt Field House to win the Western final, 64-58, and prepared to head to Hershey for the state title game two nights later. The condensed schedule was taking its toll.

"We really didn't get to enjoy it," Intrieri said. "(WPIAL executive director) Chuck Heberling wanted us to bring our suitcases to the Meadville game and leave immediately for Hershey. But I didn't want to see us lose to Meadville, then watch our kids unpack their suitcases. So we left Friday."

By then, Cavaliers fans had worked themselves into a frenzy. But they didn't anticipate what would happen in the wee hours of the morning following the Meadville game. Defending state champion Carlisle had just defeated Ridley, 62-45, at the Harrisburg Farm Show Arena. Fearful they wouldn't get tickets for the finals in Hershey, Thundering Herd fans drove all night to Kiski Area High School to buy tickets for the big game.

That left many Cavaliers fans worried about getting tickets themselves. Comcast Cable 3 of New Kensington announced that the state championship game would be carried live. So Cavaliers fans got rooms at the Clarion Hotel of New Kensington and made plans to watch the game live.

What a packed Hersheypark Arena crowd saw was unexpected by many. The Cavaliers, heavy underdogs, had Carlisle on the ropes, outscoring the Thundering Herd, 14-4, in the second period to take a 28-20 halftime lead. Kiski Area's defense, despite a severe height disadvantage, held Carlisle to just 1-for-7 from the field during the second period.

Carlisle began to assert its big height advantage and cut Kiski Area's lead to 38-37. With the score tied at 49-all, Carlisle called a time out with 23 seconds left.

Everyone expected Billy Owens, who would go on to stardom at Syracuse University and the NBA, to get the ball for the final shot.

Instead, unheralded Orlando Roebuck was open near the basket and scored with 5 seconds left to give the Thundering Herd a 51-49 victory.

Kiski Area gave all it could give. The scene in the Cavaliers' locker room afterwards was unforgettable. The team was so physically and emotionally drained from giving a maximum effort that some of the players just couldn't move. Others stared at the wall in disbelief that they had come up short.

Carlisle would go on to win two more PIAA titles and Owens finished his high school career as the third all-time leading scorer in state history with 3,299 points. He also set a record of 129 career games, a mark that still stands.

Kiski Area didn't win anything that season, except the admiration of basketball fans everywhere for their effort.

There was one other footnote for that 1986 state final, it was the last Pennsylvania high school game played without the three-point field goal.

PIAA Class AAAA Finals
March 22, 1986 at Hersheypark Arena

Score by quarters: Kiski Area   14   14   10   11 - 49
Carlisle   16   4   17   14 - 51

Individual scoring: KA: Ken Tardivo 7 0-1 14, Asayan Jordan 0 0-1-0, Joel Hansen 0 0-1 0, Tony Petrarca 7 3-5 17, Adam Petrosky 2 0-0 4, Denny Wuyscik 3 6-8 12, Eric Shaffer 1 0-0 2. Totals: 20 9-16 49.

C: Billy Owens 5 9-12 19, Paul Blackburn 0 0-1 0, Michael Owens 4 1-2 9, Orlando Roebuck 1 0-1 2, Garrett Palmer 2 0-0 4, Shawn Hodge 6 5-5 17. Totals: 18 15-21 51.

Rebounds: KA: Wuyscik 8, Shaffer 5, Tardivo 5. C: B. Owens 17, Palmer 10.

Fouled out: C: Palmer. Attendence: 7,191.

Credit: Valley News Dispatch

This is the scene in the Kisk Area locker room following the 51-49 loss to Carlisle. Denny Wuyscik (left) and Tony Petrarca are physically and emotionally drained.

Credit: Valley News Dispatch

Kiski Area's Denny Wuyscik tries a shot against Carlisle on March 22, 1986 at Hersheypark Arena, where Kiski Area nearly pulled off a mammoth upset.

chapter 39

JUST A HOMETOWN GUY

Though he made his mark and gained his riches in pro football on the West Coast, Greg Meisner never forgot his roots. "Every time I came home, I'd see the sign 'Welcome to New Kensington' and that sign meant so much to me," Meisner said before he moved back to Western Pennsylvania permanently.

"Every game I played, I played for my community and the great athletes who played here before me," he added.

During his days in Los Angeles, when Meisner was asked where he was from, he always answered New Kensington instead of just saying the Pittsburgh region.

Meisner should include himself on the list of great athletes. While at Valley High School, he was a three-year letterman as a tight end and defensive end.

His most memorable game for Valley came on Sept. 17, 1976 season when the Vikings had an away game at Kiski Area. After years of being pounded by the Cavaliers, the Vikings finally built their program so it could compete with Kiski Area in the Foothills Conference.

Tired of the cramped visitors quarters in the corner of Davis Field, the Vikings warmed up in New Kensington, took the bus and headed up Route 56 and arrived practically at game time when everybody was wondering what had happened to the team. Valley won, 14-10, thanks to a superb goal-line stand late in the game. Meisner got to the Cavaliers ballcarrier on three of the four downs to preserve the victory. It marked the third time in four seasons that Valley had knocked off the mighty Cavaliers.

Later in 1976, he was named to the AP all-state second team defense and played on the Big 33 West team in 1977. Perhaps more important, he was selected All-Scholastic first team by the Philadelphia Bulletin. In wrestling, he was a state champion as a senior in the heavyweight division and, in track, was fifth in the javelin at the PIAA meet.

But football, obviously, was the ticket to fame. Although considered by modern standards an undersized athlete, he was highly sought-after by major colleges. It appeared to be Pitt all along, but West Virginia made a major move for Meisner late in the recruiting process. In fact, Meisner verbally declared for the Mountaineers the night before Letter-of-Intent Day, but, in matter of hours, relented and signed with Pitt, along with Valley teammate Benjy Pryor. At Pitt, he bulked himself up and became part of a Panthers major recruiting class that went 39-8-1 over four seasons. Meisner bulked up with a unique training regimen. One exercise was to run the railroad tracks in New Kensington and Arnold with a railroad tie or a log on his shoulder. He also would go to his family's camp and chop down oak trees with a hand-axe to stay in shape.

His work habits were so impressive that he saw action in eight games as a freshman in 1977 and contributed four sacks, 13 tackles and five assists, earning a starting job for good as a sophomore.

Pitt went 11-1 in Meisner's junior and senior seasons. He lists as his greatest college thrill beating Penn State two consecutive seasons at Happy Valley. The 1980 team finished No. 2 in the country. Only a bad quarter at Florida State midway through the season kept the Panthers from playing for the National Championship. Pitt's 1980 team had 51 players that were either drafted, signed as a free agent or offered tryouts by an NFL team. In Meisner's case, he was chosen by the LA Rams in the third round of the 1981 draft. He quickly found his mentor, fellow lineman Jack Youngblood, long an NFL stalwart. His first start as a Rams member came on a Monday Night Football game against the 49ers. MNF was a much bigger deal then, compared to now. Meisner would go on to play eight seasons with the Rams, including the 1985 NFC title game when the Rams lost to the Super Bowl-bound Bears at chilly Soldier Field.

"I got into the locker room afterwards thinking we fell one game short of the Super Bowl, and we might not get that close again," Meisner said. "And we didn't."

After eight seasons on the Left Coast, Meisner signed as a Plan B free agent with the Kansas City Chiefs and played under defensive coordinator Bill Cowher. His 11th and final season was in 1991 with the New York Giants.

Meisner finally reached his goal of returning to Western Pennsylvania in 2006 as head coach and athletic director at Hempfield High School. The Spartans have been riddled with injuries since then and Meisner has had difficulty getting a full compliment of players on the field at once.

Hempfield is one of the most difficult places to coach in the WPIAL, and Meisner certainly has his challenges. The school is the fourth largest in the WPIAL but the area is riddled with different factions and refuses to work towards a common goal. The nefarious school board there seems to take pride is firing coaches almost on a whim, and appears to relish the creation of unsettling situations that don't benefit the children of the district.

Credit: Valley News Dispatch

Defensive tackle Greg Meisner of the LA Rams visits Valley High Memorial Stadium on Oct. 1, 1987 during the NFL players strike.

chapter 40

ZERO.....ZERO.....ZERO

There was nothing but goose eggs for teams that faced the 1943 Aspinwall Cavaliers.

Aspinwall was undefeated, untied – and unscored upon in its historic campaign.

It was the first and only time in A-K Valley history and only the fifth time in WPIAL history that a school performed that unique trifecta.

No team has done it since.

The Cavaliers, or the 'Asps' as they were conveniently known to newspaper headline writers with limited space, rolled to the WPIAL Class B title, defeating Pitcairn on Nov. 20, 1943.

Winning football was nothing new at Aspinwall. The 1921 team had a 7-1-1 record, with the loss coming to Tarentum and the tie with Glassport.

WPIAL membership began in 1923. From 1926-30, Aspinwall compiled a 38-3-5 record, including a 10-0-0 season in 1928. After three losing seasons from 1931-33, Aspinwall put together 12 winning seasons, including the unstoppable '43 outfit. During those 12 seasons, the Cavaliers were 77-14-13.

The 1936 team went 8-1-1 record, with the tie coming to Class A Etna and the loss coming to South Fayette, 20-7, in the 1937 WPIAL title game.

Here is a rundown on the memorable 1943 season under head coach Art 'Mac' McComb:
- Aspinwall 19, Apollo 0. Jack Donohue scored the first touchdown of the season in the second period at Apollo and Wally Reisch tallied in the third. Dave McCafferty concluded the scoring with Bob Malec adding the extra point.
- Aspinwall 22, Shaler Twp. 0. The Cavaliers scored in every quarter against a much smaller Shaler school. The post-World War II building boom wouldn't come to Shaler for another several years.
- Aspinwall 27, Freeport 0. Lou 'Sonny' Yakopec was the star of the game on the losers' field. Yakopec, who hailed from

Harmar Township but attended Aspinwall because of the college preparatory courses offered, scored two rushing touchdowns and threw a pass to Mel Thompson for another. Malec scored the final touchdown for the Asps and added three PATs.

- Aspinwall 20, Oakmont 0. Previously-undefeated Oakmont fell victim to Aspinwall as Malec scored two touchdowns and Yakopec added the other.
- Aspinwall 26, Millvale 0. Similarly-undefeated Millvale was eliminated from the WPIAL title chase with the loss. Malec scored three touchdowns and reserve fullback Thompson the final tally after McComb began to substitute liberally.
- Aspinwall 28, Verona 0. An 80-yard run by Agnew highlighted the decisive victory over visiting Verona. Yakopec, Malec and Donohue also joined in on the scoring barrage.
- Aspinwall 26, East Deer 0. The Asps traveled north on Route 28 to Creighton Field and cruised to the seventh victory of the season. Malec scored two touchdowns for the Cavaliers as Donohue and Agnew added insurance touchdowns.
- Aspinwall 27, Belle Vernon 0. The farthest road trip of the year for the Cavaliers was successful as Aspinwall accumulated 10 first downs as Yakopec and Malec each crossed the goal line twice at Marion Field.
- Aspinwall 26, Etna 0. All that stood between Aspinwall and a date in the WPIAL finals was the Rams, a rival since 1915. Malec scored two touchdowns in the second quarter on runs of 10 and 15 yards. Yakopec added a 3-yard scoring burst while Thompson's touchdown put the finishing touch on the big victory.
- Aspinwall 24, Pitcairn 0. A crowd of 7,000 fans packed Graham Field in Wilkinsburg for the WPIAL title clash. Aspinwall anticipated some difficulty with the Railroaders, running out of the then-novel T-formation. The quarterback was Walter 'Pete' Antimarino, who would go on to become one of the greatest coaches in WPIAL history at Gateway High School.

Malec and Yakopec scored two touchdowns apiece in what

was termed a hard-hitting contest. Aspinwall's legacy of no points given up was in jeopardy as Pitcairn advanced to the Cavaliers 2 in the second half, but a goal line stand preserved the unscored upon legacy.

Aspinwall had outscored the opposition, 245-0.

But the Cavaliers weren't through yet. In 1944, Aspinwall repeated with a 20-6 victory over East Pittsburgh in the WPIAL championship game.

Aspinwall had a final glory period from 1949-53. In that time, the Asps posted a 35-11-1 mark. The 1950 team finished the regular season 8-0-1, with the tie coming against Etna. The Cavaliers, however, fell to Masontown, 20-6.

Aspinwall's final team in 1960 struggled to an 0-9 record before students began attending the newly-formed Fox Chapel Area High School. By that point, the high school football landscape was changing drastically.

For over 50 years, the power in WPIAL football was concentrated in the old, urbanized riverfront communities, like Aspinwall. Boroughs and other municipalities sponsored school districts free for students who lived there. Others living outside the boroughs and cities that did not have a high school paid a tuition to enroll where they saw fit.

In Yakopec's case, he lived in Harmar, which had no school district. He had the choice of going to either Springdale, Oakmont or Aspinwall.

As the 1950s came to a close, the state Department of Education was on a mission to cut the 2,000 Pennsylvania school districts by about 75 percent. The newly-configured school districts would serve a defined area.

In Fox Chapel's case, the school district would serve Aspinwall, Fox Chapel and Blawnox boroughs, along with O'Hara and Indiana townships.

In 1969, Sharpsburg High School closed and joined the Fox Chapel system.

Of all the schools Aspinwall played in 1943, the only one still intact is Freeport. Belle Vernon Borough High School, which appeared on Aspinwall's '43 card, was an original borough school district that merged with North Belle Vernon to form Vernon High.

Credit: Courtesy Fox Chapel Area School District

The Aspinwall Cavaliers return home with a parade to the stadium after defeating Pitcairn for the WPIAL title.

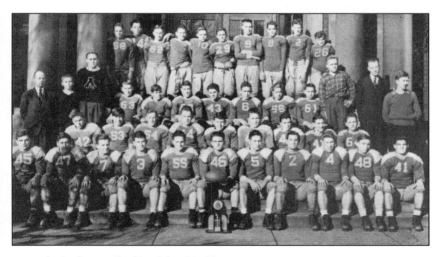

Credit: Courtesy Fox Chapel Area School District

The 1943 Aspinwall team, which was undefeated, untied and unscored upon, is pictured with the WPIAL trophy in front of the team.

Credit: Courtesy Fox Chapel Area School District

This is the WPIAL trophy awarded to Aspinwall High School in 1943.

chapter 41

THE BELL TOLLED FOR MANY

It was said that during the post-World War II era, everybody in town went to see Bell Township High School football games. With the population listed as 2,800 those days and attendance hitting 2,000, that notion was just about accurate. And those watching the Lions play, particularly in 1948-51 era, had plenty to cheer about.

Bell still holds the Alle-Kiski Valley record with 28 consecutive victories. Leechburg won 23 in a row from 1964-66 and Burrell and New Kensington ran off 24-game winning streaks. But in more than a half century, no one has equaled Bell's feats.

If today's standards were in effect then and the three wins against junior varsity teams from larger schools were counted, Bell's streak would be 31.

It wasn't like the Lions had a large student body to choose from, either. There were barely 100 students in the high school that took in students from rich farmland and small, industrial villages such as Salina, Tintown, Slickville and later, Avonmore.

The average graduating class at Bell was in the 30s. The Class of 1952 boasted 44 students after Avonmore was added to the system.

On Oct. 16, 1948, the Lions dropped a 7-6 decision to the Youngwood Railroaders. Bell wouldn't lose again until Sept. 5, 1952.

The streak started with an 8-0 victory Oct. 23, 1948 against Avonmore. A victory over The Kiski School's junior varsity occurred a week later. The season ended on a happy note with a 6-2 victory over Penn Claridge.

The 1949, '50 and '51 seasons featured undefeated campaigns under the leadership of coach George Hamilton. Bell rang up victories week after week.

"It was a great feeling, each week was an attempt to keep the tradition going," said fullback Charles 'Buster' Brewer in a 2001 interview with the *Valley News Dispatch*.

Schools had to schedule games on their own in those days. Bell was part of what was called the Little 6 Diadem, which sounds more like a group of medical treatment facilities than a football conference. The grouping consisted of Bell, Washington Township, Apollo, Saltsburg, Elders Ridge and Ligonier.

Bell took on all challengers.

Bessemer High School had been undefeated in 1949, and the Cementers were cruising along in 1950 until Bell handed them a loss. Avonmore became part of the Bell Township system in 1950 after the Indians' program struggled. Dick DeSimone and four other boys blended in well at their new school.

Bell played its home games along the present Tinsmill Spur at what is now the Salina Exit. Starting in 1950, the games were moved to Avonmore Borough.

"I fit in with what they had," DeSimone said. "Ed Meighan came up to help coach Bell, and we ran the same offense."

The then brand-new T-formation was run to perfection, with the Lions outscoring their opponents 380-28. Bell averaged 330 yards per outing behind a backfield that consisted of Brewer, quarterback George Markuzic and halfbacks Kenny Keller and Jimmy Ripple. In 1950, Ripple ran for a 92-yard touchdown, two 80-yarders and a 72-yard romp.

Keystone Keller

The keystone of the powerful Bell attack was Keller, who along with DeSimone, was all-WPIAL. The halfback rushed for 1,121 yards in 1949, 1,352 in 1950 and 1,385 in 1951 for a total of 3,858 career yards. That's good enough for third place in A-K Valley history behind Lucas Heakins (4,276 yards) who played for Riverview from 1996-98 and Brandon Williams (4,214 yards), who played for Valley from 1994-97.

Keller earned 12 varsity letters at Bell, excelling in football, basketball and baseball. He went on to play at the University of North Carolina and scored the winning touchdown in the 1955 Blue-Gray all-star game.

Keller then moved on to the NFL and was the leading rusher for the Philadelphia Eagles as a rookie in 1956.

DeSimone played at Clemson, but because of injuries and a redshirt year, he never got to play against Keller.

The Final Stretch

The 1951 season started with victories over East Pittsburgh and Derry Borough. Apollo thought it had a chance to end the streak in Week Three, but Brewer threw for a touchdown and ran for another as Bell prevailed, 24-7.

Victories followed against Sewickley Township, Saltsburg and East Deer. The Lions escaped West Newton with a 20-13 victory, preceding a 38-6 win over Ligonier.

Only Elders Ridge was standing in the way of a third straight undefeated season. A 6-0 Bell victory Nov. 3, 1951 was subdued by a tragedy. Rams all-WPIAL player John Yuhus sustained a broken neck during the contest and died several months later from pneumonia.

The only setback for Bell those three seasons was a lack of Gardner Points under the old WPIAL rating system used to determine the top teams from each classification. The Lions lacked sufficient points under the system and never got to play for a WPIAL title.

Overall, from 1947-51, Bell rang up a 33-6-2 mark.

The streak ended as Hopewell rolled past the newly-named Bell-Avon High School to start the 1952 season. Ironically, Hopewell also ended Braddock's 56-game unbeaten streak in 1960.

Bell-Avon would win just three games over the next two seasons. High school football, and the world for that matter, was changing – and changing rapidly. Since the early part of the 20th Century, high school football power was concentrated in the riverfront communities of the Pittsburgh region and the small coal mining towns. As the mines closed, the inexorable suburban development outside Pittsburgh continued to have an impact.

For many years, the WPIAL consisted of Class AA for the largest schools, Class A for the medium-sized schools and Class B, for the smallest schools like Bell. In 1954, West View High School became North Hills, recognizing the huge population shift to Ross Township. It went from Class A to AA. Also in 1954, Braddock High School moved from Class AA to A, marking the first time one of the older, riverfront mill towns dropped in classification. By 1956, long-time Bell-Avon rival Derry Borough was merged with Derry Township to form Derry Area and Youngwood was swallowed up by the gigantic Hempfield Area consolidation. One by one, Bell-Avon's foes were disappearing from the scene, forcing the school to fill its scheduling voids. Bell was forced to play larger schools like Kittanning. When Bell-Avon did find new smaller schools to play, like East McKeesport and Bridgeville, soon those schools were being swallowed up. East McKeesport was part of the East Allegheny combo and Bridgeville merged with Clark to form Chartiers Valley.

It soon became apparent that Bell-Avon would be part of the Kiski Area consolidation. Bell-Avon went out a winner, though, compiling a 5-3-1 mark under coach John Toncini.

Bell-Avon's last football game was on Nov. 4, 1961, a 35-0 triumph over Elders Ridge.

Credit: Bell Township 1952 yearbook.

Bell set its sights on a third straight undefeated season in 1951 with coaches Ed Meighan, Dick DeSimone, Kenny Keller and coach George Hamilton.

Credit: A–K Valley Hall of Fame

Kenny Keller of the 1956 Philadelphia Eagles warms up in Hersheypark Stadium with the Milton Hershey Middle School in the background.

chapter 42

THE IMPROBABLE RUN

The Highlands High School basketball program had a rags-to-riches run that culminated with a WPIAL Class AAA title on March 3, 1995.

The Golden Rams, heavy underdogs to perennial contender Blackhawk, shocked the WPIAL basketball world with a 58-56 victory at Duquesne University's A.J. Palumbo Center. A 10-foot, one-handed runner by Greg Koprivnikar proved to be the winning shot.

The thrilling moment culminated an improbable climb from the bottom to the top. Highlands had lost 41 games in a row during the early 1990s, finishing the 1991-92 season with a 1-23 mark. The school district was ready to make a change in its basketball coaching position, and Highlands simply went across the street to St. Joseph High School to hire Rich Falter, who had just coached the Spartans to a WPIAL Class A semifinal appearance several months earlier.

Highlands made some progress in Falter's first season, compiling an 8-16 mark. The next year, the Golden Rams went 14-9 in Quad-A. The highlight of the season was a victory at Penn Hills, breaking the 55-game home winning streak by the Indians on Senior Night.

Things seemed to be moving in the right direction, but Falter had to replace three starters as the 1994-95 season got underway, due to the graduation of Jeff Karacia, Jason Braun and Scott Virag. Koprivnikar and Jeremy Earnhardt were returning, and that gave Falter a solid nucleus as the duo was two of 11 returning lettermen. The new starters were Kirk Witucki, Kevin Mason and Mike Braun. Top reserves off the bench would be Ed Jenkins and Aaron Rea.

On the opening weekend of the season, a problem would surface that would become ongoing as the season wore on. Highlands just couldn't get past North Catholic. Highlands lost to the Trojans at the Somerset Tip-off Tournament. Two weeks later in the Section 6-AAA opener, the Golden Rams trailed, 45-36, at the end of the third quarter. Highlands started the fourth period with a 12-3 run to come to within 49-48 with 4:31 left in the game. But 34 seconds later, an altercation broke out after a battle for a rebound. The action moved away from the key to the scoring table, then to the benches. Even then 47-year coaching veteran Don Graham took a tumble. Earnheardt and Orlando Russell-Ryan were both ejected.

Aaron Rea came off the bench after Mason fouled out and hit a trio of 3-pointers, but North Catholic held on for a 64-59 victory. By Jan. 20, a 73-64 loss to the Trojans would be the third of the season to North Catholic. Lamar Calhoun had 30 points to lead the Trojans on the infamous auditorium stage up on Troy Hill.

But Highlands was beating everyone else. In the first section game between Highlands and Valley in five years, the Golden Rams fired in 14 3-pointers in an 81-63 victory. Highlands canned five 3-point shots in the second period en route to that win. Koprivnikar poured in 26 points and Witucki added 19. Highlands (12-2) would finish a game behind North Catholic (13-1) in the section race. The Golden Rams would be seeded seventh and North Catholic third.

In the playoff opener, Highlands won it first playoff game in seven seasons and its first Class AAA playoff game in 26 seasons with a 73-59 victory over defending WPIAL champion Beaver Falls. Up next was a Saturday afternoon quarterfinal encounter against No. 2-seeded Jeannette at Greensburg Salem High School. The Golden Rams started shooting as soon as they got off the bus and ended up with a 96-78 win over the Jayhawks in one of the highest-scoring WPIAL playoff games of all-time.

But Highlands was getting some help just above in the Class AAA bracket. Seton-LaSalle took the measure of North Catholic, 56-46. That meant Highlands would avoid playing the Trojans for a fourth time.

In the semifinals, the Golden Rams got by Seton, 60-53, to earn a berth in the finals at Palumbo Center. At the same time, Blackhawk was manhandling Chartiers Valley, 67-48, at Robert Morris College's Sewall Center behind Jim Cantamessa's 27 points. But as the Blackhawk team returned to the school, point guard

Ryan 'Archie' Miller sprained an ankle on the curb where the bus had discharged. That would have a major effect on the title game three nights later.

On to Palumbo Center

Even with Miller hobbled – he would get treatments at 6 a.m. on game day – the Cougars were the prohibitive favorite. Blackhawk was making its fifth title game appearance in the past six seasons and had considerable big-game experience over the Golden Rams. The previous season, the Cougars lost in double-overtime to Beaver Falls in the WPIAL finals.

Meanwhile, Highlands was making its first finals appearance in school history.

Blackhawk led, 20-11, at the end of one quarter. But Highlands started the second quarter with an 11-0 run en route to a 26-8 advantage in the quarter to lead at the intermission, 37-28. But Blackhawk wasn't finished. Even with Miller unable to reach the scoring column, the Cougars outscored the Golden Rams, 15-5, in the third period to lead, 43-42. The final quarter was a back-and-forth affair, with Highlands opening up a seven-point lead with 2:00 remaining. Blackhawk's J.T. Haskins scored 10 of his 14 points in the fourth quarter to keep the Cougars close. Cantamessa, the 6-foot-7 center, tipped in a missed foul shot with 30 seconds to go to tie the game at 56-all. Instead of calling a time out, Falter merely directed the Golden Rams to call the "Victory" play. Koprivnikar dribbled up the floor, setting up the four corners offense, letting the clock run down to 10 seconds.

With seven seconds left, Koprivnikar made a cross-over dribble driving the lane. Cantamessa's huge frame had jumped out to stop Koprivnikar. But Koprivnikar fired a shot over Cantamessa's head and the shot banked into the hoop with 0:03 showing on the clock. Blackhawk tried a desperation shot, but it misfired and it set off a wild celebration in Harrison, Fawn, Brackenridge and Tarentum.

End of the Big Climb
Highlands 58, Blackhawk 56
March 3, 1995 at A.J. Palumbo Center

Highlands	11	26	5	16	-	58
Blackhawk	20	8	15	13	-	56

Individual scoring: H: Michael Braun 5 0-0 10, Jeremy Earnheardt 3 1 0-0 9, Kirk Witucki 0 2 0-0 6, Greg Koprivnikar 4 1 4-6 15, Kevin Mason 2 0-0 4, Aaron Rea 0 2 1-2 7, Ed Jenkins 2 1 0-0 7. Totals: 16 7 5-8 58.
B: Ryan Miller 0 0-0 0, Steve Lodovico 2 0-0 4, Jim Cantamessa 4 3-4 11, J.T. Haskins 5 4-5 14, Jeremy Huber 9 1-4 19, Brett Parkhill 1 2 0-0 7. Totals: 21 2 8-13 58.

Credit: Valley News Dispatch

Highlands coach Rich Falter and his trusty clipboard are carried off the floor after the Golden Rams defeated Blackhawk for the 1995 WPIAL Class AA title.

Credit: Valley News Dispatch

Greg Koprivnikar talks with the media as he's being carried off the floor after sinking the winning shot against Blackhawk on March 3, 1995.

chapter 43

A BASEBALL REVOLUTIONARY

When the New York Yankees had their farewell ceremony to old Yankee Stadium in September 2008, the event had some local flavor.

Long-time Springdale resident Joe Page was among the posthumous honorees of the all-time great Yankees who performed in the Big Apple.

Page helped revolutionize baseball during his time with the Yankees (1944-50). He was an early relief specialist whose efforts helped bring about today's methods of using a pitching staff. In Page's era, relief pitchers were banished to the bullpen if they were ineffective as starters or were recovering from injuries. Page was born in Cherry Valley, PA, in 1917 and moved to Harmarville in 1920. He started his pro career in Butler with the Yankees' affiliate and moved his way up the chain to Augusta, Ga., and Newark, N.J. before crossing the Hudson River to The Bronx. An American League all-star in his rookie season of 1944, Page set a record in 1946 with 14 victories in relief, a record that lasted until 1959. His best season was 1949 when he went 13-8 with a 2.58 ERA, yielding only 113 hits in 135.1 innings.

Page capped the season with the Babe Ruth Award, the equivalent of today's World Series MVP as the Yankees defeated Brooklyn in the Fall Classic.

He finished his career with the Pirates in 1954. Page's career record was 59-50. In World Series play, he was 2-1 with seven appearances.

After his playing days, Page owned the Rocky Lodge Tavern near Ligonier, Westmoreland County. He died on April 21, 1980 in Latrobe at age 62.

Page was part of the A-K Valley Hall of Fame's first induction class in 1970.

Credit: A-K Valley Sports Hall of Fame

Springdale's Joe Page climbs out of the bullpen at old Yankee Stadium.

chapter 44

FROM A COW PASTURE TO A WPIAL FOOTBALL TITLE

From its humble start, the Knoch High School football program won the WPIAL title in 1978 and the school's athletic program overall is well-regarded throughout Western Pennsylvania.

There have been three other trips to the finals as the school is approaching 250 football victories. Knoch has made the WPIAL playoffs 15 times.

But no one should forget the trials and tribulations associated with the early days of the South Butler County School District. On Sept. 15, 1956, Knoch, then known as South Butler County Joint High School, took the field against Shenango High School and sustained a 41-0 loss. That same day, groundbreaking ceremonies were held on land bequeathed to the school district by William and Eva Knoch, to be used for a new high school near the border of Saxonburg Borough and Jefferson Township. The first year of the school was actually a carryover from the former Winfield-Clinton High School.

Saxonburg students, along with those from Winfield, Clinton, Penn and Jefferson townships, came on board to inaugurate the program. Unlike other school consolidations, none of those areas, individually, had football.

"It was quite an eye-opening experience," said John Masarik, Knoch's first head coach. "We had no practice field, and that area had never experienced football. We were limited in the equipment we could buy – it was an uphill battle all the way."

The new team had 14 players and there was little flat land by the old Winfield School for the team to practice on. No goal posts – so no kicking team practices.

There was no home field. All Knoch home games in the beginning were on the road. A week after that first game with Shenango was an encounter scheduled against another first-year school, Richland, now known as Pine-Richland. That resulted in a 27-0 setback. It was amazing that the team actually won two games the first season with victories over Moniteau and Karns City to go 2-3.

In 1957, Knoch used Butler's Pullman Park for a 'home' game against East Brady while the new high school was under construction. When Knoch High School opened its doors in 1958, there was no football stadium, though the team used a pasture from an adjacent farm to practice for an eight-game road schedule. Said Masarik in a 2006 interview with the *Valley News Dispatch:* "We literally had to get the farmer to move his cows so we could practice. We had all kinds of ruts to overcome, cow pies, you name it."

After a 2-6 record with exclusively road games, Masarik gave the school board an ultimatum: "get us a place to play, even if it means playing in the middle of Dinnerbell Road."

Industrialist Carl Jones of Penn United, also a school board member at the time, was instrumental in getting a home field. Finally, on Sept. 28, 1959, Knoch Knights Stadium opened before a sellout crowd. Richland's Bill Habay scored the new stadium's first touchdown on an early 71-yard run.

Denny Seybold scored Knoch's first TD in the second period of a game eventually won by the Rams, 34-21. Masarik's final goal in the early years was for the school to move from District 9 to the WPIAL.

In 1964, Knoch left the Butler County League for the Allegheny Interscholastic Conference and the program has never looked back.

Masarik left for Highlands after 13 years and was replaced by Bob King, who had led Freeport to the 1963 WPIAL title game.

Karrs Drives the Program

In 1976, Tim Karrs, son of legendary coach Johnny Karrs was brought in. The younger Karrs was a quarterback for Har-Brack, played for the University of North Carolina Tar Heels and spent part of 1969 on the Cleveland Browns roster.

Karrs piloted the Knights to their first WPIAL playoff berth, losing to Farrell. But by 1978, Knoch was in the WPIAL title game. The Knights had lost only to Freeport, 14-13, in the second week of the season. Knoch was unstoppable after that, defeating Mars to sew up the AIC North title.

After a rare open date in Week 10, Knoch won its first playoff game of all-time, a 26-14 decision over Beth-Center at Norwin Stadium. The victory started a tradition, of sorts, in Saxonburg. Upon arriving back from the playoff game, the players and band set up and marched down Main Street in triumph with an impromptu midnight parade.

The following week, a date with 11-0 Leechburg loomed at Butler High Stadium. Karrs switched Knoch from a 4-4 defense to a 4-3 in an attempt to neutralize Leechburg's wishbone offense. But the Blue Devils led, 14-13, before a pass interception by Brian Dietz resulted in the decisive touchdown.

It was on to Pitt Stadium for the finals against heavily-favored Beaver Falls. Knoch wasn't getting shown much respect, as the Knights had to dress at the Pitt Field House and walk over to Pitt Stadium while Beaver Falls and the Class AAA game contestants Penn Hills and Blackhawk all got to dress at the stadium.

That only seemed to fire up the Knights. But Dwight Collins, who would later go on to star at Pitt and with the Minnesota Vikings, ran 30 yards up the middle on the first play from scrimmage, and all the prognosticators looked smart.

But it was all Knoch after that. Karrs went to power formations in the second half as the Knights overwhelmed the Tigers after that. Knoch brought WPIAL gold back to Saxonburg. The line of Jeff Lassinger, Todd Tudor, Peter Albert, Mark Noah and Chris Galbreth paved the way for quarterback Don Griffin and running backs Dietz, John Rebhun and Buddy Durand.

It proved to be the final game of Beaver Falls coach John Bruno's illustrious career. As for Karrs, he would lead the Knights back to the WPIAL title game the following year. The Knights lost the 1979 opener against Burrell via a forfeit because of a teachers strike in the South Butler County school system. A 7-7 tie against Freeport in Week Two merely set the stage for another exciting conference run. The Knight shut out their final four regular season opponents.

The playoffs began with a 10-0 victory in a rematch against Freeport before what is believed to be the third largest crowd ever at Highlands High School. The Knights defeated Union Area, 13-2, to return to the title game. But the Knights lost to Seton-La Salle, 12-0, stopping Knoch's streak of five games without yielding a touchdown. Seton-La Salle was coached by future Steelers football operations head Tom Donohoe.

Karrs would leave Knoch after that game for an assistant's job at Appalachian State. He later returned to the Keystone State to coach at Clarion University. But he returned to the high school ranks in 1991 with Titusville High School before returning to Highlands a year later.

Larry Kunselman took over the Knoch program and led the Knights to the 1981 Class AAA title game, starting with a shocking, 24-18, victory at Aliquippa to open the postseason. The Knights then blanked Penn-Trafford, 14-0, to make their third WPIAL title game appearance in four seasons. But the Knights lost a heartbreaker, 12-7, at North Allegheny High School. The Knights had the ball on the Bobcats 4, but couldn't score. Knoch was a roll, making the playoffs 12 times in a 16-year stretch. The Knights made the 1992 WPIAL Class AAA title game at Three Rivers Stadium under the late Paul Giesey, losing to Blackhawk, 20-0, after upsetting Montour, 3-0, in the WPIAL semifinals at Butler.

Credit: Valley News Dispatch

The Knoch Knights Stadium press box, a school wood shop project, made its debut on Oct. 2, 1969.

chapter 45

KINGS OF THE DIAMOND

The first team to win a WPIAL title at Kiski Area High School was the 1966 baseball team. On June 20, 1966, the Cavaliers defeated Gateway, 4-2, at Forbes Field as local TV viewers saw something seldom seen.

It was only the fourth season of the school's existence, so the school system wasn't really new.

In fact, the baseball team was together for quite a while. They started out winning a title in their Little League days in Vandergrift. By 1964, the team won in the Connie Mack division of youth baseball on a team coached by Vandergrift resident and former Phillies farmhand Bob Foreman.

The Connie Mack team traveled to Harleysville, near Philadelphia, to win the state title. Because of that, the high school team, coached by Harold Egalsky, was quite optimistic as the season approached.

The team started their indoor workouts in February, so they were ready to go when the season opened. The Cavaliers defeated Tarentum, 5-3, in extra innings late in the regular season to secure the Section 9 crown.

Kiski Area didn't have to travel far for its first playoff game. The Cavaliers met local rival Har-Brack at Freeport Borough Field. The Cavaliers pulled out the victory in the bottom of the seventh. First baseman Joe McCain belted a single with the bases loaded to win it. It was McCain's fourth hit in four at bats.

"I thought that game was the turning point," Egalsky said in a 1991 *Valley News Dispatch* interview. "We had to come from behind an inning earlier."

The team's late-inning heroics continued into the next contest against Swissvale. The Cavaliers tallied four runs in their last at bat to win, 7-5. Once again, it was McCain getting the winning hit, scoring Larry Linkes who had just tripled in two runs. McCain lined a single over Swissvale's five-man infield, designed to try and cut off the lead run.

Following that was a 6-2 win over Beaver Falls, the team that had lost to Arnold the previous season in the WPIAL championship game. Up next was a semifinal round encounter against Ellwood City at Butler's Pullman Park.

In a recurring theme of the playoffs, Kiski Area came from behind as winning pitcher Bill Tress knocked in the game-winning RBI.

As Kiski Area headed to Forbes Field for the title game, one key ingredient was missing – the coach. Egalsky was in Bloomington, Ind., taking pre-scheduled tests mandated by the State Department before traveling to the Soviet Union.

"Even though it was during the Cold War, the trip gave me an opportunity to study the Russian language," said Egalsky, who received a fellowship grant for the trip while working toward his Master's degree.

Assistant coach Al Veselicky took over the team and guided the Cavaliers to a 4-2 victory in a game that was televised on WQED Channel 13. Tress improved his record to 11-0 on the season and finished off the Gators in unforgettable fashion. He whiffed Gateway's John Russo to record his 100th strikeout of the season and set off a celebration of Kiski Area players on the rock-solid infield of Forbes Field.

Those watching on TV got a rare chance to see the inside of Forbes Field. Pirates home games were not televised because Pirates general manager Joe L. Brown expressly forbid any home television of Bucco baseball, believing it would hurt the gate. It wasn't until 1977, the year after Brown retired that viewers in the Pittsburgh region ever got to see the Pirates live on Pittsburgh-based television.

The five-game playoff tourney was spread over 21 days, enabling Tress to pitch each game. There were no state playoffs at the time, nor were there any pitching limitations. Because of no state playoffs, the WPIAL had the freedom to schedule the title game during Pirates road trips.

The Cavaliers received their WPIAL trophy while dining after the game at the Hotel Webster Hall in Pittsburgh's Oakland section, just a couple of blocks from Forbes Field.

The championship was in the middle of a great run by A-K

Valley baseball teams.

Arnold won it 1965, followed by the Kiski victory. In 1967, Kittanning brought home WPIAL baseball honors.

The feat followed several other WPIAL baseball titlists from what now comprises the Kiski Area School District. Bell Township won the WPIAL baseball title in 1943 and Vandergrift won in back-to-back fashion in 1948-49.

The entire 1966 Kiski Area baseball team was inducted into the school's Hall of Fame in Sept., 2009.

Here is the Kiski Area 1966 baseball team, the school's first team to win a WPIAL title.

chapter 46

MORE THAN JUST A DOT

For years, the small community of Verona has used the slogan "A Spot That's More Than A Dot."

It touts the one-half square mile borough as something more than just a little dot on the map.

And in 1962, the dot ran the length and breadth of the WPIAL. The Verona High School Panthers, from one of the smallest schools in the entire state with only 72 boys in the top 3 grades, brought home the WPIAL Class B football championship with a 12-6 victory over Apollo at Ken High Memorial Stadium.

Only a decade earlier, there was talk about dropping football at Verona. The program had lost 28 consecutive games and interest was scant. But coach Joe Zelek quickly righted the ship. After the long losing streak ended with a 22-20 victory over Millvale on Nov. 6, 1954, Zelek led the team out of the gridiron wilderness with a 6-2 record in 1955.

That set the stage for the most successful period in school history from 1960-63 when the Panthers accumulated a 30-4-1 record. Including the tail end of the 1959 season, Verona posted winning streaks of 17 and 14 games in that era.

The highlight of that run was in 1962, when Verona won all nine regular season games and defeated Apollo in the title game. Expectations going into the season were high, but depth was, and remains today, a problem in the small schools. In Verona's case 35 of the 72 boys in the school, almost half, came out for football. Still, Zelek had to teach the players two positions on each side of the ball.

Ordinarily, rivals played each other last, but Verona and Oakmont for many years started the season with one another. The three weeks of training camp leading up to the opening game had fans in the Twin Boros raging with anticipation. Followers from each team would 'spy' on the opposite team and then report the findings to their coach. In Oakmont's case, there was a canvas along the chain-link fence surrounding Cribbs Field in Verona. Oaks fans would have to sneak a peak under the canvas to see what was going on.

Zelek and Oakmont coach Chuck Wagner would get a laugh out of the findings of the unofficial scouts.

"We saw people looking under the fences, but I had a real good relationship with Chuck and Elmer Gross before him," Zelek said in a 1992 interview in the *Valley News Dispatch*. "We knew what each other were going to run."

Verona started its championship drive with an 18-6 victory over Oakmont, followed by a resounding 39-12 win against Edgewood. But the win in Week Three over WPIAL contender Snowden (now known as South Park) gave Zelek the feeling that his team was a WPIAL title threat.

The problem was with the WPIAL's Gardner Point System, where the top two teams that finished with the highest number of rating points would compete for the title. By mid-season, it appeared that Verona wouldn't have enough Gardner Points to make the final two, so Zelek, also Verona's athletic director, hastily arranged a game with East Huntingdon the week after the regular season was slated to end. The winner of that game would be ensured of enough Gardner Points to qualify for the one-game playoff.

The Verona offense was designed around do-everything quarterback Garry Lyle. The defense was built around linebacker Harold Mauro. The team attracted a huge following for games at Cribbs Field, and on the road.

Victories over Millvale, East Deer-Frazer, West Mifflin South made the Panthers 6-0. Next up was a game against a first-year school, Franklin Regional. The school was a merger between Franklin Township and Export high schools. Verona won that one Oct. 21 game with ease, 21-0. Franklin Regional, also called the Panthers, was feeling the effects of a fourth consecutive road game.

Up next on the schedule was Verona's first night game of the season at Sharpsburg. The unfamiliarity of playing under the lights caused a sluggish start for Verona. Ultimately, a strong second half paced the Panthers to a 19-0 victory to go 8-0.

By then, Apollo was the leader in Gardner Points and it became apparent that the Verona-East Huntingdon winner would oppose the Striped Tigers for WPIAL honors. Neshannock and Northwestern (now known as Blackhawk High School) were undefeated but would lack sufficient Gardner Points unless Verona and East Huntingdon would play to a tie.

In what amounted to a WPIAL semifinal, Verona came from behind to defeat East Huntingdon, 14-7, before a crowd estimated at 7,000 on a soggy field located near the assembly plant which once housed SONY and Volkswagen.

The WPIAL selected New Kensington on Nov. 16 as the championship game site for the first matchup between two local schools since Ken High played Har-Brack in 1947.

Art Williamson scored early in the second period for Apollo and the Tigers' hard-hitting defense sidelined both Lyle and backup quarterback Ed Lyons. Zelek had to turn to freshman QB Cy Greeve who flawlessly handled the offense to two series until Lyle recovered enough from a hip-pointer to return to the lineup. Lyle threw a 27-yard touchdown pass to John Bouch then scored on a 6-yard keeper early in the second half to clinch the biggest victory in Verona history. The Panthers returned home to a noisy throng and impromptu parties that lasted into the wee hours of the following morning.

Mauro was selected to the 1962 all-state team and played at Indiana University. He was in the lineup when the Hoosiers represented the Big 10 in the 1968 Rose Bowl.

Lyle went on to become the first black All-American player at George Washington University and played nine seasons with the Chicago Bears.

Zelek, along with Mauro and Lyle, are members of the A-K Valley Sports Hall of Fame. When Zelek was inducted in 2000, his following from Verona was one of the biggest in the hall's 40 years of induction ceremonies.

Zelek died in 2001.

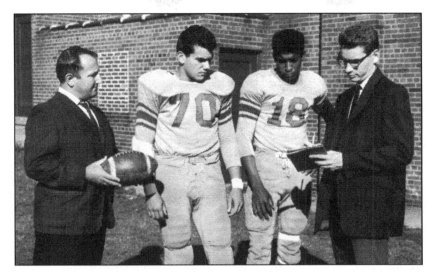

Credit: Courtesy Riverview School District

Verona coach Joe Zelek, Harold Mauro, Garry Lyle, and assistant Carl England plot strategy.

chapter 47

FROM ARNOLD TO THE NATION'S CAPITOL

Even though Al DeMao didn't play football until his senior season at Arnold High School, it didn't stop the center/linebacker from being named to the top 70 Redskins players of all time in 2002.

DeMao and the 69 others were honored on Oct. 27, 2002, as part of the franchise's 70th anniversary celebration at FedEx Field. The only other centers selected to the all-time team were Jeff Bostic and Len Hauss.

DeMao played for the Redskins from 1945-53, snapping the ball to one of the NFL's all-time great quarterbacks, Slingin' Sammy Baugh.

Albert Marcellus DeMao entered the world as a Leap Year Baby – born on Feb. 29, 1920.

While he played for some independent football teams as a youngster, including a sandlot team sponsored by a drug store, DeMao finally hooked on with the Arnold team in 1937. Arnold compiled a 4-3 record that season, including a 6-0 victory over Springdale.

His play that season was good enough for Duquesne University, then a Division I school, to take notice. DeMao was a member of the Dukes from 1939-41 and was set to graduate from Duquesne. But World War II intervened, and all resources turned to the war effort. DeMao returned to Duquesne to receive his diploma after the war.

A War Hero

The Redskins drafted DeMao in the 9th round of the 1942 NFL draft.

Soon after the attacks on Pearl Harbor, where fellow Arnold native George Leslie was the first Pennsylvanian killed in the attack, DeMao joined the Navy. He quickly rose to a lieutenant, and was part of the D-Day invasion on June 6, 1944. He made nine courageous landings on Normandy Beach in what has been called

The Longest Day. One time, a landing plank was stuck. DeMao got out of the boat and dislodged the plank with brute strength while bullets whizzed overhead.

Future Hall of Fame coaching legend Paul 'Bear' Bryant inked DeMao to a contract with a $250 signing bonus. That's a paltry figure compared to today's extraordinary bonuses.

DeMao joined the Redskins at mid-season in 1945, playing in the last five games of what was in time for an eventual playoff matchup with the Cleveland Rams.

Cleveland won that game, 15-14, before moving to Los Angeles.

For his last seven seasons, DeMao served as a team captain and played at center and linebacker – NFL players generally went both ways in those days. But DeMao is most famous for snapping to Baugh.

DeMao and Baugh were the only Redskins from the early, post-World War II era to be named to the all-time team. He made his first Pro Bowl appearance in 1950. After making the Pro Bowl for the second time in '52, he announced his retirement. But the 'Skins persuaded him to come back for a final season.

In Nov., 1952, he was honored with an Al DeMao Day at Griffith Stadium against the Steelers. He received a boatload of gifts, including a brand-new Pontiac.

In 1957, he founded the Redskins Alumni Association.

DeMao died on Feb. 1, 2008 of pneumonia at the Baltimore Washington Medical Center, Glen Burnie, Md.

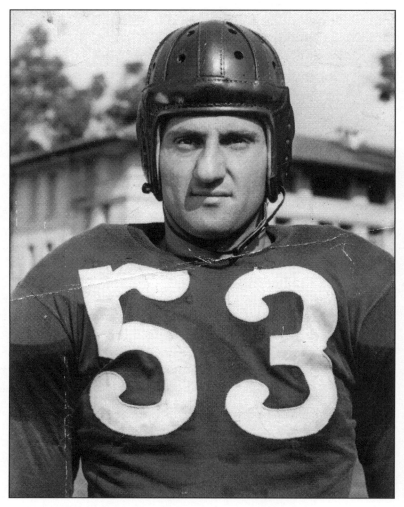

Credit: A–K Valley Sports Hall of Fame

Arnold native Al DeMao played seven years with the Washington Redskins after his heroic deeds performed on D-Day.

chapter 48

SAVING THE BEST FOR LAST

Tarentum High School went out with a bang.

The Redcats, in their final season of existence, won the WPIAL basketball title before the school was combined with Har-Brack to form Highlands. On March 12, 1968, Tarentum defeated Albert Gallatin, 74-58, at Pitt's Fitzgerald Field House to win the WPIAL Class B title.

With merger mania at its peak during the 1960s as the state Department of Education drove to reduce the school districts in Pennsylvania from about 2,000 to the current 502, Tarentum and Har-Brack tried their best to hang on.

The communities, by then suffering a population loss, didn't want to lose their identity – as did many across the state. One concoction had Tarentum, Fawn Township, Frazer Township and East Deer Township forming one school, while Har-Brack and West Deer would be left alone. East Deer, in fact, had much demographically in common with Tarentum. The two municipalities met on the west end of Tarentum, and East Deer, at one time, played their big home football games at Dreshar Stadium on Saturday nights, so the school systems had worked together for many years.

Not good enough, said the state. In fact, the Department of Ed threatened to sue Tarentum and Har-Brack if they didn't dance to the state's merger music.

It had become apparent that the 1967-68 school year would be the last for the separate districts. The fortunes of the football teams from the two separate districts had been sagging of late, but Har-Brack was still one of the top basketball programs around and Tarentum, after an injury-riddled football season, was hoping to make a big splash on the hardwood.

In the 1966-67 campaign, Tarentum finished with a pedestrian 6-6 mark and was 8-13 overall. Freeport won the Section 21-B crown and made it to the WPIAL finals before losing to Turtle Creek. Many considered the Yellowjackets the pre-season favorites.

The last thing a small school could afford was injuries, and Tarentum seemed to have plenty of them. The leading scorer from the previous season, Joe 'Skip' Guyaux, fractured his wrist during the football season where Tarentum, for a time, was down to its fourth-string quarterback. Guyaux wasn't ready to return for the start of the basketball season, but by the time he did, Jim Tench suffered a season-ending back injury.

Tarentum posted only a 5-5 record during the December exhibition season, but veteran coach Ted Timashenka detected a spark and thought the team could jell as the season went along. He was right, as the Redcats breezed through the section that consisted of Freeport, East Deer, West Deer, Oakmont and Verona. Tarentum clinched the section crown with an 83-49 win over East Deer. In that game, Guyaux became the school's all-time leading scorer, eclipsing the 1,000-point mark

The Redcats were in the WPIAL postseason for the first time since 1963 when they lost a section tie-breaker game to Springdale at the Pitt Field House. Only section winners were admitted to the WPIAL playoffs at the time. The last outright section won by Tarentum was in 1957 when the Redcats defeated Freeport in a tie-breaker game.

Despite a 9-1 finish in the regular season, the WPIAL Basketball Steering Committee wasn't impressed, seeding Tarentum 11th in an 11-team tournament field.

In fact, Tarentum got a lower seed than teams that had to go through a section tie-breaker. But the Redcats started their 11th and final trip to the WPIAL postseason with a 63-42 victory over Peters Township.

But next up was Rankin, the No. 1-seeded team and the favorite for the WPIAL title. The Jackrabbits had all-stater Jerome Flowers and Matt Furjanic, who would later coach Woodland Hills High School and Robert Morris College.

Tarentum center Chet Teklinski brashly told a reporter that Tarentum would beat Rankin. But many from the Tarentum-Fawn Township area didn't share the same feeling as 200 tickets from Tarentum's allotment went unsold.

The Redcats rolled out to a 20-9 lead at the end of one quarter. But Rankin continued to peck away at the lead until tying the contest in the third period. The Jackrabbits took two brief leads late in the third quarter, but Bruce Nichols got hot in the fourth period, scoring six points as Tarentum kept pace.

With the score knotted at 58-58, Norm Moser canned two free throws with 1:22 left in the game to give Tarentum the lead for good, eventually winning by a 63-60 margin.

Next up on the schedule was a date with California Area in the semifinals at Pitt. The Trojans were fresh off a 64-50 over Knoch in the quarterfinals.

Tarentum handled California, 60-53, to advance to the title game for the first time.

Just like the Rankin game, Tarentum was ready to play and quickly jumped out to a lead over the Colonials. But Albert Gallatin fought back to tie the game at 52-all. The Redcats, however, reeled off an 11-0 run to finally take control of the game. Guyaux came up big on the WPIAL's biggest stage with 31 points and 20 rebounds.

Said Timashenka:"It was a proud moment of my life. We believed in ourselves and I'm not sure a lot of other people did." A big celebration took place when the team finally returned to the West End of Tarentum – remember, there was no Route 28 Expressway at the time and the team had to wend its way back home along old 28. The band, majorettes and student buses were escorted throughout the community by police cars and fire department trucks.

Tarentum wasn't as successful, however, in its initial PIAA appearance, losing to Homer Center, 81-65. Guyaux finished with 1,130 career points.

Tarentum wasn't done winning WPIAL titles. Two months later, Guyaux and Moser combined to win the WPIAL doubles tennis championship. In the team competition, Tarentum, once the winner of 30 straight section matches, faced Mount Lebanon in the tennis team title and lost, 3-2.

"Most of that year, in fact, to me was bittersweet," Guyaux said in a 2008 interview with the *Valley News Dispatch*. "What we did in basketball and tennis for a small school and small community was exciting, but we all understood the inevitableness of it all." Tarentum's last athletic event was a baseball game on June 1, 1968, as the Redcats won at Shannock Valley, 8-2.

Credit: Valley News Dispatch

The Tarentum Redcats celebrate the 1968 WPIAL Class B title with Joe 'Skip' Guyaux and coach Ted Timashenka.

Credit: Valley News Dispatch

The newly-crowned WPIAL Class B champion Tarentum Redcats are paraded through downtown Tarentum on March 18, 1968.

chapter 49

AIDING IN THE TRANSITION

Prior to the creation of Holiday Park, Ramparts and other suburban-type settings, Plum was once a conglomeration of coal-mining towns and areas where natural gas drilling was important like Renton, Logans Ferry Heights, Barking, Unity and others.

In the 1950s, Plum was a rapidly-changing community. The coal mines began to close, the natural gas wells were capped and more and more farmers were selling their land to residential developers.

Plum started out as a township in 1788. Settlers observed plum trees along a creek that was soon named Plum Creek. In 1956, the municipality changed its status from a township to a borough. Because of the bourgeoning population, a new high school building was opened at its current site in 1961, replacing the old school, now known as George Pivik Elementary School.

In 1980, Plum became the first A-K Valley high school to play in all four football enrollment classifications.

During that time of transition in the 1950s, Plum fans were brought together by the exploits of three multi-sport athletes – Vic Zucco, Joe Naunchik and Frank Marchlewski.

Vic Zucco

Zucco graduated from Plum in 1953 after a stellar career in football, basketball and track.

As a running back, he was named all-Allegheny Valley Conference in 1952 when the Mustangs were 6-2-1 playing in the WPIAL's Class B, then the league's smallest enrollment classification. He held the school's rushing and scoring records for many years. In track, Zucco won the WPIAL title in 1952 in the long jump, the 100-yard dash and the 220. Plum won the team title at the WPIAL meet, the first WPIAL title of any kind for the high school, which first opened its doors in 1939.

Zucco also placed four times in the PIAA meet before heading to Wayne State University in Detroit on a football scholarship. He set the WSU record of 228 yards rushing and used his blinding speed to score on touchdown runs of 76, 55 and 52 yards in one game.

When Wayne was no longer a Division I school under an NCAA reorganization, Zucco transferred to Michigan State where he played both offense and defense for the 1956 Spartans. He was chosen to play in the 1957 Senior Bowl and the North-South Shrine all-star games.

Zucco was drafted in the fifth round of the 1957 NFL draft by the Bears, the 60th overall choice. He was a defensive back for legendary coach George Halas. On Nov. 3, 1957, he recovered a fumble against the Los Angeles Rams and ran 43 yards for a touchdown at the LA Coliseum.

On Aug. 15, 1959 as Vince Lombardi made his debut as head coach of the Green Bay Packers in an NFL pre-season game at Milwaukee County Stadium, Zucco intercepted a pass from QB Lamar McHan with 23 seconds left in the game to preserve an 18-16 victory for the Bears.

He retired after four NFL seasons and has been a successful businessman in Northwestern Michigan, where he operated a ski lodge for a time.

Joe Naunchik

Naunchik, who grew up in the Logans Ferry Heights section of town, was part of the 1956 graduating class, the final one under the banner of Plum Township High, before the name was changed to the Plum Borough School District.

Naunchik was team captain for the Mustangs in baseball, football and basketball. He quarterbacked Plum's outstanding football team in 1955 under coach Willie Rometo. The Mustangs went 7-1-1 with only a tie to Freeport and a 7-6 loss to Oakmont blemishing the record. After high school, Naunchik was awarded a football scholarship to Arizona State, but instead signed with the Pittsburgh Pirates. After a three-year baseball career that included 271 games and stops in Salem (Va.), San Angelo (Tex.) and Dubuque (Ia.), Nauncik returned to college, where he set the stage for an outstanding coaching career that lasted 38 years – 25 as a head coach.

After several years as an assistant, Naunchik took over the head coaching job at Plum in 1970 as the program was struggling mightily. By 1974, Plum was in contention for the Keystone Conference title and a WPIAL playoff berth before losing to Southmoreland on the next-to-the-last week of the regular season.

But Plum's breakthrough season came in 1975 when Plum won the Keystone title, the first of three consecutive conference titles and trips to the WPIAL playoffs. He went to Pitt from 1979-82, coaching tight ends such as John Brown, who made the heroic catch in the 1982 Sugar Bowl.

But Naunchik left Pitt in 1983 and went back to the scholastic ranks, taking over as coach/athletic director at Hempfield High School. Naunchik led the Spartans to the WPIAL playoffs in 1985.

That same year, the New Kensington-Arnold School District was looking for a football coach/athletic director and asked Naunchik to list the job specifications. While Naunchik was listing a duty roster, he discovered the man they were looking for was none other than himself, the same person who was making the 76-mile round trip daily from Arnold to Hempfield.

By 1988, Naunchik had led Valley High School to the WPIAL playoffs as a conference champion. After five seasons at Valley, Naunchik went back to the classroom and looked to right the Fox Chapel program after another legendary coach, Chuck Wagner, left.

In 1996, he led his fourth different school to the WPIAL playoffs. He retired after a WPIAL Quad-A semifinal appearance in 1997 with the Foxes.

Frank Marchlewski

Marchlewski graduated in 1960, the next-to-the-last class at the original high school building.

During his time at Plum, Marchlewski lettered in football, baseball, basketball and track. He won four letters in football, including an all-WPIAL lineman award, the Valley Daily News first team lineman and earned a scholarship to the University of Minnesota.

Marchlewski played in the Big 10 Conference with the Golden Gophers under coach Murray Warmath. He lettered three years for Minny as a center, and so impressed Warmath that he later named Marchlewski center of the decade.

He was also named an honorable mention All-American.

Marchlewski was selected in the fifth round by the Los Angeles Rams in the 1965 NFL draft, the 60th player taken overall. He was part of the same draft that included fellow Western Pennsylvanians Joe Namath (Beaver Falls), Jim Nance (Indiana Area) and Bo Scott (Connellsville).

In the NFL, Marchlewski's career spanned six seasons with the Rams, the Falcons and later, the Bills. The best pro team Marchlewski played on was the 1969 Rams, who got off to an 11-0 start under Hall of Fame coach George Allen. After the Rams lost their final three games of the regular season, quarterback Roman Gabriel, who was making a movie called *The Undefeated* at the time, said they might change the name of the movie to simply *11-3*.

In the playoffs, Marchlewski played in what was the final postseason of the original NFL before the NFL/AFL merger officially took place in 1970.

After football, Marchlewski was employed by the Genessee Brewing Co. for 33 years.

Credit: A-K Valley Hall of Fame

Frank Marchlewski played for Plum before heading to the University of Minnesota.

Credit: A–K Valley Sports Hall of Fame

Vic Zucco was a multi-sport athlete at Plum Township High School and played for the Chicago Bears.

Credit: Valley High School program

Joe Naunchik was head football coach/athletic director at Valley High School in 1987. Naunchik led four different high schools to the WPIAL playoffs.

chapter 50

WINNING LIKE A GALE-FORCE WIND

Few teams live up to their nicknames, but in the case of the Harmarvillle Hurricanes, the remarkable soccer club blew past opponents like a gale-force wind.

The Hurricanes won national championships in 1952 and '56, then known as the Open Cup. In 1999, the name was changed to the Lamar Hunt U.S. Open Cup.

No matter what the symbol of soccer supremacy was called, Harmarville was a constant contender. From 1947-63, the Hurricanes compiled a 340-60-36 record - a percentage of .850.

The kicker to the whole thing was the fact that Harmarville played in relative obscurity. The Pirates and the Steelers were pretty bad. Hockey fans had only the minor league Hornets to root for and Pitt was sporadically good in football. About the only winner was the Duquesne University Dukes basketball team – and the Harmarville Hurricanes.

There was no local television to speak of and soccer battled for, much like now, attention from other sports. Still, many fans didn't realize they had a nationally-renowned team in their midst.

While other clubs from around the country stacked their teams with ringers, Harmarville was purely Western Pennsylvania. Some pro and collegiate teams today like to describe a hard-nosed style as blue-collar, but Harmarville truly was blue collar. The players worked in coal mines, steel mills and factories and were grizzled war veterans. Many of the players, particularly from the Springdale area, brought the game of soccer to the A-K Valley area when they emigrated to the United States.

One of Harmarville's rivals was Beadling, hailing from a small coal mining community in Upper St. Clair. Most of the region's mining towns fielded soccer clubs, with athletes being recruited with well-paying jobs in the mines or with mining companies in return for playing for the soccer club.

One of the brightest stars of the Harmarville heyday was Lou 'Sonny' Yakopec. A 1944 graduate of Aspinwall High School,

Yakopec also was a member of the U.S. Olympic teams in 1948 and 1952, scoring the winning goal in the '52 game.

Harmarville beat the Philadelphia Nationals, 7-5, on an aggregate goal-total in a home-and-home series. Yakopec's name appears on the 1952 Open Cup trophy which is on display, along with other memorabilia, in a second-floor showcase at the Pittsburgh Indoor Sports Arena, Harmar.

Much of the memorabilia was on display until 1999 at the National Soccer Hall of Fame in Oneonta, N.Y. Yakopec also holds the distinction of playing on a U.S. all-star team that took on Mexico in Mexico City.

In 1953, Harmarville lost to the Chicago Falcons in the title match. But it was a different story in 1956, also a home-and-home series where the Hurricanes defeated Chicago Schwaben, 3-2.

Harmarville fell behind, 2-0, in aggregate goals. But reserve Harry Pitchok and Tom Craddock scored to force overtime. The two clubs played 52 minutes of overtime before George Resavage clinched the cup with eight minutes left.

Estimates had the crowd at 5,000 people at Chicago's Consumer Field for the '56 championship. Earlier that same year, the Hurricanes gained national prominence in a *Sports Illustrated* article by Myron Cope.

The following the club had shriveled up after the '56 campaign and Harmarville died in 1967. The reason – television.

With the increasing popularity of televised pro football into the 1960s, it was difficult for Harmarville to compete, since most of their games were on Sundays.

Resavage said the death of the local coal industry and soccer also are interrelated.

Credit: A-K Valley Sports Hall of Fame

Lou 'Sonny' Yakopec boots the ball away at the Harmarville Hurricanes soccer field. Yakopec & the Hurricanes won the 1956 national title. Note the top of the Oakmont-Hulton Bridge in the background.

Gone, But Not Forgotten

Here is a list of now-defunct football schools and their all-time records:

SCHOOL	YEARS ACTIVE	W	L	T	PCT.
Apollo	1898-1915, 1917-1968	224	216	43	.509
Armstrong Central	1990-1992	11	19	1	.367
Arnold	1921-1966	179	200	30	.472
Aspinwall	1907-1960	236	145	41	.619
Bell Twp.-Avonmore	1929-1961	129	130	23	.498
East Deer-Frazer	1939-1968	128	113	13	.520
Elders Ridge	1931, 1937-41, 1945-68	92	140	19	.397
Har-Brack	1924-1967	225	152	33	.597
Natrona	1921-1923	8	5	3	.615
Natrona St. Joseph	1930-1934, 1946-1947	10	26	2	.278
New Kensington	1906-1966	253	197	40	.562
Oakmont	1919-1970	218	182	32	.545
Parnassus	1909-1930	79	62	17	.560
Tarentum	1906-1967	269	212	46	.559
Vandergrift	1912-1961	192	190	26	.503
Verona	1921-1970	156	216	27	.419
Washington Twp.	1929-1965	105	151	21	.410
West Deer	1944-1968	79	145	11	.359

The All-Staters

Here is a list of all A-K Valley football players named to the wire service all-state teams. The Associated Press (AP) annual teams started in 1939 and continues to the present. The United Press International (UPI) selected teams from 1952 to 1984.

1940 AP second team	Bob 'Sonny' Davidson	Tackle	Tarentum
1942 AP second team	George Vasilopus	Back	New Kensington
1945 AP first team	Ray Newman	Tackle	New Kensington
1946 AP first team	Tony Kotowski	End	New Kensington
1947 AP first team	Renaldo Kosikowski	Guard	New Kensington
1947 AP first team	Harold Vestrand	Back	New Kensington
1947 AP second team	Dick Tamburro	Center	New Kensington
1947 AP second team	Ed Modzelewski	Back	Har-Brack
1948 AP first team	Willie Thrower	Back	New Kensington
1948 AP second team	Renaldo Kosikowski	Guard	New Kensington
1948 AP second team	Dick Modzelewski	Tackle	Har-Brack
1950 AP first team	Rudy Mattioli	QB	Har-Brack
1950 AP second team	Vic Kolenik	End	Leechburg
1952 AP second team	Ricky Wagner	Tackle	Har-Brack
1953 AP & UPI first team	Chester Gilchrist	Back	Har-Brack
1953 UPI second team	Bob Brodhead	Back	Kittanning
1953 UPI second team	Rich Ross	Back	Vandergrift
1953 UPI third team	Rich Racchione	Tackle	Vanderfrift
1953 AP third team	Dick Hunter	Back	Leechburg
1954 AP first team	Paul Widmer	Guard	Har-Brack
1955 AP third team & UPI first team	Fran Dobrowolski	End	Har-Brack
1956 UPI second team	Nolan Jones	Back	New Kensington
1957 UPI first team & AP second team	Nolan Jones	Back	New Kensington
1962 AP third team	Harold Mauro	Center	Verona
1963 AP fourth team	Charles 'Chip' Young	Back	Freeport
1964 UPI second team & AP third team	Phil Booker	Back	Kiski Area

1965 AP second team	Ron Cecil	Tackle	Oakmont
1965 UPI third team	Dennis Morabito	Tackle	Kiski Area
1967 AP & UPI first team	Jack Dykes	Tackle	Kiski Area
1968 AP & UPI first team	Dennis Booker	Fullback	Kiski Area
1968 UPI second team	Robbin Schindhette	Tackle	Kiski Area
1968 AP second team	Mike Spires	Tackle	Burrell
1968 AP second team	Paul Yakulis	Center	Kiski Area
1969 AP first team	Terry Factor	Linebacker	Highlands
1969 AP second team	Bill Chada	Off End	Highlands
1969 UPI second team & AP third team	Clair Wilson	Halfback	Kiski Area
1969 AP third team	Rob Noble	Def. End	Kiski Area
1970 AP first team	Rich Kaminski	Def. Back	Kiski Area
1970 UPI first team	George Geier	Center	Kiski Area
1970 AP second team	Rich Kamisnki	Halfback	Kiski Area
1970 AP second team	Don Tarosky	Def. Back	Kiski Area
1970 AP third team	Phil Bonello	Off. End	Leechburg
1971 UPI first team & AP second team	Mike Milito	ILB	Kiski Area
1971 AP third team	Andy Peters	Guard	Fox Chapel
1971 AP third team	Russ Clark	Center	Kiski Area
1971 AP third team	Tom Giotto	Def. Back	Kiski Area
1972 AP & UPI first team	Russ Clark	Center	Kiski Area
1972 AP & UPI first team	Jim Henderson	ILB	Kiski Area
1972 AP first team	Frank Ballina	Def. Back	Freeport
1972 AP second team	Joe Stone	Off. End	Kiski Area
1972 AP third team	Steve Earley	Off. Tackle	Kiski Area
1972 UPI first team & AP third team	Mike Hansen	Running Back	Kiski Area
1972 AP third team	Joe Bushovsky	Linebacker	Kiski Area
1973 UPI first team	Kim Sypula	End	Highlands
1973 AP third team	Paul King	Off. Tackle	Kiski Area
1974 AP first team	Dan Leri	QB	Freeport
1974 AP & UPI first team	Kevin Thrower	Running Back	Valley
1974 AP & UPI second team	Steve Kiragas	ILB	Plum
1974 UPI second team & AP third team	Frank Gaydos	ILB	Kiski Area

1975 AP & UPI first team	Bob Smart	Guard	Plum
1975 AP first team	Larry Shepard	LB	Kittanning
1975 UPI second team	Don Tomporoski	Guard	Freeport
1976 AP & UPI first team	Benjy Pryor	Tight End	Valley
1976 AP first team	Dave Blotzer	Center	Plum
1976 AP second team	Greg Meisner	Def. End	Valley
1976 UPI first team & AP third team	Angelo Fasano	Def. Back	Kiski Area
1977 AP first team	Frank Rocco	QB	Fox Chapel
1977 AP & UPI first team	Leo Wisniewski	Def. End	Fox Chapel
1977 UPI first team & AP second team	Ed Skerl	Guard	Plum
1978 AP first team	Dan Rocco	Def. Back	Fox Chapel
1978 AP second team	Anthony Collecchi	ILB	Kiski Area
1981 AP UPI first team	Bobby White	Linebacker	Freeport
1981 AP second team	Bill Callahan	Running Back	Valley
1981 UPI first team	Bill Callahan	Def. Back	Valley
1981 UPI first team & AP second team	Lee Hetrick	Linebacker	Highlands
1981 AP third team	Eric Crum	Def. Back	Highlands
1982 AP first team	Tom Brown	Running Back	Burrell
1982 UPI first team & AP second team	Mitch Frerotte	Linebacker	Kittanning
1984 UPI first team & AP second team	Chris Thorpe	Running Back	Fox Chapel
1985 AP first team	Rush Hodgin	Guard	Fox Chapel
1985 AP second team	Jeff Christy	Running Back	Freeport
1985 AP second team	Dennis Wuyscik	Def. End	Kiski Area
1985 AP second team	Harvey Kemp	Def. End	Valley
1986 AP first team	Chip Nitowski	Off. Line	Highlands
1986 AP first team	Jeff Christy	Linebacker	Freeport
1986 AP second team	Tom Hornack	Def. Back	Burrell
1987 AP second team	Mark Shemanski	Linebacker	Burrell
1988 AP Big school second team	P.J. Killian	Def. Back	Fox Chapel
1988 AP Small school first team	Eric Ravotti	Linebacker	Freeport

Year/Team	Name	Position	School
1988 AP Small school first team	Carl Johnson	Def. Back	Valley
1988 AP Small school second team	Keith Oconis	Off. Line	Deer Lakes
1989 AP Small school first team	Jody White	Linebacker	Freeport
1990 AP Big school second team	Mike Halapin	Def. Line	Kiski Area
1990 AP Big school third team	Lewis Lawhorn	Def. Back	Kiski Area
1990 AP Small school second team	Dave Viszlay	Off. Line	Freeport
1990 AP Small school third team	Brian Kurn	Def. Back	Freeport
1991 AP Big school first team	Cliff Stroud	Def. Line	Highlands
1991 AP Big school third team	Jay White	Running Back	Valley
1992 AP Big school third team	Doug Ostrosky	Def. Line	Fox Chapel
1992 AP Big school third team	Nick Reiser	Linebacker	Knoch
1992 AP Big school third team	Bill Coury	Def. Back	Valley
1992 AP Small school second team	Andy Crocker	Off. Line	Freeport
1992 AP Small school third team	Ron DeJidas	Def. Back	Freeport
1993 AP Big school first team	Doug Ostrosky	Tight End	Fox Chapel
1994 AP Big school second team	Don Snow	Def. Line	Knoch
1994 AP Big school third team	John Shikella	Kicker	Knoch
1994 AP Small school third team	Jason Cappa	Tight end	Riverview
1995 AP Big school first team	Ben Kopp	Off. Line	Valley
1995 AP Big school third team	Craig Johnson	Def. Back	Valley
1995 AP Small school first team	Seth Hornack	Def. Back	Burrell
1995 AP Small school third team	Joe Kurtik	Off. Line	Burrell
1995 AP Small school third team	Jason Gregg	Def. Line	Burrell
1996 AP Big school third team	Tom Coury	Def. Line	Highlands
1996 AP Small school first team	Randy Gilbert	Def. Line	Riverview
1996 AP Small school second team	Ben Erdeljac	Specialist	Riverview
1996 AP Small school third team	Billy Daugherty	Wide Receiver	Leechburg
1997 AP Big school first team	Brandon Williams	Running Back	Valley
1997 AP Big school second team	Steve Lindsay	Off. Line	Fox Chapel
1997 AP Big school second team	Tim Sasson	Def. Line	Fox Chapel
1997 AP Big school second team	Chad Killian	Def. Back	FoxChapel
1997 AP Big school third team	Joe Manganello	Off. Line	Plum
1997 AP Small school first team	Lucas Heakins	Specialist	Riverview
1997 AP Small school third team	Kent Crytzer	Specialist	Freeport
1997 AP Small school third team	Billy Daugherty	Kick Ret.	Leechburg
1998 AP Big school second team	Matt Morgan	Off. Line	Plum
1998 AP Big school third team	Chad Ryan	Def. Line	Highlands

1998 AP Small school first team	Lucas Heakins	Running Back	Riverview
1998 AP Small school second team	Anthony Zurisko	Kicker	Springdale
1999 AP Small school third team	Jeremy McCorkle	Tight end	Freeport
2000 AP Big school third team	Donny Booker	Linebacker	Valley
2002 AP Big school third team	Greg Hutcherson	Wide Receiver	Kiski Area
2003 AP Class AAAA first team	Scott McKillop	Linebacker	Kiski Area
2003 AP Class AAAA second team	Adam Gunn	Def. Back	Kiski Area
2003 AP Class AA second team	Zach Wolfe	Tight End	Ford City
2003 AP Class AA second team	Jarrod Miller	Linebacker	Apollo-Ridge
2003 AP Class A second team	Lucas Cox	Def. Line	Springdale
2004 AP Class AA first team	John Brown	Off. Line	Burrell
2004 AP Class AA second team	Tyler Henderson	Running Back	Burrell
2004 AP Class A first team	Shane Steffey	Off. Line	Riverview
2005 AP Class AA second team	Tyler Henderson	Running Back	Burrell
2005 AP Class AA second team	Aaron Brown	Specialist	Burrell
2005 AP Class AA second team	Tyler Santucci	Linebacker	Valley
2005 AP Class A second team	Andrew Bosman	Kicker	Springdale
2006 AP Class AA first team	Robert Law	Off. Line	Ford City
2006 AP Class AA second team	Toney Clemons	Wide Receiver	Valley
2007 AP Class AAA first team	Tim McNerney	Running Back	Knoch
2007 AP Class A first team	Ryan Hohman	Linebacker	Springdale
2008 AP Class AAAA first team	Miles Dieffenbach	Off. Line	Fox Chapel
2008 AP Class AAA second team	Jeff Sinclair	Defensive Back	Highlands

WA